HUMAN RACE 4.0

THE SCIENCE OF GETTING AHEAD IN THE NEW WORLD ORDER

Shu-Tze

PARTRIDGE

Library of Congress Control Number:		2020903229
ISBN:	Softcover	978-1-5437-5673-9
	eBook	978-1-5437-5674-6

For permission requests or engagement inquiries write to the author, address, "Attention: Human Race 4.0 Inquiries" at shutze.tan@alignzassociates.com.

Cover design by Shu-Tze Tan
Cover page image source: www.123rf.com

1st Edition: January 2021
Edited by: Shu-Chien Law

Print information available on the last page.

To order additional copies of this book, contact
Toll Free 800 101 2657 (Singapore)
Toll Free 1 800 81 7340 (Malaysia)
orders.singapore@partridgepublishing.com

www.partridgepublishing.com/singapore

THE BEST WAY TO PREDICT OUR FUTURE
IS TO CREATE IT.
—— Abraham Lincoln

A major pandemic of the century has struck the world again.
On top of that, smart technology is rapidly invading our lives,
dramatically changed the way we live, work, play, and connect.

While life is becoming faster and more convenient,
humans' wellbeing and mental health are deteriorating.
Some are losing jobs to COVID-19 and
technological advancement.
Others are facing difficulty keeping pace with the sudden changes.
Most importantly, we seem lost.

Is our livelihood being threatened? Are our days numbered?
How do we survive the post-pandemic era
and smarter, faster machines?
The good news is, by reprogramming our
physical and psychological DNA,
WE will thrive!

This book is about how we can:
- Redefine Humans and Being Humans in the New World Order
- Grasp Nature's Laws and Universal Principles
  to Grow from Good to Great
- Apply Proven Systems to Increase Agility,
  Resilience, and Entrepreneurial Spirit
- Gain Insights from our Forefathers to
  Rethink the Meaning of Life
- Tap into the Human Spirit within us
  and Go Forth Courageously

AGILITY is the ability to identify,
change, and adapt continually
to the evolving environment while delivering values.

• • •

An **AGILE** living organism is characterised as

RESILIENT
The flexibility to spring back and recover
from failure and adversity, repeatedly.

MENTALLY TOUGH /GRITTY
The capacity to stay on course to achieve long-term goals,
despite obstacles and criticisms.

CONNECTED
Being mindful and aware of one's surroundings and
has the ability to stay actively engaged.

DETERMINED
The courage to press forward and take action
in fear and doubt.

ADAPTABLE TO CHANGE
The propensity to grow and the eagerness to learn
new ways of thinking, feelings, and doing.

CONTENTS

PROLOGUE

IMAGINE A WORLD half occupied by artificial intelligence and half by humans, living, working, playing, and interacting with one another. We are in that world now. An era where machines and humans are connecting and collaborating to create new realities every day. It used to be a world we once knew is coming, and we need to get ready for. However, nature has it her way and push everyone into it with the COVID-19 pandemic.

Cloud computing, the Internet of Things (IoT), Artificial Intelligence (AI), and smart technology have sped the change to this new normal. The world is moving faster, easier, simpler, and, to a large extend, cheaper. Innovations are mushrooming every day, accelerating at an exponential rate which humans have not experienced before.

Smart machines are now gathering, monitoring, analysing massive data to predict, prescript, and execute complex solutions at a pace many times faster than any human could. These machines are self-learning, self-correcting, and implementing decisions autonomously across the world, free of human intervention. Artificial superintelligence is now learning, perceiving, understanding, and functioning almost like humans, but with immense speed and accuracy, minus the emotional and bias barrier human has.

"Change or die!"

"Change faster than the change, or risk of being left behind!"

These are phrases often cited by world leaders and business consultants. The pace and complexity of change have created high Volatility, Uncertainty, Complexity, and Ambiguity (VUCA) in the new world today. Boundaries and old beliefs are being challenged every minute. Human morals are being tested in every possible way. Collective individuals are becoming more influential. Words coming out from the mouth of an individual can be more potent than any institutions or governments.

Human wellbeing, however, seems going in the opposite direction. Mental health is deteriorating globally at an accelerating speed. Anxiety, depression, and bipolarity have become a common disease in our society today. Suicide, violence, and public displays of anger are soaring. Loneliness has reached epidemic proportions, even though humans are more connected than ever with smart technologies. And the COVID-19 pandemic, which caused major lockdowns globally, escalated this disease by many folds.

The calls received by the mental health and emotional support centres have risen sharply in recent years even before the COVID-19 pandemic. Similarly, the suicide rate is rising. Why has humanity's eudaimonia worsened while the world is becoming smarter?

Is the human race endangered? Are our life and livelihood threatened? Headlines of the layoff, foreclosure, bankruptcies, poverty are flashing in the news every day. As unemployment rates are rising, smart machines are replacing more jobs.

On top of that, questionable behaviours are emerging, especially amongst the people with influence and in positions of power. Overnight fame and wealth rose with borrowed reputation, borrowed trust, and borrowed wealth. Meanwhile, the income inequality gap is widening. The big corporations are getting bigger, while more people are getting poorer. Global debts have jumped more than four times since the Great Recession, while recovery seems implausible.

HUMAN RACE 4.0: The Science of Getting Ahead in the New World Order is a book about how we could move forward post-pandemic with increasingly more machines smarter and faster than us. It is a book about how we can reprogram our physical and psychological DNA to do so.

Throughout our life journey, we have not been spared the trials and tribulations life brings. Nature makes sure of it. Those who can take full control of their physical and mental wellbeing, and their surroundings, are more agile, resilient, and adaptive towards the unprecedented changes in life. But they must play by nature's rules. The ones who could not, would be left behind and eliminated by nature. Who will get ahead? Who would be eliminated? What is nature's selection criteria?

However, while nature would take its course, we can still redesign the course of our life. When we take ownership of what we are becoming, we begin to tap into our inner power and the wealth of resources around us. When we do that together as one, we will reach new heights and live a meaningful life.

"Human Being" is different from "Being Human." The ways our eyes read and process these words now and our mind assign meanings to us, we are humans. Being human is more intricate than being a human. It is the cognition, emotion, and choices we make deliberately to achieve a desirous outcome, yet influenced by our background, childhood, life experiences, and surroundings.

Humans are the complex output of life. Our ability to connect with others at the human level: their needs, dreams, disappointments, fears, and hopes are more crucial, especially in a world full of smart machines. Rethinking the purpose and meaning of being human is, therefore, critical.

How do we do that? The secret lies in our innermost being, and the abundant resources nature provides to us. As humans, we have more than 100 billion brain cells, forming trillions of connections between our inner world with the outer world. Coupled with that, it is also nature's will for energy——the source of life——to transmute from one form to another, creating meaning and bringing joy to life.

While smart machines might be replacing many functions held by humans before, there is still an enormous lot of the universe we have yet discovered. We are living in an exciting time, privileged to have more than 200,000 years of recorded life lessons from our ancestors, guiding us through every revolution and evolution.

Also, many great philosophers, scientists, inventors, and artists in the past have left us with priceless insights into the way nature works. They have discovered the science to achieve whatever we desire. Like Isaac Newton's laws of motion and the behaviours of particles explained by quantum physics which give light to how we can systematically make our desires and dreams come true.

Scientists and philosophers throughout the centuries have found empirical evidence of how universal principles work for us, with us, and against us, even if we are not aware of that. And, after many excruciating painful experiences they have gone in life, they concluded, "Since nature never breaks its laws, we must not."

In a society getting smarter every day, there are two different thoughts on how we could get ahead in life: the logical, scientific, goal-oriented, quantitative approach; and the emotive, psychological, heart-oriented, "soft," qualitative approach. However, as psychologists and scientists, neuroscientists, and artificial intelligence engineers, are working together, we are gaining an advance discovery into the untapped potentials in the humans' DNA and minds.

Hidden behind the rules, principles, logic, and mathematics, is the unspoken magical force which is the nature's gift to the human race. These forces ignited the spirit in humans during the worst of time throughout the centuries and helped us survive the impossible. We must, therefore, find that perfect marriage between these two thoughts, and learn to work with logic and emotions, purpose and profit, science and art again, like many philosophers, scientists, and artists in the past did.

Leonardo Da Vinci, who was famous for many of his paintings, was a polymath, a renaissance man who conceptually invented the self-propelled cart (the car), aerial screw (the helicopter), flying machines (the aeroplane) and many more. His years of anatomical studies of humans and animal bodies helped him produce monumental improvements to his paintings, as he understood how the bones, tendons, and muscles move beneath the naked skin.

Our goal is to rethink humanity, life, purpose, principles, and habits in the new world order. How do we live purposeful even if we did not find our purpose? Why must we live a principle-centred life, while the principle is a double-edged sword which can also work against us?

Thomas Edison, who was famous for not giving up in inventing the electric light bulb, said, "I have not failed 10,000 times. I've just found 10,00 ways that won't work." We might go through many trials, especially as the world is renewing itself after the great reset. We must redefine our purpose as humans amongst the smarter and faster machines.

Perhaps, this is the time we must explore many foreign perspectives which used to irk us. Perhaps this is the time we revisit many ideas we used to reject and ask ourselves, "WHY NOT?" Those who could predict the future can "see" what lies ahead. Those who are courageous enough to step out of their comfort zone are better prepared. Those who are willing to embrace the change now grow faster and prosper more.

We are living in an extraordinary time. We must grow beyond who we used to be for a new world that needs a new human being. While the smart world represents a world full of smart technologies, it is also an era where we should focus on the humans. Hence, this era is also known as the human age.

WHO IS THIS BOOK FOR

WE HAVE ENTERED, the beginning of a new civilisation. The pandemic has pushed the reset button and forced every one of us to rethink about life. It has also caused chaos to our social-economic system. We have to reexamine how do we achieve our desire for our family and loved ones in this new world. We do this by starting with the end in mind.

Our goal is to increase the human in us systematically with the help of smart technologies, to fill our needs to protect and provide for our family and create a meaningful and joy-filled life.

As sons and daughters to our parents, fathers and mothers to our children, partners to our spouse and business associates, leaders of our communities and countries, we are at the forefront of change to prepare our love ones of the new reality.

While we are still riding towards the turbulent aftermath of the pandemic, the ability to adapt and get ahead of the change in the new normal is of paramount importance. Whatever shifts we have experienced so far, that is just the beginning. Most of what we were before are no longer relevant. Ideas that may work well today could become obsolete in a matter of a few weeks.

Boundaries are being tested every second. New rules are formed every minute. We simply must learn on the fly while advancing into the unknown future without the certainty of what lies ahead. We have witnessed that in the way leaders around the world switched between approaches to keep the pandemic at bay.

The last time an unprecedented event which affected millions of lives in human history was way back in the early 1900s. World War I in July 1914 to November 1918 killed more than 22 million people. While the war was still raging, the Spanish flu pandemic broke out in February 1918 and killed more than 50 million people. That pandemic lasted more than twenty-four months till April 1920. Thirty years later, World War II broke out in the 1940s and killed another 60 million people, including 6 million Jews. That pandemic and wars have left many parts of the world in Europe and Asia in ruins.

In preparation to rebuild the world economy while the World War II was still ongoing, 730 delegates from 44 allied nations signed the Bretton Woods Agreement on 22 July 1944 to set up new rules to regulate international monetary systems. That agreement became part of the World Bank Group today.

When this book was published in late 2020, we were still fighting the COVID-19 pandemic. A microscopic virus which has no respect for who we are and how we feel has crippled the world. The second and third wave surged again in October 2020, crashing the world's hope for a speedy recovery.

Who would have imagined a day when more than two-thirds of the 39,000 planes globally were grounded for months, millions of office space left empty, and hundreds of country borders sealed? Who would have believed we would come a day when theme parks, hotels, shopping malls, cinemas, and restaurants shut their doors to customers, and people were told to keep a distance from one another for an unseeable period?

On top of that, the race to adopt smart technologies into a new way of working, living, and doing business is acceleration speedily. The adoption rate in using smart technologies has never been so swiftly before. The pandemic has made many impossibilities possible. In times of crisis, innovations and inventions exploded. Work-from-home and home-schooling which were once frowned upon are now the new norms. Regulators and politicians are approving processes that used to be said, "impossible."

Winston Churchill once said, "Never let a good crisis go to waste." The race to create new solutions is on. This crisis on top of smart technologies which are easily accessible now has provided an exceptional opportunity for many people to create values in uncharted grounds.

Therefore, as humans, we need to develop a new way of thinking, being, and behaving. The characters and competencies we need to have in the new world are different from the past. Furthermore, it is our responsibility for transforming ourselves, the humans, and paving the way for our future generations, as our forefathers have done for us.

One of the most common questions people ask today is, "How do we move ahead after a global pandemic, in a world where smarter and faster machines than the humans are rapidly replacing us, and in a turbulent time when the world order is changing?!"

Human Race 4.0: The Science of Getting Ahead in the New World Order, is a book which explains how a new world order is replacing the order we were so familiar with. This book also aims to systematically decode how humans are constructed internally and connected to our surroundings externally. By that, we can reprogram both our physical and psychological DNA to get ahead and still, creating a meaningful and joy-filled life, in whatever circumstances surrounding us.

Smart machines will continue to replace many functions used to perform by humans. They are processing both non-linear and unstructured data which give birth to many new algorithms we have not thought of before. That has helped us discover many newer innovations faster. Smart machines can also perform millions of tasks while making improvements all the time, without the physical and emotional barriers humans have.

With the faster capacity to analyse data and execute decisions, the performance of smart machines surpasses humans in many ways. They are increasing productivity, efficiency, and accuracy by many folds, and reaching close to zero mistakes. It is not surprising that companies today much prefer smart machines than humans. If they do not, they would be left behind.

On top of the autonomously smart machines today, artificial neural networks, a computing system designed to simulate the way the human brain analyses and processes information, is already mimicking humans brain activity. Artificial superintelligence (ASI), machines with "self-aware" with capabilities far superior to humans and is capable of operating morally like a human is already in the pipeline. But could machines eventually evoke emotions, needs, beliefs, and desires like humans? Would it come to a day when superintelligence robots overthrow and enslave humans?

Despite all the smart machines and superintelligence technologies, they are created through the studies and imitations of the anatomy, physiology, and psychology of humans, including the neural networks, cognitive patterns, emotional filters, perceptions, and human moral code. However, there is still a whole universe in the deoxyribonucleic acid (DNA) and minds of humans yet to be explored.

Although science can explain how nature works, it cannot explain why it works the way it does. Engineers and neurologists generally agree that, while we have decades of the study done to understand how the human brain and mind operate, we know about 10% of the total function. And we only discovered less than 10% of the molecular elements in DNA.

While we know our DNA determines our physical being and how our conscious mind influences behaviours, we have not yet understood why it processes the way it is. We know how to be more knowledgeable, skilled, competent, and increase motivation, raise the human spirit, but we do not understand why our brain processes information the way it does. While we know our personality, traits, intuition, and conscientiousness are encoded in our DNA, we do not know how it is encoded there.

Many scientists conclude there must be a "Creator" who holds the answers to the many questions we still do not have answers yet. There must be a higher being than us who ensures everything in life exists as it is, the one who empowers the entire ecology and gives life to forms. It is not surprising, too, 90% of Nobel Prize winners between 1901 and 2000 believe in the existence of God. Those who do not eventually acknowledge there must be a higher being to explain many of the life phenomena we still wonder.

There is still much to discover about the universe and "human" in us. Although we do not yet know precisely what the future might look like and who we will become, many scientists, economists, and philosophers have already reimagined the new human being and being humans in the new reality.

And, perhaps, when artificial superintelligence and humans integrate, we will understand God, matter, the universe, and humans better. Meanwhile, since Genesis, the beginning of life, humans have been finding new ways to manipulate tools to improve lives, we will continue to find new ways to advance in the new world.

SYNOPSIS

THIS BOOK is constructed in three parts: A New World order, The Human Race, and The Race of Being Human.

Part 1, A Smart New World, consists of three chapters. Chapter 1 gives an overview of how innovations have triggered industrial revolutions and improved productivity, hence, affecting the world economically, politically, and socially since the mid-18th century.

By the turn of the 21st century, the world has entered into the 4th industrial revolution, or IR 4.0. And as with the last three revolutions, innovation and evolution accelerated. But the industrial revolution this time is different. The 4th industrial revolution is the epic of all, affecting every industry in every aspect of life, at which speed we have yet seen. On top of that, the 2020 COVID-19 pandemic has brutally pushed everyone into a light-speed change, metaphorically and literally.

In chapter 1, we will have a glimpse of how the new world order would look like, with a deeper understanding of what is causing the light-speed change. We will also gain a more comprehensive view of how all these changes are reshaping geopolitical and social-economic relationships in the world. Every sector, including agriculture, manufacturing, supply-chain, healthcare, retail, finance, and technology, have been disrupted.

In Chapter 2, we will dive more in-depth and explore how the industrial revolution transforms civilisation. While smart machines communicate and work together with other machines and humans, new forms of social interactions, norms, and agreements are emerging. New economic giants in the world are rising to replace the old ones. Governments and formal institutions seem losing ground to corporations and individuals.

Technological innovation has always been focusing on increasing productivity, efficiency, and quality of life. Yet humans have never felt so helpless and emasculated as we are today. Why is that happening? What is the root cause? How can we curb that? We are racing against time to fight a plague bigger than COVID-19––the deterioration of the humans!

Chapter 3 will bring us back to our centeredness. Although we have access to extensive education and opportunities in our fingertips today, only 59% of the world population have access to the internet and internet tools can do so. Moreover, for those who can, we are being bombarded with enormous amounts of information which deter us from our core purpose.

We also have to deal with escalating cyber-security problems, frauds, and scams, which will be amounting to an estimated loss of tens of billion dollars worldwide by 2022! On top of that, there are many online marketers selling ideas to anyone they can reach globally. How do we differentiate what works and what won't? How can we tell a genuine from the fakes? How do we distinguish realism from make-believe?

On the bright side, we have abundant resources to guide us today. We are blessed to be living in a time when we have many historical records, wisdom from the past, words from the wise, and nature's will to show us the way forward. The truth is, while the approaches we choose to get ahead might change over time, our purpose and needs as humans remain the same since life exists.

Part 2 of this book, *The Human Race*, is about the human being in us; how our mind and our physical brain work together. In Chapter 4, we will take an anatomical and physiological tour into our inner brain. We seek to understand how our brain is constructed and pre-programmed to work with the outer world. By comprehending the structures and functions of our brains, we gain better insights on ways to reverse our physical DNA to increase our agility and resilience to adapt in a fast-changing world.

In Chapter 5, we will take another tour into our psychological being, the way our subconscious and unconscious minds work all the time to influence our conscious mind and physical being. When we bring to our awareness the hidden minds, we can rewire our psychological DNA to get ahead.

Finally, we will examine how our mind systematically shapes the physical world. The reality of our circumstances is first created in our mind. We can train our mind to realise our desires and dreams systematically and physically. In other words, we will use a scientific approach to make the "Law of Attraction" work in our favours.

The knowledge about human beings is different from being human. Part 3 of this book, *The Race of Being Human*, focuses on how we can become a better human. Through the Internet of Things and cloud computing, we are becoming a mega global citizen. We can connect and collaborate with anyone globally to realise our desires and dreams together.

As Aristotle said, "The whole is greater than the sum of its parts." When we come together as one entity, we will break through many barriers and create new possibilities. The multifaceted composition of perceptions, beliefs, ideas, values, hopes, faith, and love opens up a new wealth of resources we have never seen before.

Our ability to interact, relate, negotiate, and assimilate foreign views is crucial for survival and thrive in the new world. The ability to connect at the humanly, psychological, and emotional level has become a priceless asset in a smart, logical, and mechanical world. Our ability to work through perceptions, emotions, needs, values, and prejudices to achieve common goals is more valuable than any technology combined.

And last, but not the least, who we have become originated from our inner being and influenced by the world. The results of our lives have everything to do with the world views we hold, the values we embrace, the decisions we make, and the actions we take. Every one of us is given the gift of freedom to choose, despite the surrounding circumstances. When we systematically understood and reprogrammed our physical and psychological beings; when we do so with appreciation and respect for nature's will, we could re-create in the new reality. Throughout the history of revolutions, wars, and nature-induced disasters, those who did play a significant part in forming the world we are in today. And so, we will.

PART 1

A NEW WORLD ORDER

1

A NEW REALITY
THE HUMAN ERA

---

*Industrial revolution was another one of those
extraordinary jumps forward in the story of civilisation.*
— Stephen Gardiner

TEN YEARS AGO, I came across the story of a businessman who wanted to give two of his sons $1 million each. He also let them choose how they would like to receive the money: a lump sum of $1 million, or a penny a day, doubling each day for 30 days. The first son decided to take the $1 million in a lump sum and get on with his life. So, the businessman gave him a lump sum of $1 million and sent him off.

As the second son, he chose to receive a penny a day and double each day for 30 days. The businessman gave him a penny on the first day, two pennies on the second day, four pennies on the third day, and doubled every day for the next thirty days. On the fifteenth day, the second son received only a total of $163.84. On the twenty-seventh day, he only received a total amount of $671,008,64. But, on the thirtieth day, he received $5,368,709.12! That is more than $1 million by five times. If the businessman decides to continue giving to the son, the amount would have doubled to $10,737,418.24 on the thirty-first day and exceeded the $1 billion on the forty-first day!

1

That doubling effect is from a well-known mathematical equation called "Double a Penny a Day". Small, insignificant actions, when performed consistently over time, produce the compounding effect that leads to massive results.

Similarly, the way we spend our time and energy has the same compounding effect on our lives. If we were to eat the best burger in town for dinner every night, we might overlook the impact to our waistline on the first few days. But imagine that extra layers of fat under our skin, in our body after a few weeks of having a burger for dinner every night. On top of the health risks that come with it too! When we put ourselves in a positive environment and engage in empowering activities: investing in continuous learning, reading well-researched books, spending time with solution-oriented people, setting and achieving goals, we will be better prepared to get ahead in life.

We are experiencing the compounding effect of evolution today. The advancement of technology has reached an epic level. The speed of innovation over the centuries has increased and is accelerating expeditiously. On top of the 2020 pandemic, smart technologies have altered most of how we used to live, work, and do business.

The world has become a gigantic, intertwined, boundless, complex being, with smarter, faster, and more fluid technologies. Artificial Intelligence (AI) tools and assistants have become easily accessible and more affordable. Anyone can design solutions at a ground-breaking speed with many smart tools available to us online.

Our world is also becoming smaller through the convergence of collective effort and, simultaneously, growing larger through the divergence of variety. Every one of us has the whole world in our hands now.

In megacities like Shanghai, people can buy almost anything and access to all types of services through their smartphone. Super app like WeChat allows us to pay bills, transfer money, shopping, order food, hire rides, book movies, train, or airline tickets, buy insurance, or make an investment.

News goes viral in seconds as people share what they see and capture with their phones through social media much faster than traditional news channels. The world of the internet has allowed for the wealth of information to be exchanged among billions of users worldwide.

Megacorporations are trying their best, using machine learning to moderate conversations amount the community in social media twenty-four hours a day, seven days a week. Marketers, public relations, governments, companies, and collective individuals are using massive data collected from social media to reprogram and manipulate public perception.

The indoctrination of ideas is just a click away, both for the good and evil. All happening now with the accelerating development of a tiny computer chip which can be found in every machine and device we use today.

POWERED BY SMART CHIPS

In 1965, one of Intel's co-founders, Gordon Moore, noticed that the numbers of transistors per square inch on the integrated circuit chip had doubled every two years since the chip was invented in 1959. The processing speed in processors has increased twice as fast every two years while the cost is halved. As innovation advances, Moore said, this doubling of processing speed and minimisation of size every two years will continue indefinitely. His observation is known as Moore's Law.

Today, the numbers of transistors installed in a single chip are doubling up every 18 months. Advanced manufacturing and advanced materials have made this possible. Chips in every device we are using are getting smaller. Apple launched its latest Macbook and Mac Mini in November 2020 with the latest M1 chip, a

5-nanometre chip packed with 16 billion transistors. Nanochips as tiny as 2.5-nanometre, named as the "Smart Dust" packed with more than 30 billion transistors, is already in the research stage, scheduled to be ready between 2024 and 2027. Putting it into perspective, a nanometre is one-thousandth of a millimetre, and the diameter of a human deoxyribonucleic acid (DNA) is round 2-nanometer. Imagine what else we can do with chips almost the size of our DNA.

The need for more powerful chips has climbed sharply over the years as the demand for faster processors to operate devices packed with every possible function we can think of is skyrocketing. Today, chips are transmitting billions of data in nanosecond intervals. Our need for speed is intensifying exponentially.

Imagine how many data transmission takes place in every autonomous vehicle, sensing and responding trillions of data from other vehicles, the road ahead, curbing at the side, moving animals and running children, the temperature and potholes on the road, and the rain, dust, flying objects directly across the windscreen. Multiply that by millions of vehicles and other machinery that is an immense amount of data transmitting every second. And we need powerful chips that can operate processes at extremely high speed to do that.

The research and development for faster and smaller chips remain the centrepiece of smart technologies today, with the sole to quicken operating processes. It is the same with the many innovations preceding that, the single more important purpose of innovation and invention is to find new ways of increasing productivity, efficiency, and effectiveness. Evolution of chips, just like the advancement of technology, will continue until humans discover newer, faster, more cost-efficient ways to operate machines and robots.

Transistors in the chips are electrical switches that can be switched on or off like switches for light bulbs. That allows and blocks electrons to pass through, hence, creating the binary code language of 1 (on) and 0 (off). All computers before quantum computing use binary systems because it is safer and more reliable, and use the least amount of circuitry which require the least amount of space, energy, and cost.

Today, transistors for electronic chips have reached a level that would be too thin to prevent the electrons from penetrating. When that happens, electrons can disappear from one side and appear on the other, creating a quantum tunnelling effect. In other words, the transistor could not generate 0 (off) anymore when it is no longer thick enough to block electrons from passing through.

To solve this problem, engineers have begun to use photons or light waves to create photonic or optical transistors. Since photons of different wavelengths do not interact, it is possible to multiplex or combine several input signals into a single common line output to transport them simultaneously over a single fibre.

With that, the optical transistors can switch signals a thousand times faster than electron transistors. And, photons do not consume electricity and do not generate heat when they travel. Therefore, photonic integrated circuits are more energy-efficient than electron transistors. That also means, with photonic chips, our machine no longer need cooling systems.

While Moore's Law on electronic chips might come to an ending, but the doubling up of processing speed continues with "light-wave" optical chips. That would be the next giant step in computing, including the 5th generation or 5G network. We can now say, the world is changing at the speed of light, figuratively and literally.

The continuing betterment in integrated circuit chip technology is the reason for the emergence of smarter, faster, smaller, and cheaper technologies today. Including many of the machine, robot, hand-held devices, wearable, and sensors we are using now. By combining supercomputers, cloud-computing, artificial intelligence, big data, and the Internet of Things, we have entered into a new reality where the blurring lines between physical, digital, and biological spheres. That is why we are said to have entered into the 4th industrial revolution now.

Some of us are just beginning to experience the dawn of industrial revolution 4.0. Yet, some have wholly embraced smart technologies in every aspect of their lives, in the way they work, live, play, and communicate.

Meanwhile, we will be entering into another "newer" reality we have yet experienced when every smart device and machine in the world is fully integrated and interconnected. And when artificial superintelligence replaces artificial intelligence. That "newer" reality will completely change the way we protect and provide for our loved ones, connect and relate with one another, create and co-create together.

Like all revolutions in the past, the industrial revolutions change the way we receive education, do business, work, play, transact, and communicate. It will change every fibre of our society at the individual level, communities, and governments; economically, politically, and societal all around the world. Revolutions will continue to cause evolutions in civilisations and humans.

The next crucial question would be, what exactly is the industrial revolution 4.0? What would the world look like at the advance level of the industrial revolution 4.0? What role would we, the humans play in a superintelligence, automated world, half-filled with machines smarter and faster than us? How do we prepare ourselves for the new reality? To answer these questions, we will go back to the history of the industrial revolution in the 18th century and examine the effects on social contracts in Chapter 2.

INDUSTRIAL REVOLUTIONS

The 1st industrial revolution, or also known as the age of mechanical production, happened after the Medieval Era, at the beginning of the early modern society. It started in the middle of 18th century in Great Britain and spread to the rest of Europe and America from 1760 to 1840.

The 1st industrial revolution was a period in which everything that was done by hand during the pre-industrial era was revolutionised with the invention of water and steam power. The invention of mechanical tools powered by water and steam began. The factory system started to develop. The rural agricultural society also began to give way to industrialisation and urbanisation. Trades, businesses, and living standards among the peasants began to rise.

Meanwhile, ships and trains powered by steam revolutionised human movement and accelerated expeditions across the oceans. Factories sprouted like mushrooms, and new communities start forming around them.

As the 1st industrial revolution took shape in the early 19th century, many unskilled cheap labours flowed into the city to earn a living. Working conditions were terrible and unsafe. Children as young as five years old often worked in shifts of twelve to fourteen hours, alongside with the adults, and were often abused and tumbled upon.

The industrial revolution also increased the concentration of material wealth among manufacturers and traders. Wealth began to change hands from the upper-class, the aristocrats with hereditary rank and title, to the middle-class, the bourgeoisie who were more concerned with the value of property and preservation of capital to secure their economic supremacy in society. That caused a powerful force for societal shift. The middle-class society began to gain more power over the country rulers and aristocrats.

Image 1.1: The Industrial Revolutions

INDUSTRY 1.0	INDUSTRY 2.0	INDUSTRY 3.0	INDUSTRY 4.0
Mid 18th Century	Mid 19th Century	Mid 20th Century	Early 21st Century
Mechanical Production Age	Science and Technology Age	Information and Digitization Age	Smart Technology and Human Age
Water and Steam power	Electricity, Railroad Telephone	Computers, Internet Information Technology	Internet of things Artificial intelligent 3D, advance materials
Mechanized productions, Rural to urban, Governments go global	Mass production, Companies go global	Automated production, Individuals go global	Intelligent, flexible Personalize, customized Autonomous machines
Manual labor replaced by machinery	Cities and communities expanded and connects	Automation increases productions	Lines between physical, digital and biological realms blurred

Adapted from www.123rf.com image

As inventions and innovations continued, the 2nd industrial revolution, also known as the age of science and technology, began in the1870s. It lasted until the mid-19th century, primarily in Britain, Continental Europe, North America, and Japan. The enormous expansion of railroad networks, electrical energy, and telegraph lines later significantly improved connectivity, communication, expedited the widespread technological adoption. Mass migration of humans and ideas became possible and faster. That has facilitated the growth beyond a few concentrated cities. More companies began to expand globally.

The 3rd industrial revolution, also known as the digital revolution, began in the second half of the 20th century, in the 1950s. It is also known as the Information Age. It started with the first computer, Electrical Numerical Integrator and Calculator (ENIAC), which was introduced in 1946 by Dr John Mauchly and J. Presper Eckert.

That was followed by the invention of the integrated circuit in 1959, followed by the internet in 1960, personal computers in

1974, and the world wide web in 1989. Digital technology was born along with information technology systems and led to faster global interactions.

Significant changes took place with the transition from analogue electronics and mechanical systems to digital systems. Rapid advancements in computing power, using logic processors, and information technology led to the digitalisation and the automation of production.

As technology grew and became cloud-enabled, megacorporations started to globalise supply chain, and that set the stage for a newer way of producing, processing, exchanging information, and raising productivity and productions to a whole new level.

Digitalisation impacted every industry simultaneously, transforming every way every industry is connecting with the others, paving the way for the succeeding industrial revolution.

INDUSTRIAL REVOLUTION 4.0

The 4th industrial revolution is also widely known as the "Smart Age" is a time when technologies have become smarter, faster, and more efficient than humans. The 4th industrial revolution took automated production to a whole new level. A time when the internet, robotics, artificial intelligence, augmented and virtual reality comes together and blurs the lines between physical, digital, and biological spheres.

Smart machines now autonomously find solutions, form, and execute decisions with minimum or no human involvement. Physical and emotional barriers do not hinder these machines humans have. Productivity and efficiency increased sharply, while mistakes and wastage minimised dramatically.

Smart machines are accessing massive data, communicating with other machines, and humans in a cyber-physical system (CPS) today. Physical-world integrating with computing networks and creating new realities beyond the physical world. Hence, we have autonomous automobile systems, industrial control systems, and many other robotic systems managed by computer-based algorithms.

We now have a computer-generated simulation, an artificial three-dimensional environment in which we can immerse virtually. City planners and factory builders can have a realistic view of their project layout virtually, allowing them to study how each building or equipment fits into and responds to the environment before physically constructing it.

House buyers now can step into their new house and decorate every room virtually before making purchase decisions. Medical professionals today have a more complex, three-dimensional view of human anatomy as they diagnose what is going on with their patients and give a more accurate prognosis.

The cyber-physical system has also allowed for virtual conferencing, performance arts, career fairs, trade shows, travelling and tours, and securing sales of properties and cars a reality to millions of clients while they were staying at home during the global pandemic lockdowns.

In addition to cloud-based processes or cloud computing, and the Industrial Internet of Things (IIoT), smart technologies with artificial intelligence connect every aspect of manufacturing, from the point of sourcing of raw materials and production, through to sales and last-mile delivery to end-users.

Increasingly, more manufacturers are going direct to consumers (D2C), cutting through distribution channels in the middle. On top of that, straight-through-processing are eliminating the entire value chain in the middle, and hence, opportunities and profit margins of distributors significantly. Jobs that used to require humans to generate records, reports, issue purchase orders, invoices, bills, verify, approve, and monitor machines instantly displaced with smart technologies.

Furthermore, as technology becomes more flexible, masses of consumer data are being collected and analysed. That has allowed for customisation of personalised solutions without limiting consumers to one-size-fits-all predefined selections.

Artificial intelligence has also activated innovations like genetic sequencing and editing, biotechnology, miniaturised sensors smaller than human deoxyribonucleic acid (DNA), three-dimensional (3D) printing, 5th generation network (5G), and blockchain. That impacts every industry and every aspect of life we can imagine.

Engineers and scientists from various fields are now working closely together, combining and integrating their intelligence to innovate and invent more tools to increase the quality of work and life. Organ-on-a-chip (OOC) or artificial organs which mimic vital human organs and the cell environment is one such example. Micro-fabrication and tissue engineers have developed the artificial organs––micro-devices as small as an AA battery, and contributed substantially to medical field drug testing.

By using artificial organs, drug tests can be carried out without endangering animals and humans. That has also brought the possibility for personalised and self-serving medicines into reality soon. Micro-devices like these reduced costs and accelerated scientific research furthermore. Meanwhile, scientists have also started imagining ways to kill and remove cancer cells and repair DNA with nano-robotics; artificial superintelligence robots smaller than our red blood cells which can 'swim' in our blood veins.

Inspired by the evolutionary theorem and how humans receive and process information in the brain, scientists have incorporated the genetic evolutionary algorithm into artificial intelligence. Evolutionary machine learning is optimising themselves, with a generic population-based metaheuristic, computer science and mathematical optimisation algorithm.

Through the process of natural selection, the genetic evolutionary algorithm artificial superintelligence machines can modify and generate new decisions, and eliminate previous generations of decisions without humans intervention. The evolutionary machines perform millions of tests and retest on every possible algorithm it can "think of" to get better results progressively at speeds much faster than humans. And because the evolutionary machines do not have feelings, it won't feel "hurt" by failed tests like humans, they can move on quickly to test out the succeeding algorithm they can think of.

Companies like DeepMind, Google Brain, OpenAi, and many emerging artificial intelligence companies are accelerating innovation with evolutionary machine learning algorithms. Smart computer systems today are capable of performing tasks used to require human intelligence, including visual perception, face, voice, and tone recognition, as well as language translation.

Smart technologies are also solving more challenging and complex problems better than humans. We now have artificially smarter and faster, self-improving, self-optimising, self-learning, and a self-adapting machine working and living with us.

How is the industrial revolution 4.0 different from 3.0 and 2.0? I usually like to explain the various industrial revolutions by this simple analogy, "If we use paper and pencil, we are still in 2.0. If we use any form of digital tools, including our smartphones, we are in 3.0. When ALL the smart machines and devices and materials are connected and combined, shared via cloud-computing; when we rely on the smart tools to autonomously share, analyse, formulate and execute decisions 24-7 without our inputs, we are in 4.0."

There are still innovations we have not yet anticipated. When the 5th generation network (5G), which transfers data 100 to 250 times faster than the 4th generation network (4G) is in place, we will enter into another realm of reality. With low latency, we can experience real-time response without delay, transmitting trillions of bits of data worldwide.

Imagine being able to experience a live-streamed of a full-scale symphony orchestra performance by a hundred musicians playing simultaneously from different parts of the world without experiencing the lagging. Animators and illustrators from all over the world can work on an artwork concurrently. Surgeons from various locations can conduct robotic surgery on the same patient remotely. The 5th generation (5G) network will shift us out of the new normal we just got in today.

In a more advanced level, neuroscientists and artificial intelligence engineers have started working on artificial consciousness while we are still puzzled with how consciousness is created and works. Many neuroscientists hold the view that consciousness is an emergent property of the brain, generated by the neuronal consciousness correlations (NCC). They believe the neural changes happen in relation with specific experience with the environment, caused by neuronal complexity, and perhaps without any adaptive value.

Precisely what is the emergent property, how it emerges, and from which a specific neuronal process? That still up for debate.

However, with artificial consciousness, self-optimising machines selectively structure information received, optimise self-analysis, and execute decisions according to the specific goals that the machine has formulated before that. Therefore, forming perceptions of the world and creating representations of the surroundings by itself.

In other words, artificial consciousness is imitating the functioning of human consciousness, minus the disempowering emotional state. Artificial superintelligence does that by combining logic with various possible forms of human emotions, fears, values, and needs. Then, it generates weighted decisions and executes the decision systematically without being affected emotionally to achieve predefined desired outcomes.

We are still at the dawn of understanding how human consciousness works, and for that, there are still limitations to how scientists and engineers develop artificial consciences. But whatever we could imagine in the past has become to pass.

What would be the future of humans when artificial superintelligence machines started to shape their consciousness, intuition, and moral code like humans? Will artificial superintelligence robots become our law enforcers? Will smart technologies one day overrule and enslave humans? How do we ensure they behave ethically?

I met the chief data scientist of an international bank a few years ago who said, data scientists have access to an immense amount of highly sensitive data that can raise or destroy a country, or the world. The character of data scientists is more critical than their smartness and skills. It is like all other professions. Mind-set and heart-set must supersede skill-set.

As the saying goes, "Great power comes with great responsibility," if we want to ensure the smart machines remain ethical, we, the humans must first, be ethical. We must use the power brought to us with smart technologies conscientiously for the benefit of the human race. Virtue, therefore, must become the centre of who we are becoming in the new world order.

That brings us to the next question, amid these rapid changes after the great reset by the 2020 pandemic, and a world powered by artificial superintelligence machines, how do we move forward?

NEW HUMAN ERA

As smart machines are getting more intelligent, taking over many jobs performed by humans before, it seems like there will be less job opportunity for humans. The Future Jobs Report by World Economic Forum projected, by 2025, automation will replace around 85 million jobs. But, 97 million jobs are predicted to emerge concurrently. However, just as in any change, the skills-set, mind-set, and heart-set required in the new world are different from what most of us have today.

The hard skills like deep analytic skills, complex problem-solving, knowing which technology to use, are in demand. But the more critical skills are in the soft skills, including self-management, face up to the pressure of the rapidly changing and ambiguous environment, and working with people including understanding the needs and challenges humans face through different life-cycles and life-stages. Josh Bersin, the founder of Bersin by Deloitte, said, "The future of work has little to do with technology, artificial intelligence, or algorithms. It is all about people and organisations and how we work with them."

Many companies today are urging their employees to be more agile, resilient, and have the entrepreneurial spirit, to be more self-driven and adaptive to an uncertain and unknown future. They want their employees to be more creative and innovative and able to find solutions and new ways of doing things independently while having the foresight to make the right decisions. Companies are also wanting their employees to work together and formulate common goals, to take on full ownership and be responsible for the results of their actions.

As smart technologies automate manual repetitive tasks, integrating workflow across all functions, and standardising infrastructure with self-serving tools accessible to all, the future of work requires us to be a well-rounded innovator with sophisticated ability to collaborate cross-functionally, and responsible for end-to-end delivery together.

No matter how smart we are, if we never know how to work with people, we will never succeed. People skills——the ability to understand human emotions and deal with people in their inner world——are crucial in the new world where smart technologies are taking care much of our outer world tasks.

Most of us would have worked with people who are ingenious, innovative, and smarter than most, but failed to create desired results. We have also seen how discussion can get heated and quickly turn south, and how anger flares when emotions are high. All these happen because, as humans, we live in two worlds: the outer world, the surface where behaviours can be seen and words can be heard; and the inner world, where values, beliefs, and emotion hide.

Dealing with people and their inner world is more challenging than working with the outer world. Learning to elicit and understand the inner world is more difficult than acquiring skills to handle technology and processes. Human minds are much more sophisticated and complicated than machines.

Napoleon Hill said in his book *Think and Grow Rich*, "Thoughts are things, and our mind is a powerful tool when thoughts are mixed with the determination of purpose, persistence, and a burning desire." Many psychologists, neuroscientists, and philosophers, including Socrates, John Locke, and Jim Rohn vouched our minds create our reality in physical form. Emotion is a form of energy and energy that can transmute and transform matters and forms.

Hence, everything we think of in our mind and believe about the world will create our reality in physical form. That is why it is said our subconscious and subconscious minds, which are below our awareness level, control over 90% of our decisions, and therefore, the results in our life. Hence, to get ahead amidst uncertainty and the unknown, we must learn to deal with the fear and pressure in the inner world of humans.

Piyush Gupta, the CEO of DBS Group, the most innovative banking and financial institution in Singapore in the 2010s, said, "The skills we need for the future are soft skills. We will need philosophy, psychology, and emotional science because the biggest challenge in society is to reinvent the rules of society." And if I may add to what he said, the studies of history, economics, and political science, provide us valuable insights on how humans thrive through every adversity and adversity in the past.

That said, we are blessed to be in a time without the lack of know-how and wisdom to get ahead. Humans have withstood and emerged better from centuries of the worst sufferings brought by the technological, political, and economical revolutions, as well as wars and nature-induced disasters. Every revolution has caused evolution of civilisation. At the epic revolution of technological today, where superintelligence machines are already working independently of humans, it is, perhaps, a new era of humans.

As human beings,
our greatness lies not so much in being able to remark the world,
but in being able to remark ourselves.
— Mahatma Gandhi

2

A NEW ORDER
SOCIAL CONTRACT

All human beings are born free and equal in dignity and rights.
They are endowed with reason and conscience
and should act towards one another in a spirit of brotherhood.
— Universal Declaration of Human Rights

A FEW YEARS AGO, I met an elderly gentleman from the United States at a business seminar. He is Ray Keller. Ray was seventy years old when I first met him. He came from a family of farmers. When he was a young boy, he would spend his days riding far and wide with his father, grandfather, and few other older men to search for lands for farming. What they would look for were forests rich and fertile with full-grown trees and many woody plants with rivers and streams flowing through the land.

When they found a fine piece of land, they would spend many months to fell the trees by using only hand tools, axes and saws, digging up massive root nets, and turning the ground over with wooden wedge-shaped implements pulled by oxen. The work was laborious, and the hours were long, with a lot of moxie and muscle.

Moving forward a few decades later, the farming industry changed drastically. Machinery is being deployed. And today, we witness miles of agriculture lands remotely monitored and managed with smart technologies. Irrigation, fertilisation, and pest control are now being managed autonomously with minimum human inputs. Drones and remotely controlled Global Positioning System (GPS)-enabled machinery is being used to scan, plant, fertilise, and harvest crops.

Farmers today are well-educated. Many of them armed themselves with the knowledge of modern technology, environmental sciences, social media, entrepreneurial acumen, and agricultural and plant biology. They have access to massive real-time data and rely on smart technologies to monitor climate change, control greenhouse effects, detect vulnerabilities and corrosion in devices, and maintain hardware autonomously with minimal human inputs.

Ray also shared, as technology advanced and innovation was changing the agriculture industry, some adapting quickly and others don't. Those who adopted new technology early expanded their farms by many folds, and some became farmers who own many lands internationally and supplied their products to their clients globally. Some moved downstream, and many became wholesalers and distributors for the products from the farmers. But those who could not cope with the change left the industry altogether.

According to Ray, the term "innovation disruption" is not a new word coined this century. It has been around for many decades before our time. He also explained how innovation is a character that has always been around since life exists, and innovations continue to disrupt and replace existing methods. That is why change is constant, and it's part of life.

Since life has existed, humans have been manipulating and improving tools to make hunting, collecting, farming, distributing, and preserving food better, faster, and easier. The pace of innovation which disrupts and affects every aspect of human life today, has increased expeditiously.

Smart technologies and machines are changing the industrial and business landscape every day. Machines are deployed to monitor, measure, and manage almost everything, anytime, anywhere.

Wearable devices tracking vital signs in the human body are used to ensure workers work in highly dangerous and hazardous areas for their safety, especially in sectors like oil and gas depots, quarries, construction sites, underground, deep sea, jungles, war zones; industries dealing with heavy machinery and highly explosive materials.

In logistics, supply chain and retail operators are optimising and improving inventory control with a microelectromechanical system (MEMS), tracking every product movement and safety from the shelf in production facilities to boxes, pallets, and transport containers to the shelf of the retail store.

In a mature model, the manufacturer-to-consumer (D2C) has reduced the middle distribution channels significantly. Manufacturers connect information relating to product movements from the point-of-sale directly back to their original equipment manufacturers (OEMs) or suppliers. The D2C has dramatically reduced a massive amount of inventories, risks, and works in between the entire value chain. Bringing consumer pricing down. This has also lowered margins for mid-stream business and job opportunities.

Smart technology plays a crucial role in the life sciences and healthcare industry as well. It has strengthened collaboration between health professionals to improve the speed and accuracy in diagnosis, prognosis, and treatment.

During the 2020 pandemic outbreak, China uses supercomputers with machine learning, a form of artificial intelligence to analyse hundreds of images generated by computed tomography (CT) to identify COVID-19 patients. According to Dr Xu Ba, a lead scientist at the Tianjin Medical University, a task like this would usually take an experienced doctor about 15 minutes to go through 300 images generated by CT scan. But the artificial intelligence diagnostic tool only takes about 10 seconds to do so.

That device, located at the National Supercomputer Centre in Tianjin, has helped many medical professionals quickly distinguish between patients infected with the novel coronavirus and those who frequently suffer from pneumonia or other diseases. During the outbreak, more than 30 hospitals in Wuhan and other cities accessed the system via cloud-computing and received results from computers and mobile phones.

Smart technologies are already being used to identify, monitor, and recommend solutions. Eventually, smart technologies, including advanced materials and 3D printing, would enable the production of tailor-made and individualised medicine according to the patient's typical condition and genetic profile.

In a paper published by researchers at the University of California, Berkeley, the implantable tracking chip for monitoring health is already in the pipeline. Potentially, the neural "Smart Dust", smaller than the smallest human blood cells, could be scattered into the human brain to monitor and control brain function.

The global market value of digital healthcare is expected to reach $511 billion by 2026, according to Acumen Research & Consulting, a market research firm. Specifically, in the field of mobile health, wireless solutions, and telemedicine to increase self-managed care and independence of patients.

Many organisations have invested their resources in healthcare technology and services, including megacorporations like Apple, Amazon, Alibaba, and Alphabet, Google's parent company.

Andrew Paul McAfee, a principal research scientist at the MIT's Sloan School of Management, said, "For thousands of years, from horizontal to the discovery of steam power and electricity, human history has changed. Today we have artificial intelligence to overcome many limitations humans have.

Artificial intelligence technology works faster than humans without emotional barriers and biases and without needing time to rest and recover like humans. Artificial intelligence captures all forms of data, linear and non-linear, structured and unstructured, in milliseconds, making calculation decisions more complicated and complex than humans could.

Artificial intelligence collects and processes trillions of data from around the world in minutes, recognising subtle patterns in the overwhelming amount of data that humans tend to overlook. Machine learning in artificial intelligence stays up to date with the current field every minute and every second, keeping us, humans, informed with the latest updates and recommend solutions to us, and even autonomously ascertain and execute the best solutions without humans' interventions.

Deep learning in artificial intelligence helps humans make in-roads into intricate work humanly impossible. It offers us the opportunity to optimise our professional and private lives. When we adopt artificial intelligence and intelligent assistance into our life, we increase the betterment of our jobs, businesses, and life. When we work with smart technologies, life can become more meaningful and joy-filled in this new reality.

Artificial intelligence will further boost productivity in critical sectors like healthcare, agriculture, telecommunications and finance. In September 2018, McKinsey reported that artificial intelligence has the potential to create a $13 trillion growth in the world economy by 2030, expanding gross domestic product (GDP) by 16%.

In China alone, artificial intelligence is expected to boost the country's economy by 26% over the next 13 years, adding $7 trillion to GDP. China is already well ahead of its goal of becoming a $150 billion global leader in artificial intelligence by 2030. Looking at the way China has handled the coronavirus pandemic, it has demonstrated maturity in adopting smart technologies to solve mega problems.

ATTRIBUTES OF "SMART" WORLD

There are three key attributes which continue to change through every revolution. These attributes are the reasons for the evolutions of civilisation and our reality. The attributes are speed, width, and depth.

1. **SPEED**

   The most obvious change we are encountering today is speed. The speed at which we interact, collaborate, transact, or start a business has jumped many folds compared to two decades ago. The pace of change has accelerated with the constant development of chips found in all devices available today, and the speed of change will increase many times more compared to what we are experiencing now.

   Meanwhile, multi-disciplinary and cross-functional collaborations have also significantly increased the imagination, creativity, and innovation globally. 3-dimensional (3-D) printing has gone beyond prototyping, rapid tooling and additive manufacturing, enabling manufacturers to produce longer-lasting and safer products in large quantities, faster and cheaper, by using advanced materials.

   GitHub is one of the prominent examples of people around the world gathered to solve issues together. As an artificial intelligence-powered open-source hub, GitHub provides hosting services to software developers worldwide, so they can jointly discover, share, build, and solve problems for their clients.

   GitHub is the largest host of source code in the world today. As of January 2020, GitHub already has over 40 million users, with more than 100 million repositories. There are already over 2.9 million businesses and organisations use GitHub, including the world's leading companies, Facebook, IBM, Bloomberg, Walmart. On a monthly subscription model, GitHub connects businesses and developers who seek and offer solutions.

Developers from around the world work together around the clock to develop solutions, and hence, requiring shorter lead times. Collaboration at global scales like that has significantly reduced development costs and increased production quality and speed, exceeding the talents any organisations could hire.

Education, one of the oldest industries, is also experiencing a high pace of change. In May 2012, Harvard University and Massachusetts Institute of Technology (MIT) founded EdX, a non-profit entity, offering mass open online courses (MOOC) to students around the world. Universities like Stanford, Harvard, MIT, University of Pennsylvania, the University of Texas at Austin, Tsinghua University in China, the National University of Singapore, and many others learning institutions offer their courses on EdX.

Through this collaboration, higher education has become accessible and available to the larger population at a fraction of a cost. They are benefiting especially those who did not have the financial means to continue their studies before, including the poorest of the poor around the world. Those who are hungry to improve their life have a better opportunity to advance themselves today.

During the pandemic, many countries, including countries in South America, Africa, India, Indonesia, United States, Russia, Australia, implemented nationwide and partial school closure. 9 out of 10 children from 190 countries had their schooling affected by the pandemic. More than 1.6 billion children and young people were affected. Major exams like Cambridge International Examinations (CIE), International Baccalaureate Exams, Advanced Placement Exams, SAT and ACT administrations were moved online or cancelled.

In a matter of weeks, the way students learn changed. Learning from home remotely or digitally via email, Whatsapp, live stream, podcast, television and radio broadcast, online learning, and pre-recorded videos surged overnight. However, about one-third of the students affected have no access to any form of remote learning tools. That creates a significant impact on preparing them for the future. The World Bank estimated a $10 trillion loss of earning from this while the entire world economy is desperate for growth.

In ensuring the growth of the world economy, we must prepare our future talents, leaders, and entrepreneurs. Before the pandemic, ed-tech has been growing steadily to $18.66 billion and more industry by 2019, reading out to as many children as possible to allow them to learn and gain future skills. Investment in ed-tech is expected to reach $350 billion or more by 2025.

Similarly, more companies and adults are choosing online learning, especially for programs that focus on top executive, professional skills, and passion-driven topics. E-learning platforms like Coursera, Udemy, and Udacity are making global resources available to all online, self-determined, lifelong learners. As of December 2019, the mass online open courses platforms have recorded over 900 universities, 110 million students, 13,500 courses, and 850 micro-references.

According to a report by Business Wire, Udemy, the largest global marketplace for online learning and teaching has experienced a huge jump in global demand in responding to the pandemic. Udemy witnessed a 425% increase in customer numbers, a 55% increase in instructor courses and an 80% increase in usage by companies and governments.

The rapid adoption of home-schooling and learning from home online, shifting away from in-person conventional classroom learning and training, have brought a significant benefit to those who can access them. That has also reduced travelling, accommodation, venue cost, and location bound. Many learning institutions and organisations have already introduced e-learning and online webinars as part of their offerings during the pandemic.

Meanwhile, there have been many researchers found retention rate of online learners who learn at their own pace is higher. Online learners can repeat lessons they need more help and skip areas they are well versed in. There are also online learning institutions like Khan University use machine learning to assess student mastery level to move them quicker off areas they are good at and make them spend more time on areas they need more practice.

Many organisations believe the new ways of learning and training will stay even after the world has recovered from the pandemic, having experienced the benefits of online learning first-hand. And, more companies have also started searching for ways to attract, select, and hire self-directed learners and talents beyond the walls of universities and formal education certifications.

The pandemic has accelerated the adoption to the new way of life, work, and education at a much faster pace than before. In a short few weeks, schooling-from-home and working-from-home became a new norm. However, the speed of adoption also comes with its adverse effect. Not everyone can adapt quickly due to structural and social-economic challenges. The impact is more severe for disadvantaged children and their families. The inequality gap was immediately felt when offices and schools doors were shut and forced us to move to online instantly.

2. BREADTH

Another attribute that can be felt in the smart world is breadth. As smart technologies accelerated the speed and ease of connection, communication, and transactions worldwide, new business models emerged. Direct-to-consumer models, all-in-one solutions, and subscription-based models are dominating the world of business today.

Meanwhile, megacorporations are getting bigger. Companies Google has grown from a search company into a $1 trillion global artificial intelligence powerhouse, joining Apple, Microsoft, and Amazon in the trillion-dollar race before the pandemic. Google has expended its reach into cloud services, biotechnology, life science, broadband internet, internet, and autonomous technology on top of its involvement in urban innovation and countering extremism.

Amazon is another company that has grown from a humble online bookstore to e-commerce services, web services, application program interface (API), and cloud computing, and became the largest online retailer in the world. Amazon has since acquired shoe retailing, grocery, robotics, business insights, social media, space, film, music, video, and the latest, health services, making them the biggest provider of third-party-seller services.

In addition to the breadth of portfolio expansion, many technology companies are moving into providing all-in-one solutions that can solve almost every problem that anyone could face on a day-to-day basis.

WeChat by Tencent is one such example. WeChat was launched in 2010 as a messaging application for sending texts, voice messages, and photos to friends and family. Today, customers can use WeChat for making purchases, gaming, money transfers, set doctor appointments, lodge police reports, book airlines, train, or movie tickets, taxi rides, pay bills, and make investments.

Once users become accustomed to the simplicity and convenience of an all-in-one super app, they would not need to download and use separate applications. That increases customer loyalty, fends off competition, and boosts brand loyalty. Many financial institutions and payment gateway companies today are following their footsteps, building super app whenever possible.

Breadth also means the ability to understand the context, relate to it, and connect with others. In a highly interconnected and interdependent world today, inevitably, we will break away from individuality. We can no longer be great on our own or stick to a single view without taking into account perspectives unfamiliar to us.

We can learn this from an English teacher in China, Jack Ma. Ma has never written a single line of a programming language but has built a multibillion-dollar conglomerate of the internet, e-commerce, payment platforms, financial services, and cloud technology eventually. He is an excellent example of someone who has always been curious and allows himself to seek and absorb foreign ideas to his thoughts.

When Jack Ma was a teacher, he spent nine years volunteering as a tour guide and pen pal to foreigners. During that period, he learned about the trading activities emerged outside of China. In 1995, he and some friends founded the first website providing information about China after he visited the United States and experienced the Internet for the first time. Today, Alibaba Group is the largest of its kind after Amazon, with a market capitalisation of over $800 billion in October 2020.

Perhaps in the new world order, we need to be like Leonardo Da Vinci and few of his peers and masters before and after his time; a polymath, a renaissance man, having knowledge that spans across several areas to solve complex problems. Perhaps we must become the architect of life, a well-rounded creator, pulling various smart tools together, working with multiple fields, to discover new ways forward. We have to be able to see the big picture, creative, innovative, and also systematic, practical, analytical, and critical. On top of that, in a new world, we must have originality.

Perhaps, to get ahead in the smart new world, we must acquire knowledge of all trades and working with masters of various fields to develop solutions together. The ability to lead ourselves, negotiate, and influence each other, to reason and co-ideate is beyond mastering technical skills. If fact, research has found 80% of success is due to the psychological factor. Only 20% of success is from technical skills. In a light-speed changing world, we must be resilient, flexible, and tolerate stress.

Meanwhile, also having the confidence to strategise, lead, design, while possessing a holistic view on how we fit into the ecosystem become critical. The ability to work with multiple functions and fields to produce new ideas has become a necessity. When we are open to ideas that challenge us many times, we grow and expand beyond what we can imagine today. When we become competent in analysing, selecting, and integrating relevant perspectives into our system, we transform and find new ways to achieve common goals together. Hence, being the best and the fittest today is no longer measured by smartness and fastest, unless our business' winning strategy is in pioneering.

Another critical observation we must note is this, while we are going through a time when we would go through many trials and errors, we must be resourceful. We must have the resources to be agile and nimble. Megacorporations like Alphabet, Amazon, Alibaba, Apple can invest in more in researches and venture into fields beyond their original core business because they have accumulated excess resources to do so.

In a letter to shareholders, Amazon founder Jeff Bezos said, "If we don't fail more, we are not taking enough risks." As failed drain resources, including the energy and time, companies must have accumulated abundant resources to do so.

Many renown investors like Warren Buffett and Ray Dalio invest more than 90% of their net liquid assets in safer assets which provides more stable returns to counter inflation and increase wealth. Only 5% of their net liquid assets are invested in research and development, start-ups, or companies with potentials to generate high returns.

In practical terms, it is, therefore, vital that we grow our resources needed to explore widely and to deal with potential failures without slipping into the red. These resources would include the courage to embrace the adversaries despite fear, the environment we are in, people we are with, and the ability to grow and manage our relationships, health, finances, and wellness.

3. **DEPTHS**

On top of the light-speed change and growth in breadth, the other key attribute that is evolving is depth. As we begin to gain a deeper understanding of the world with the help of smart technologies and artificial intelligence, we gain new knowledge and discover a whole new world of possibilities.

Scientists and engineers today are manipulating complex materials at the microscopic level and using newly found properties to create advanced materials. They are working at the atomic and molecular levels to create unique, fabricated matters. One of such examples is the bioplastics produced from renewable biomass like vegetable fats, oils, corn starch, wood chips, sawdust, and recycled food waste.

The additive manufacturing, the process of combining different materials to invent new objects, is another example that emerges from going deep. Engineers and scientists have found ways to break down the properties of materials including acrylonitrile butadiene styrene (ABS), nylon, glass-filled polyamide, silver, titanium, steel, wax, photopolymers, polycarbonate, and many more into fine powder form. Then by using 3-D printers to rebuild components layer by layer through the combinations of these materials. Hence, producing production materials faster at a more cost-effectively manner compared to using natural raw materials.

Imagine what we can do with more materials discovered at a microscopic level where we would not be able to do so before.

When scientists and researchers gain deeper understandings of the nature and behaviour of matter and energy at the atomic and subatomic levels, we will be operating at the quantum level. For this reason, we can say we have entered a new realm of reality.

When we go deeper into any matter, we discover a whole new world of possibilities. This principle applies to life itself and is also the basis for putting this book together. The purpose of this book is to explore and exploit the opportunities' life offers us by understanding the external world around us and the internal world inside us.

Neuroscientists and artificial intelligence engineers are now working together to gain a deeper understanding of humans' physical and psychology being, in a structural, systematic, and scientific manner. When we know exactly how our brains and minds work together and influence our inner and outer world, we gain new insights on how to deal with our thought, emotions, beliefs, and behaviours to get towards what we want. Moreover, the excitement and joy of having deeper understandings of nature and its meaning to us, around us, about us, and within us, give us life.

Going deeper or becoming more precise in what we do takes effort. It requires commitment and perseverance, it requires dedication, and concentration, it requires patience and passion. It also exposes the aspects of life that are unfamiliar to us; hence, creating fear, causing scepticism, and inflicting uncertainty. It is not surprising then, in this new transition into the new reality, will challenge many of the beliefs and norms we were so accustomed.

Meanwhile, it is the consistent cumulation of the little actions and achievements that make significant success happen. Hence, depths take times to build. When we have depth, we become the go-to-person because of the years of consistency, experiences, and specialisation. In other words, despite the light-speed change we are experiencing today, consistency in what we do daily will give us certainty and bring us forward. Our daily deliberate actions today will determine the life we will have tomorrow.

With a better understanding of the attributes, we can better predict how the new world order would demand and how we can best prepare ourselves.

UNCONVENTIONAL RULES

At every gathering of living organisms, there are unwritten codes of conduct which are considered acceptable by its members. The unwritten codes are social rules which guide behaviour, provide order, and shape relationships. Most people abide by these rules to maintain harmony and gain acceptance, connections, and collaborations.

Social rules or social contracts change over time as society evolves, primarily through revolutions of any kind. Sometimes, when the existing rules cease to serve society, the members of the community rise to force the rules to change. This may cause social unrest in the process as people start coming out and marching on the streets to ensure their voice are heard. The march will continue to grow as anger began to build up and eventually resulting in a demonstration, protest, riot, and developed into civil war if the rules remain the same.

We had witnessed that even in recent years when people in Hong Kong assembled in the streets for almost two years, started with the demand for the withdrawal of the extradition bill and transparency in elections since the Umbrella Movement. We had also observed the Black Lives Matter Movement started with 20 million people in the United States advocating for non-racially motivated violence against black people, when an African-American man was killed by a police officer who pinned him down and suffocated him. That movement spread globally in a period of weeks. We have also seen thousands of young Thais in Thailand gathering on the street for a peaceful march despite the pandemic, demanding for the removal of the military-government and reform the administration of the country.

John Locke, the most influential of Enlightenment thinkers and the father of liberalism, said, "If the government failed to protect the people's rights, its citizens would have the right to overthrow that government." His words profoundly influenced Thomas Jefferson more than a hundred years later, as he was drafting the United States Declaration of Independence.

In the new world, smart machines will inevitably co-exist with humans. We are already dependent on smart technologies like our phones to connect and collaborate. On top of that, smart technologies will also analyse, predict, formulate solutions, and execute decisions for us. Leaving us, humans, ample time to do what we want and interact more.

The way we interact is also changing. Open-source, crowd-based solutioning, and co-creating are a new way forward. Co-ownership and the decentralisation of power from the few to the many are on the rise. When the members of society become more interdependent, the common rules become more apparent and observed. As the world becomes a mega global citizen, local rules will be challenged by generally accepted practices and enforced by its members.

Another significant change is the increase in organisations and individuals moving away from the mainstreams. Payments and fund transfers are taking place outside of the formal and highly regulated financial institutions. Alibaba's Alipay, Apple's Apple Pay, and Tencent's WeChat have created a "virtual financial world" of their own outside of the conventional financial systems, with transaction fees almost negligible. And fundamentally change the way how consumers spend money, save, borrow money, and invest. Ant Group's annual payment transactions in 2020 of $17.6 trillion have already exceeded Visa and MasterCard combined.

Ant Group, Alibaba's fintech, expected to raise $34.5 billion would have been the largest public offering for sales in history, exceeding that of Saudi Arabia's state oil company, Saudi Aramco's $29.4 billion public sales. While Ant Group public sales were abruptly halt by China's regulator just days before the company was set to start trading on 5 November 2020, but the world has already started embracing new ways of financial services in a large scale.

Moving out from the conventional systems has opened up opportunities for billions of "unbankable" people who did not have access to the most basic financial services previously. There were 225 millions of "unbank" people just in China. Micro-transactions, micro-payments, micro-financing, as well as micro-investments, are now available to poor and marginalised. Allowing micro-entrepreneurs to get into business more easily. Providing opportunities to people living in the most rural and remote parts of China, India, Russia, Brazil, Indonesia,

Today, Alipay and WeChat are the two payment giants that control nearly 90% of the market in China alone. However, with the recent suspension of Ant Group's public sales, regulators and central governments are beginning to scrutinise financial models and risks behind fintech companies. Many fintech companies are providing financial products and services, particularly in the area of credit lending, financing, insurance, and investment to sub-prime customers and businesses without unsecured financial facilities. These increases the default and longevity risks—similar risks to the United States subprime mortgage crisis in 2007 to 2008, which causes the Great Recession.

Another emerging "off-mainstream" organisation is the peer-to-peer (P2P) community. Peer-to-peer was originally intended for the process of files or information shared directly between computer systems on the network without going through a central server. Today, peer-to-peer communities are mushrooming rapidly as people with common goals come together voluntarily, without formal regulation or mediation by conventional institutions like the central banks, law firms, or regulators.

There are many peer-to-peer communities set up for trading, sharing, lending, insuring, and investing, and also peer-to-peer home-share and ride-share. There are many peer-to-peer groups using platforms like Facebook, Telegram, Whatsapp groups, or more organised hubs like GitHub to connect its members.

Interactions among the people in peer-to-peer groups typically have little to do with rankings or hierarchies. To some extent, peer-to-peer groups are leaderless. Members in the community come together and agree on commonly observed ground rules among its members. Most members will behave with respect, trust, and goodwill.

These communities also subtly and naturally eliminate, alienate, or dissolve those who have not behaved appropriately. More often than not, a natural selection process will take place. The ones who could not 'fit' in or find themselves not benefiting from the group will eventually remove themselves from the group before being asked to leave.

There are commonly-unspoken, universally-accepted rules that govern us. The collective evaluation of qualitative contribution to the purpose of a group determines superiority. Members who are regarded to be of good character, contributing, collaborating, and having the ability to deliver results are highly desired.

Just like the quote from the Universal Declaration of Human Rights, those who possess the desired qualities will gain greater respect and, therefore, sought after. That brings us to the next crucial topic on reputation.

REPUTATION

The most important factor in a relationship is trust––believing and relying on one's capability. And trust has a lot to do with the reputation of a person. While reputation is a subjective qualitative perception of one's brand, character, truthfulness, and action, it is an essential key to success. Hence, we cannot ignore the general perception, opinion, or beliefs of someone or something in a community. Yet, we also cannot allow naysayers and haters to sway us away from our goals.

An admirable reputation gives us a competitive advantage and is necessary, especially in a gig economy. In a world where more jobs are becoming task-based, project-specific, pre-defined timeline of delivery, as compared to conventional full-time, permanent employment, we are constantly being re-evaluated. Marshall Goldsmith, in his book, *What Got You Here, Won't Get You There* said, the success and accomplishment we have achieved until now, is not going to get us ahead. We must evolve and grow continuingly to get ahead.

Reputation has a lot to do with credibility, the level to which we can trust someone. Every one of us is being assessed by others, whether we like it or not. When we meet someone for the first time, we put on our best behaviour to create the first good impression. We are forming others' perception of us. When we introduce a new friend to our close friends or family members for the first time, the level of interaction and empathy are social judgment. We can't avoid that. When we apply for a credit facility, the lender will check our credit scores to assess the level of our 'trustworthiness'. The higher the credit rating we scored, the higher the chances of us being offered the facility, and sometimes, with a better interest rate too. In other words, reputation is the new currency.

Our reputation has a direct influence on our personal and professional success. And, today, our reputations are being monitored from all angles, physically and virtually, offline and online. The pressure to live by the commonly expected ad accepted behaviours has increased with the enforcement by the social structure and smart technologies today.

We no longer have only our parents, school teachers, and bosses watching over us, we also have the whole world's eyes on us too. Companies already conduct reference checks and also using social media to screen job seekers with the help of artificial intelligence before making hiring decisions. We "Google" to check on others' profile and background before engaging with them. We seek users' reviews before making a buying decision.

In the year 2020, the government of China implemented a "social credit system" to standardise its national reputation. Through mass surveillance, state media, and big data analytics, the government monitors the behaviour of its citizens and businesses.

Like the banks' credit scoring system on customers, the social credit system covers a wider range of behavioural ratings on individuals, companies, and government institutions. Including the way they behave in public areas, queuing for their turns in the train station, their behaviour when they are on the road, also promptness in paying taxes, loans, school fees, and other services. Those with high social credit scores will enjoy more benefits, like access to first-class public services, better schools for their children, exclusive seats in public transport, and elite accommodation areas.

In December 2019, the government of China had also announced the use of artificial intelligence in regtech or regulatory technology, in the state tax administration systems to detect fraudulent behaviours, to track down businesses who cheat on taxes.

Some felt China's social credit system violates human rights, yet, humans have already been assessing each other formally and informally since civilisation began. Moreover, the public already act like the ethic enforcers today, using their smartphones to video-record inappropriate public behaviours, whether we agree with unsolicited recordings or not.

Credibility––the ability to do what we say, in a pleasant and socially acceptable manner––is our personal branding. In a world where individuals and businesses increasingly have access to massive data, credibility becomes more crucial.

Credibility ratings have gone beyond formal regulators and institutions into the hands of individuals. Peer-to-peer evaluation is already in e-hailing, e-accommodation, e-service, and e-commerce platforms. Most of us would prefer product sellers and service providers who have more positive reviews or more stars from other users. We are willing to pay a higher premium for reputable and credible brands. Similarly, sellers and service providers also rate if we are an ideal purchaser.

However, whether we have the "eyes" on us or not, our reputations should be based on the choices we make and how we choose to behave even when no one is watching. That is integrity. And, we build our reputation from home; our character, relationship, household, health, and the way we manage our resources and finances. For the way we do anything is the way we do everything.

So, the next question we should ask is, how do we live under the pressure of all these perceptions and still thrive under pressure? In the next section, we will study how great leaders grow 10X more than the average despite the economic downturn, fatal decisions, lawsuit, and negative news slapping on them.

GREATNESS

In October 2001, Jim Collins published *Good to Great*, a book with six years of research with his colleagues. The team combed through more than 40 years of business performance from 1,000 plus good companies. After sifting through more than 6,000 articles and 2,000 interview transcripts, they found the secret behind companies who went from "good" to "great" and grown 10X more than the average. The book, *Good to Great*, became a best-seller with more than four million copies sold.

In their research, Collins and his team found that the main reason large companies grow ten times faster than their peers are that, they "choose to be great" deliberately, regardless of the circumstances around them. They do not allow uncertainty and an inability to predict the future accurately to determine their fate. They decide to face the brutal facts about themselves and their circumstances without justification.

"Greatness" was not a function of circumstances, but a matter of conscious decision and discipline. It is a personal decision to raise the bar and become a better version of ourselves every day. In other words, preparing for the future to stay ahead is not a coincidence; it is a choice. And, we are free to make the same conscious decision to move forward in any circumstances we face by being aware of the choices we make every day, because every choice comes with an equal multitude or more, rewards and consequences.

According to a study by Ray Dalio, the founder of Bridgewater, great leaders like Bill Gates, Elon Musk, Muhammad Yunus, and more, are independent thinkers. They do not let anyone stand in their ways of achieving their audacious goals. They are extremely resilient. Their need to achieve their desire is stronger than the pain of struggling to achieve it.

Collins also found through his research, we cannot make good decisions without first dealing with the brutal facts of the circumstances we are in. "We all know this, complaining about a problem without finding a solution is called whining", quoting Theodore Roosevelt. But if we face the painful truth of our situation, we can reshape our thinking, beliefs, values, emotions, attitudes, and behaviours to become better. For every problem bears the seeds of its solution.

Questions like, "What happens to my family and me when my business or job is replaced?", "do I have a risk mitigation plan for my income source?", "What is my plan B?", "How do I prepare my children for their future?" forces us to face the brutal truth of life. And, when we acknowledge the risk of our circumstances, take ownership and become responsible by working out solutions, we start to move forward.

And we do this with faith while we are on it. "Keep absolute faith that we can and will prevail in the end, regardless of the difficulties, and face the most brutal facts or our present reality, whatever they may be." said Admiral James Stockdale, a senior naval officer.

Stockdale was a prisoner of war in Vietnam. For more than 7 years, he was tortured and tormented with the worst kind of treatment one can think. He said, that the only thing that keeps him alive is faith.

Collins and his team also found that great companies get the right people on board first, then only figure out what role to assign to them to leverage their capabilities. And that requires faith.

One of the biggest lessons we can learn from all of this is, focus not on what I should be doing, but on whom we become. When we focus on whom we are becoming, we will do the right things to become the person we want to be and hence create results. Great companies focus on "becoming great" and do whatever necessary to be great. And they remain humble, keeping their heads down to do what they need to do to be great.

Similarly, instead of deciding on what we want to "do" to get ahead, we must first decide the person we want to "become". "Who would I want to be, as the children to my parents, partner to my spouse, parents to my children, a useful and respectable person in the society?"

Once we have clarity about who we want to become, we look for people who have already become the person we desire to be. We model their belief systems, thought processes, the way they structure their life, systems and tools they adopted to get to where they are today. When we learn from others, take massive actions to grow into the person we want to be, we become a person of good character and value to society. That is how we can get ahead and achieve our desires.

So, how do we get ahead in the unknown and uncertain new world order after the great reset? Perhaps when we say, "I don't know what I want," or "I do not know what to do," we, in fact, have not had the courage to decide the person we want to become yet. Perhaps we are fearful of what others might think of us when we change. And, perhaps too, we are afraid of failing to become the person we desire to be.

Yet, it is in the "becoming" that we find our purpose. Many great men and women, including the late Mother Teresa, share this view. Having a grand vision without a personal decision to pursue greatness is worthless. The desire for a great future without the decision to grow towards greatness—becoming a better version of ourselves every day—will not help us to realise our desires and dreams. That brings us to chapter 3, how do we pursue greatness and become a "great" person.

3

AN AGREEMENT
NATURE AND THE UNIVERSE

It is not the strongest of the species that survives,
nor the most intelligent that survives.
It is the one that is the most responsive to change.
— Charles Darwin

SINCE THE BEGINNING of life, every living being has been instructed by its creator to live a meaningful and productive life, using the resources made available by nature. We are to work, produce, and populate planet Earth. We have also been entrusted to look after planet Earth by using only what we need and allowing the chance for her to rest and reproduce. Therefore, the single most important purpose of life is to "go forth and multiply."

In one of the many holy books written says, "And God blessed them, and God said unto them, Be fruitful, multiply, replenish the earth, and subdue it: and have dominion over the fish of the sea, over the fowl of the air, over every living thing that moveth upon the earth." (Genesis 1:28, Old King James Bible). The effort which every living being goes through in the course of its life, every pain and sweat, tears and joy, ultimately is to protect, multiply, and prolong life.

Most of us understand the meaning of "multiply" in the phrase "go forth and multiply." The term "go forth" is as important as "multiply". "Go forth" is a call to move forward, despite the surrounding circumstances, and the uncertainties ahead. That requires courage. A decree to face all adversity and multiply. To leave a legacy to the next generation. We multiply through giving birth or by contributing to the procreation and preservation of life.

We are in an exciting time in human history. A time when repetitive jobs and jobs that highly complex or have a great risk of endangering life are being done by smart machines, so that we can focus on more important tasks, create meaningful life together, and go home safely to our family at the end of the day. The increasing speed and ease of access to smart technologies give the world new opportunities we do not have before.

Scientists are inventing faster and smarter machines, gaining a deeper understanding of the universe and humans, and developing more materials by blurring the lines between digital, physical, and biological spheres. The world has become like a gigantic Legoland today, with too exorbitant the amount of smart tools at our disposal. We can create almost anything we could imagine.

In the agricultural industry, bioscience and biotechnology scientists are working closely with artificial intelligence engineers to discover new ways to help plants and animals grow faster, healthier, and mass-produce higher quality food. Logistics and supply chain strategists are finding new ways to optimise systems and operations, making way for manufacturers to sell their products directly to consumers.

Meanwhile, health scientists in the healthcare industry are discovering new ways to help people achieve a better quality of life by staying healthier, living longer, and enjoying happier lives. Life is becoming more comfortable and easier, giving us, the humans, more space and time to focus on what matter most. We have a better chance than before to go out and multiply, to live meaningful, and joyful lives, even to transform our careers and businesses in with the pandemic.

However, despite all the technological advances and wisdom, the mental health of humans is deteriorating. Poor mental health is one of the most common causes of morbidity and mortality worldwide. Anxiety and depression are the top two poor mental health conditions. Worried about future misfortune, feelings of helplessness, hopelessness, and worthlessness, losing interest in daily activities, experiencing fatigue, and having difficulty to concentrate are the most common symptoms of anxiety and depression.

The many studies conducted by the American Institute of Stress (AIS) show that stress at work has escalated in recent decades. A perception of having little control in life, especially in times of uncertainty, and the inability to predict the future accurately have created significant anxiety about the future, which escalated even before the 2020 pandemic. The full extent of the impact by mass unemployment, isolation, and anxiety due to COVID-19 on mental health is not yet known.

According to the Mental Health at Work 2019 Report by Mind Share Partners, nearly 60% of respondents answered "YES" to the question, "Do you feel down, numb, lose interest or pleasure in most activities for at least two weeks in the last 12 months?" 37% said their work environment has contributed to these feelings.

The World Economic Forum estimates that 275 million people will suffer from anxiety disorder by 2019. The anxiety and depression symptoms have tripled during the pandemic, especially among the marginalised people and people with fewer societal resources. The poor mental health could cost the global economy about $16 trillion by 2030.

Suicide rates, especially among young people, have also risen sharply. According to Centres for Disease Control and Prevention (CDC), the youth suicide rate among ages 10 to 24 years of age has climbed 56% between the year 2007 and 2017. The second leading cause of death for generation Z is suicide——a worse epidemic than what the millennial faced at the same age.

By the end of November 2020, Japan reported the death by suicide in October 2020 is already more than total death caused by COVID-19 in 2020. The suicide rate has soared to 2153, just in that month, in a country that did not have lockdown and with minimal impact from the pandemic compared to the other countries.

We are heading for a serious mental health crisis. What is happening to humanity in a world becomes increasingly intelligent? In a world that is supposedly getting better?

THREATS HUMANS FACE

In 1943, Abraham Maslow first presented the "Hierarchy of Needs" in his work *A Theory of Human Motivation*. According to Maslow, people are by nature driven to fulfil their needs in a hierarchical order. Starting with the physiological need, moving on to the needs for safety, love and belonging, esteem, and self-realisation.

I would regroup these needs into three main categories: protect and provide, belong and acknowledge, grow and contribute.

1. **PROTECT and PROVIDE**

    The most basic need that drives us to do what we do every day, every moment, is the need to protect and provide for people that matter to us. If we do not have a chemical disorder in our brain, we would have the instinct to protect our loved ones and ourselves from dangerous and harmful environments. We want to provide shelter and put food on the table and give the best education for our children to prepare them for the future.

    Billions of people around the world are now worried about their lives and livelihoods when the pandemic hit. Many people lost their jobs, businesses, and homes. According to the International Labour Organisation, the world has lost nearly 400 million full-time jobs in the second quarter of 2020 alone.

Image 3.1: Three Categories of Human Needs

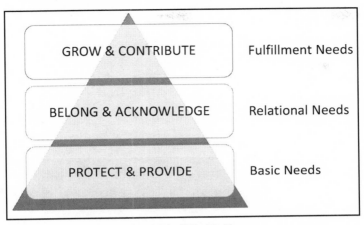

CopyRight©ShuTzeTan

As of the end of November 2020, close to 64 million people were infected with the COVID-19, and over 1.5 million confirmed deaths. The numbers were still climbing when these words were written. The World Economic Forum estimated about 1 in 10 people, or 10% of the world population, have been infected by the coronavirus. The World Health Organisation has also warned, the situation would get tougher as cases are resurging in many countries.

On top of the pandemic, the world also suffered from the worst locust attacks in 70 years, in countries in East Africa, the Middle East, part of India. Acute food shortages threaten more than five million people in Kenya alone.

Meanwhile, the world also experienced the worst floods on the Yangtze River since 1998, which had killed hundreds, forced 3.6 million people in central and southwest China to relocate, and affected a total of 54.8 million people between July and September 2020 alone.

The world has also experienced the wildest wildfires in history in parts of Australia from September 2019 to March 2020. And the wildfire broke out in California and Oregon in August 2020, destroying property and livelihood. The Arctic Circle wildfire in the summer of 2020 released record levels of carbon dioxide from ancient peat-lands, amplifying climate change.

The World Economic Forum estimated by the end of 2020, more than 265 million people could be at risk of starvation and death from starvation. In addition to the many devastating nature-induced circumstances, companies replacing human workers with smarter machines is also rising rapidly. Companies, operating manually and conventionally, are losing their customers to a new way of business quickly. Almost every day, we read of news of layoffs and bankruptcies around the world which is directly threatening the most basic human needs to protect and provide.

In many of my closed-door conversations with people working across all levels of the workforce, including executives at the top, the top concerns, when changes happen, is job security. Many people are anxious about losing their job when there is an organisational restructuring, merger and acquisition, and digital transformation effort, even before the pandemic. Yet, many people do not have a safe space to voice out their worries and discuss ways to prepare for the possibility of losing their jobs.

Over the years, companies spent billions of dollars in training to ensure their employees become better leaders and upgrade their skills to perform better. The key objectives centred around, increase productivity, service standard, revenue growth, and profitability. Today, many companies want their employees to be more agile, resilient, creative, collaborative, and have an entrepreneurial spirit to get ahead in the new normal.

However, few companies prepare their employees to face the brutal truth of potentially losing their jobs to the change, the pandemic, or smart machines. Many people do not know how to increase their income potential, manage their finances correctly, invest, and increase their financial independence. They were not trained to move from a cost-expense-income mindset to an investment-risk-return mindset, from scarcity to abundance, fear to opportunity mindset, and the grit to push forward despite the circumstances, like how a successful business owner would.

Research on "The Emerging Millennial Wealth Gap" sponsored by the Citi Foundation found that millennial in their mid-30s today earn 20% less than what the baby boomers and generation X earned when they were in their 30s, despite being better educated. Average income has fallen significantly, owing to less predictable employment, lower salary levels, higher college tuition fees, escalating inflation, and increases in jobs moving from permanent employment to short-term contract jobs. That has delayed and hampered the accumulation of wealth.

At the annual World Economic Forum Meeting in Davos, world leaders have been discussing the need to provide a universal basic income (UBI) for people living in poverty to meet their basic needs for survival and release them from the pressure of living on day-by-day basics. It is with the hope it would give them basic healthcare, basic housing, and education to release them from acute anxiety and improve their mental health. Hence, giving them a stronger foundation to find a better job, improve themselves, and advance their family's economy and quality of life.

The universal basic income could be achieved by taxing corporations more, especially megacorporations that pay almost zero income tax on trillions of revenues. Many megacorporations have structured their organisations to maximise tax incentives and receive millions of dollars in tax rebates from governments around the world instead of paying taxes. These tax incentives and rebates for big corporations created a structural problem which caused income inequality, elevated the wealth of a few at the top, and reduced the income of average person globally.

Meanwhile, living standards of the middle class have lowered in the last 30 years. House rental, house price, and college tuition fee have risen faster than the average salary, reducing the chance of millennial saving more and accumulating wealth earlier.

Concurrently, more manufacturers are going direct to consumers, squeezing out the intermediaries. Straight-through-processing and automation are reducing dependency on the middle management level. All these contribute to the shrinking middle-class level and limiting opportunities as compared to the baby boomers when they were at the millennial' age.

One of my mentors, Pak Robert from Indonesia, a banker who became a self-made billionaire and helped many people create successful businesses all over the world, once said, if we have a spare or a run-flat tyre in the car, we should have a source of asset-based income that could sustain our living expenses, so that if our main source of income stopped, we could still get on with our life. And, we must learn to invest well to fight inflation and accumulate more wealth to ride through unprecedented events.

To do that, there are questions we might need to face to move forward:

"What is my alternate plan, if my job or business disappears?"

"How much net liquid asset would I need to accumulate to generate asset-based incomes to cover my basic living and household expenses?"

"How much net liquid asset did I have now?"

"What is the net liquid asset gap between what I have now compared to what I need?"

"How much time do I have to accumulate the net liquid asset I need to achieve my goal?"

"What business could I tap into to generate asset-based income?"

"What are my skills and unique qualities that would help create solutions the world needs and would pay for?"

"How do I position and market myself?"

"What business I can start without huge capital outlay and ongoing operating cost?"

"How do I win by collaborating with my finest competitors?"

"Who can I learn from?"

2. **BELONG and ACKNOWLEDGE**

Once our basic need to protect and provide is met, our needs for belonging and acknowledge, including the need for love and recognised, will begin to intensify. The need to belong and acknowledge is a relational need. It is psychological in nature. As humans are social beings, it is only normal for us to yearn for connections, respected, and acceptance for who we are.

Living in a community, we seek to protect, provide, and seek guidance. We draw strengths from each other, and hence, it is only fair we become a worthy person to one another and a useful person to society.

Working as an organisational change consultant and career transition coach in the past, I have been tasked to deliver the news of lay-off to thousands of people for the companies I worked with. Through many of the conversations with those were laid-off over the years, this is what I have observed; the level of anxiety was highest among middle and senior management teams.

Most of us who are having worked for more than twenty to thirty years in the field we specialise in and known for would have grown to accustom to who we are in the industry we are in. We have grown ourselves and belong to a social circle where we are known for what we are good at. We have earned the recognition and respect for our contribution to the companies we represent and society we are in.

We pride ourselves for the years of hard work, achievements, and enjoy the fruit of our labours. It is only natural that our job and the brand name of the companies we worked with become a significant part of our life and identity. On top of that, we have developed solid relationships over the years with many of our colleagues, customers, and suppliers who become long term friends.

When someone got laid-off from our jobs or forced to close down their businesses, it is only natural that they experienced complete lost. Losing one of the most significant parts of who we are, which took years of pain and tears to build, devastates us. That experience of losing a job or business is likened to receiving news of a life-threatening disease, a major accident, or sudden death of our loved ones. Even if we have already anticipated the possibility of losing our jobs or businesses.

The immediate thoughts that would come to mind are, "How am I going to survive after this?" "How am I going to inform my family and others?" "What should I do next?" "Who would hire me?" "Who am I now?". These are the anxieties we face, even for those who left behind.

Over the years, I have met people who were laid-off and did not know how to break the news to their family initially. Some people would get up every morning, get dressed in their office attire, and go out of their house at the same time they did when they had their job. They would spend the rest of their days in a café and go home at the time they usually would when they were still working. The worries and fear of facing up to the response of their loved ones were too overwhelming that they could not bring themselves to tell them, they have lost their job.

What we can do in this situation like this is to help them regain their dignity as a person. We do that by providing them with a psychologically safe space to voice their fear, anxiety, and worries. Then, we guide them to relook into their identity beyond the role and job they were so familiar. We guide them to acknowledge the achievements they have had, contributions they have given over the years, and reconnect to their purpose for their loved ones.

When they began to focus on whom they can become for their children, spouse, and parents, despite the circumstances surrounding them, they began to find the strength in them to create a new opportunity, new identity, and a new sense of belongingness and recognition beyond the identity on their previous role.

Many people who have gone through the painful experiences of being laid-off or lost their business before, eventually immerged better than they were before. More importantly, many of them were humbled and changed their worldview. They eventually grew stronger relationships, career, health, and finances by leaps and bounds.

I have witnessed the same matter in grooming leaders for succession planning. Top talents who have failed badly before, either in their career or business, and pick themselves up many times after that somehow become a much better leader. They are more determined, focus, and compassionate, and understanding. While they tend to have a higher level of empathy, they do not let circumstances around them affect what they set out to achieve. They dare to fail more because they have learned how to pick themselves up before. They have found a new way to earn back their place in the society they serve.

3. **GROWTH and CONTRIBUTE**

The need to protect, provide, belong, and acknowledge are forms of "insufficient" needs that arise from the feeling of "not having enough" or "lacking something." Once these needs are fulfilled, the motivation to focus on these needs decreases, and the need to grow and contribute begins to rise.

Grow and contribution needs are the need to self-actualise, or the need to fulfil our purpose to others and the world. The need to grow and contribution is the highest level of human needs which grow beyond ourselves. It compels us to make a difference in this world, and to develop someone beyond us, to multiply and leave a legacy. It comes from our innate need to give meaningfully and to be part of something greater than ourselves. This level of need usually grows from the overflowing fulfilment and overwhelming gratitude of the lower-level needs.

The beauty of it is, grow and contribution needs are also the "lifelines" especially when lives are threatened. It gives us a sense of purposefulness and hope beyond our circumstances, for the benefit of others, and thus bringing fulfilment and meaning to life. The needs this level help shift our focus from our pain or current situation to the needs of others. That is the reason we would usually do more for those we love than for ourselves.

That is why most parents are naturally driven to do what is best for their children. The pain and sacrifice they did became negligible when their desire to do the best for their children takes precedent. Through many revolutions and wars, it is the love for the family, the community, and others that have inspired individuals to rise against all odds. It is the same love that flames the courage to overcome all threats. It is the same love beyond themselves that makes them hang on to the hope for a better future.

During the trips to the Nazis' concentration and extermination camps in Poland and Austria, as I strolled by the rows of barracks, the gas chambers, and crematoriums in Auschwitz-Birkenau and Mauthausen-Gusen camps, I sensed the same human spirit which kept the survival alive during the worst of the Holocaust period. As I poured through many books, movies, and materials on how individuals lived through extreme conditions, I felt the same faith and hope to reunite with their family again, and the same love that helped them through one of the worst massacres in the history of humans.

The parents and children who were determined to stay alive for their families held out. Many others risked their lives to help the Jews and Polish to escape the Nazi. Many more who fought to preserve the pieces of evidence from the era. All that gives us the certainty that we, the humans, will do everything we can to get ahead.

According to Abraham Maslow, the lower-level human needs to protect, provide, belong, and acknowledge must first be fulfilled before we could fulfil the higher level human need. These are the foundational needs. Otherwise, the attainment of the higher level needs would short-lived. If the foundational levels of human needs are weak, the fulfilment of human needs at a higher level will not last.

Before the pandemic widespread in 2020, many businesses and companies focused on fulfilling higher-level human needs. We spend a significant amount of effort, resources, and engaging in activities that drive engagement and create a joyful working space in hope to bring more fulfilment and meaning to work.

Simultaneously, cheerful faces, foods, activities, and travelling photos flooded the pages of Tik Tok, Instagram, LinkedIn,

Facebook and more. However, many people were suffering in silence with unmet basic and psychological needs, overcompensated with the higher-level self-actualising and fulfilment needs. Meanwhile, personal and business debts rose, overvalued businesses, startups, and lifestyle shot up. It is no wonder, anxiety, depression, poor mental health, and suicide rate escalate.

In the new world order, where business margins and incomes are reduced, it is more important than ever for us to find new ways to take care of our basic and psychological needs first. When we find new ways to protect and provide for our loved ones, we will find a new meaning and joy-filled life. As humans have lived through many evolutionary changes and emerged victoriously, we will continue to do so in this revolution of life we are going through now.

For this reason, too, we are the only species known in *Latin* as the *Homo sapiens*. We are likely the only surviving species of the genus *Homo* since life began. By the laws of nature, biological evolution, biodiversity, natural selection, elimination, mutation, recombination, and reproduction, we are likely the composition of the finest genetic code that has evolved and survived many life threats over a hundred thousand years.

As we continue to be adaptable to the continuingly changing environment, our better genes which are more flexible and resilient will last as long as life itself. And, the "less suitable" genes are likely to be eliminated.

Beyond our genetic makeup, we also have the smarter, self-learning, self-optimising machine that would become our intelligent assistant and intelligence assistant. We will continue to find better ways to survive and get ahead. In fact, throughout history, humans have been evolving and searching for the perfect formula to an ideal life.

AN IDEAL WORLD

Nature has an innate ability to learn and adapt to the surrounding environment——likewise, humans. We continually improve the way we hunt, collect, grow, distribute, consume, and preserve food by manipulating tools and improving our capabilities.

It is the same today. Parents hope their children live a better life than them and provide them with the best education they could afford. Entrepreneurs continuingly improve themselves to grow their business. Business owners find new ways to increase productivity and profitability every year. Scientists discovered new ways to understand our world, inventors inventing smarter, faster and more powerful tools to increase productivity and quality of life. At the same time, philosophers imagined an "ideal world" in which humans could live better.

The search for an "ideal" world——a world free from conflict, hunger, and misfortune——goes way back in human history. In 1516, Sir Thomas More, a lawyer, saint, and councillor to the England King Henry VII, first coined the word "Utopia" (ou-topos) to describe a perfect imaginary world. The title of the book, "Utopia" means "no place". However, because the word, "Utopia" sounds like an Ancient Greed word, "Eutopia" (Uo-topos) or "perfect place", some scholars suggest More entitled his book "Utopia" as a sarcastic way of questioning if humans can ever create a perfect world, the "Eutopia".

In his book, *Utopia* More describes a fictional island consisting of a perfect society, which is highly desirable by most. An island where the citizen processes ideal characteristics in every aspect of life, including health, religious, social, and political customs. A society where its people are all excellence in whatever they do. Everyone has a role to play, and they live to the best of their ability on this island. Everyone works hard and together and profit from their effort.

More's *Utopia* was not the first written text to describe the image of an ideal world. More than 2,000 years ago, around 375 BC, Plato wrote the *Republic,* which became the most influential work of philosophy and political theory. In that book, Plato defined justice and order as the characteristics of an "ideal city" with an "ideal community." Plato used his famous teacher Socrates, the father of Western philosophy, as the protagonist in a dialogue with the Athenians and immigrants. In that dialogue, Socrates discussed the idea of an "ideal city" with his audiences.

In that "ideal city" there were three categories of society: the guardians, the auxiliaries, and the producers. The guardians were responsible for ruling the city. They were the rulers, the philosopher-kings, who govern, protect, and bring justice to the subjects under their jurisdiction.

There were four cardinal virtues—prudence, justice, fortitude, and temperance—that became the guardians' main education, to become a rightful ruler for the city. Meanwhile, the guardians also lived simple lives to tame their greed and focus on serving others. They were also given physical training, military skills, and martial arts to ensure they remained physically healthy and strong.

The auxiliaries were the warriors, responsible for defending the city from invaders and maintaining peace in the city. They also enforced the orders of the guardians and ensured the producers obeyed. Producers constitute the largest category of society. They were the farmers, craftsmen, merchants, doctors, artists, actors, lawyers, and all other professions. The producers were not involved in the judgement but obeyed the order of the rulers. Their goal was to produce what they were best suited for.

In this ideal city, everyone, including women, received education in the four cardinal virtues, so that everyone knows his or her responsibilities, cooperates, and respects the roles of the other. To ensure that everyone was happy and accepts their predetermined status within society, Socrates invented a noble lie to keep the peace. The lie is famously known as the Myth of the Metals.

In that noble lie, Socrates would tell the citizens, "Although all of you in the city were brothers when the god was forming you. The god mixed gold into those of you who are capable of ruling, which is why they are the most honourable; silver into the auxiliaries; and iron and bronze into the farmers and other craftsmen."

What Socrates means was, there would be a creator whom Socrates calls "the god". The god placed every citizen at a specific level of society with predefined roles. The citizens should respect the god's decision and carry out their respective functions and duties to their fullest potential. Since the citizens were related by blood, they passed to their offspring the role for which they were created. If the citizens attempt to move out of or from the level they were created for, they would be going against the creator and the predetermined decisions, and therefore, will cause wrath to the creator.

Although the idea put forward by Socrates may sound absurd to some extent, Socrates wanted a world in which the citizens were satisfied with who they were and focused on what they would do best, without attempting to enter to other social categories, which would cause chaos.

The idea of an "ideal city" in the *Republic* attracted many critics. Some even claimed that Socrates and Plato had raised the ideology of republicans and socialism. Their work continues to influence much of Western philosophy, political science, psychology, and our lives today.

As the search for an ideal world or society continues, we cannot deny that to create an ideal world. We need some form of social rules in which the members of a society would agree on, and regulate their behaviour and provide them with the freedom to express.

SOCIAL NORMS

Throughout history, philosophers, and scholars, including Stoic, Thomas Hobbes, Jean-Jacques Rousseau, Lao-Tze, Confucius, and more had discussed how we could live harmoniously with ourself and others in an ideal environment. Many believe that people should have the freedom to do what they want and express themselves as they deem fit, as long as they live according to social norms.

Social norms are unspoken and unwritten rules about how we should behave. As civilisation grew, this freedom was given to the state. Social norms began to take form in rules, regulations, laws and written moral codes to standardise and regulate behaviour. When people live together amicably, there will be peace and people will be pleased. But, when they feel their rights are being threatened, they will raise to demand change. The protest, rebel, and revolt will follow if their demands are not met. There will be chaos, and in some cases, followed by riots and wars, until change happens. Then, peace will ascend when the social equilibrium and stability is reached until the subsequent discontent feeling begins to rise.

As technologies bring us from various backgrounds together, we are exposed to various social rules. Some rules have become a part of who we are. Some rules are easier to be accepted in other communities compared to ours. When a group of people challenge existing rules, boundaries are stretched. Social rules are most frequently questioned in times of crisis. Likewise, many rules were challenged with widespread COVID-19 and economic slowdown. Many rules are evolving as new rules replace the conventional ones.

There are more organisations and groups of people breaking out from the central government controls, institutional arbitration and regulations, compared to yesteryears. Decentralised technologies and platforms like blockchain, cryptocurrency, none central government regulated institutional lending, are examples of breakouts from centralised authority, order, and control. People finding ways to deal directly without regulated intermediation by a third party to ensure appropriate and proper conduct.

The continuing changes in social rules are more intense today and have reached epic evolution. Communication technologies have allowed for individuals to propagate their agendas faster than ever.

We have witnessed the rise of people in positions of power and influence that use Twitter more than the past. What is our position in all these? What is the proper thing we must do to survive, stay relevant, and get ahead?

Aristotle once said, "If one way is better than the other, then that is surely the way of nature." Nature has a lot to teach us on how we should go forth and multiply while maintaining social equilibrium. Throughout history, we have also witnessed those who choose to do the right thing, which survived and thrived through tough times. No matter how difficult the circumstances they were in, or how silly their actions might appear to others. Remember a time when Elon Musk publicly discussed the idea of autopilot car, hyper-loop travel, space travel, and colonisation of the planet Mars? Many people ridiculed him. But today, many of his ideas have become a reality. Similarly, few organisations survived through wars, pandemics, or natural disasters over hundreds of years, while many did not.

If one way is better than the other,
then that is surely the way of nature.
——Aristotle

ECOSYSTEM AND BIODIVERSITY

In an ecosystem of life, there are the biomes——the community of plants and animals with common characteristics for the environment they exist——living, interacting, and functioning as one ecological unit. Every member of the community has its own potential to adapt, change, and grow. Every member also has a specific purpose for the total sum of the whole, greater than the sum of its parts.

Meanwhile, the biomes exhibit distinct biological characteristics that are formed from response to the abiotic substances, the non-living chemical, and physical parts of the environment, which form the deserts, rainforests, or coral reefs or all other parts of a diverse planet Earth. If one element in the abiotic substance changed slightly, it would cause a disturbance to the living organisms in the ecosystem.

The living organisms can be characterised as the "producer", "consumers", and "decomposers," also known as the "reducers". Similarly, amongst the humans, some of us are the inventors, creators, entrepreneurs; most us are the consumers, users, or buyers; and some play the role as the resolvers, regulators, enforcers, or executioners.

The "producers" are organisms which produce complex organic compounds from abiotic substances present in an ecosystem. They are bacteria, algae, or plants. Producers convert non-organic sources or the abiotic component energy like the sun and store them for future use.

The "consumers" are the essential component of the ecosystem. "Consumers" are organisms that cannot fix carbon from non-organic sources. They are the herbivores and carnivores who eat other living organisms.

The "decomposers" or "reducer", like the fungi and certain bacteria species, play a critical role in breaking down dead organisms and waste matter. Decomposers are critical for any ecosystem to function. Without them, the ecosystems would be littered with dead organisms.

The health of an ecosystem is defined by the richness of the diversity of its community——the biodiversity. Bio (life) and diversity (variety) is the gigantic diversification of genetics and species of a variety of living organisms in a given habitat, including all the plants, animals, insects, and bacterial. The richer the diversity, the greater the opportunity for discovery, growth, and adaptive responses to new challenges. Similarly, the more exposed we are to various ideas, discipline, field, and culture, the more insightful we become and the opportunities we realise.

Every species continuingly evolves in responding to other species and abiotic substances or the environment. Some grow stronger and multiply more, some barely keep themselves alive and stay in stagnant without much growth, and others die, even prematurely. No matter how insignificant one may appear, every species plays a crucial role in increasing the health and productivity of the entire ecosystem.

Pope Francis put it beautifully by saying, "Rivers do not drink their own water; trees do not eat their own fruits; the sun does not shine on itself and flowers do not spread their fragrance for themselves. Living for others is a rule of nature. We are all born to help each other. No matter how demanding it is."

Biodiversity is crucial to the survival and sustainability of all life forms on our planet. Food production is depended on the biodiversity of plants, pollination, nutrient provision, genetic diversification, and disease prevention.

I have learned this from a mentor from Australia, Dr Paddy Reynolds. Dr Paddy bought a barren land many years ago and shared how he turned it into a healthy piece of land again with significant vegetation today. According to Dr Paddy, one of nature's ways to restore a barren land is by planting many species of plants repeatedly for a few years. Many plants will die in the first few years. But they become food for other plants, and so that is how the barren land heals naturally.

When a diversity of plants living together, they will fight to outright each other for survival. Some will die in the fight. But some will survive and thrive. Every living organism must scan its environment for any sort of danger continuingly and be flexible to adapt to all circumstances. Those that are most resistant to the threats surrounding them and able to absorb foreign influences into their systems selectively have the most eminent tendency to grow and multiply. That is how we should live in a diverse way of life, work, and business today with a light-speed changing environment.

The strongest and the most agile will continue to evolve, adapt, and survive, contributing to the ecological structure and function of the land, and regenerate life. The toughest of all species will also produce the most potent effects, causing others to adjust and adapt to them, and hence, change the environment and the ecosystem. The weaker species which could not quickly enough eventually die, and their offspring might be eliminated forever.

We might have read or sung of the song of the miracle of a tiny mustard seed that became a mighty tree. When a mustard seed, smaller than most grains, falls to the ground, it must fight its way through the threats of nature and the environment it is in, including the peril of weather, animals, bigger trees, and plants around it for survival. The risk of being crushed by the thunderstorms, washed away by the rain or floods, or being eaten by animals is only normal as in any ecosystem of life. If this seed survives and is resilient to adapt to its ever-changing environment, it will live and outgrow the threats.

Eventually, the tiny mustard seed will grow into a giant mustard tree with its root deeply anchored into the ground and take its rightful place, and it will change the surrounding environment. Some plants and animals around this mustard tree will be cast off or die. But some will find their way around the tree. The giant mustard tree will also provide food for other animals and plants, while others will seek shelter, or construct a home on its roots, trunk, branches, or leaves.

The diversity of the human race and how we live has many similarities with other living organisms. Inevitably, we grow with one another. We have built on ourselves a complex global network that is so interconnected and interdependent to protect, provide, and preserve life. We learn to co-exist, co-correct, and co-create with people from diverse backgrounds. We cross-pollinate our genetics and experiences and create new breeds, new perspectives, and new opportunities.

Charles Darwin summed up this natural process by saying, "In the struggle for survival, the strongest win at the expense of their rivals because they manage to adapt best to their environment," and this process is known as the natural selection.

With the advancement of today's technology, humans are now becoming a single global citizen. The widespread evolution caused by the pandemic on top of the adoption of smart machines is revolutionising every aspect of our life. Bringing significant impact on our relationship, intimacy, health, wellbeing, resources and growth.

Meanwhile, the strongest and fittest amongst us continue to impost their ideology, beliefs, and values on others. The chiefs of country, organisation, or community, are influencing the minds and actions of many, no matter who they are, whether the world favours or despises them, whether we like it or not. Perhaps, they are the ones who are most resilient, most agile, and have the highest propensity to exert themselves, no matter what circumstances surrounding them, until someone who detests them rise to oust them.

Biodiversity and natural selection have taught us to be aware of what is happening around us. Being agile and adapting faster than change is a way of life. The ability to scan and identify the surrounding changes, to anticipate and predict the future, is a vital ability to remain relevant and survive a light-speed changing world.

Biodiversity and natural selection have also taught us that, if we do not respect nature's needs for biodiversity, we will face the biggest environmental problems, as we have today. Deforestation, overexploitation, invasion, including overpopulation in a particular area, rapid urbanisation, overconsumption, pollution, and using Earth's resources more than it can replenish naturally have reduced biodiversity. These have resulted in soil degeneration over the centuries and contributed to a climax crisis at an accelerating and unprecedented rate.

What should we do today to overcome these? How do we work together to preserve the natural resources we have, stay alive, and stay relevant enough to get ahead? What would the new world need? What value can the humans bring in the new order? Answers to these questions will determine our place on planet Earth in the future.

NATURE'S WAY TO PREDICT THE FUTURE

Humans are now bombarded with news and individual opinions that are continuously screaming at us through our digital screens. Social media is flashing with shout-outs from individuals who roar most frequently to market their thoughts and propagate a movement every day. Our ability to scan and predict the future, and to assess which information is trustworthy and authentic, has become harder.

There is as much fake news created with ill intentions as there is news with a noble purpose. We need a tried and tested method to distinguish between the two. The ability to know the difference and say "NO" to many "forged-believed-world" to get the "YES" to the "truth" is a critical competency to get ahead.

The good news is, we have an advantage today. Since the earliest known form of written records in the Neolithic period in 7,000 BC to 6,000 BC, our forefathers have shared their experience, observations, and many lessons nature brought to them. These are priceless insights that life has handed down to us. Through hundreds of thousands of years, many of these records described nature's laws and universal principles through many evolutions, revolutions, the rise, and fall of civilisations over time. It is, therefore, noteworthy for us to understand the intentions and differences in the laws of nature, principles, and theories and the guiding axioms of our life.

Laws of nature, principles, and theories are three explicit statements of phenomena regarding life that could become our guides for scanning, predicting, preparing, and thriving in the unknown new world. Let us consider each of these and examine how we can apply them in our daily decisions.

1. **LAWS OF NATURE**

    The laws of nature are statements of phenomena through repeated observation and proven over an extended time. Laws of nature are not statements of "proof of a phenomenon", but the "description of a particular phenomenon." Laws of nature described a phenomenon which happens the same way, every time, without fail, throughout the centuries, and can be proven by mathematical equations. It is based directly and indirectly on empirical findings, observed, and confirmed by many people.

    For instance, the law of natural selection describes the natural process in which living organisms with certain traits favourable to their environment, are more likely to survive and produce more offspring than others. In this process, too, natural selection will eliminate biological variations that do not adapt well and contribute to the changing conditions.

    As humans are living organisms in nature, we are not spared from the laws of natural selection. Laws of nature or nature's laws are objective and exist independently of our understanding. Therefore, we must not break the nature's law. If we tried, we would only break ourselves against it.

    In the 16th century, Nicolaus Copernicus, a Polish Renaissance-era mathematician and astronomer, established the sun-centred (heliocentric) universe. In this idea that the earth, including humans, are part of a much bigger universe, and the sun being the centre of the universe. His concept radically challenged the traditional earth-centred (geocentric) view of the Catholic Church. Galileo Galilei, an Italian astronomer, physicist and engineer, later proved the Copernicus theory when he invented the telescope.

Then came Isaac Newton, who was seated under an apple tree and saw the apple fall to the ground. He wondered why would the apple fall to the ground and not fly above the tree or to any other direction. After twenty years of accumulated studies, Newton extended his discovery of gravity to the famous, Newton's laws of motion.

Newtonian laws of motion lay the foundation for classical mechanics and describe the relationship between a body or mass, the forces acting on it, and its movement as a reaction to action. These laws have a significant influence on many scientists, philosophers, and leadership theories.

The following describes how each of these laws is regulating lives.

1st Law of Motion: Law of Inertia
Any object in a state of uniform motion will remain in that state of motion unless an external force affects it.
The first Newton's law of motion is also known as the law of inertia. As a creature of habits, we have the natural tendency to get used to and become comfortable doing what we learned to do over a period until new habits are formed. We also incline to remain in our comfort zone without making deliberate changes to our state, until a force pushes us to do so, as the COVID-19 pandemic forces us to change the way we live, work, and communicate.

Similarly, those who break out from their comfort zone decide within themselves that they can no longer tolerate the state they were in. People who appear to have drastically changed their lives while they seem doing well are the ones who said, "This is it" or "enough is enough!" They took the leap of faith to step out of their comfort zone and make necessary changes for the future they want. It is no wonder, we have the saying, "No pain, no gain."

This also means every one of us lives in two worlds: the outer world and the inner world. 80% of our decisions come from our inner world or our psychological world. Hence, our reality in the outer world is actually created from within our inner world. In chapters 4 and 5, we will systematically dig into the process underlying these phenomena.

2nd Law of Motion: Law of Dynamic
The total force on an object is equal to the mass of the object multiplied by the acceleration of the object; in short, force (F) equals mass (m) time acceleration (a).
F = m*a

If we apply the same force to two objects of different masses or weights, we will have different velocities. A heavier or more massive object needs more force to move it compared to the less massive or lighter object. The speed of change is equal in weight and direction to the power imposed upon it.

In practical, every one of us experiences the pace of changes differently. Some of us need a longer time to change than others; others take a longer time to evaluate more information in considerable details before they decide to change. As human beings, we have accumulated experiences and emotional baggage throughout our life. We developed beliefs and feelings about our past and the events that had happened to us. These beliefs and feelings become our emotional baggage that shapes our worldviews, thoughts, values, and decisions, which influences our behaviour.

Over the years, we have many unsolved issues that created the feelings of jealousy, anxiety, anger, sadness, guilt, or shame. The more massive our emotional baggage is, the greater effort we need to let go and grow out from the baggage.

For this reason, increasingly, as we will be working with people of various backgrounds and experiences, we must learn to understand people at a deeper level, in their inner world. The ability to deal with people at a deeper, emotional level is inevitable and will become a valuable component in moving forward in the new world order.

3rd Law of Motion: Law of Action and Reaction
For every action, there is an equal and opposite reaction. When two bodies interact, they exert forces of the same magnitude and opposite direction on each other. This is also known as the law of cause and effect, action and reaction. It means that all forces always occur in pairs.

Everything flows in and out, rising and falling. It is like the pendulum swing which manifests in everything. Similarly, in everything we choose to do or not to do will bring the outcomes we want, and we shun. There are risk and reward, discipline and freedom, power and respect. When we act according to nature's law, we will be rewarded. If we do not do what we must do, we will bear the consequences.

Whatever happens to us today is a direct reflection of the decisions and actions we have taken or not taken in the past. The results in our lives today are direct feedback on how we chose to live our life yesterday. Every outcome corresponds directly to our actions.

The laws of motion help us understand the underlying forces in life, and give us clues on how we can ignite the power within us and around us to get ahead. These laws, directly and indirectly, determine our lives. In Chapter 4, we will delve deeper to understand how motions and emotions affect us physically, psychologically and physiologically, and therefore our outer physical world.

2. PRINCIPLES

Principles are the statement of the fundamental operating mechanism or process, proven beyond a reasonable doubt. Principles explain the process of how things work. They are not statements of evidence, but explicit descriptions of procedures. Because principles are more universally accepted and applicable on a philosophical basis, they are therefore considered legitimate across all cultures, ethnicities, and faiths. For example, the golden rule which every religion teaches, "Do to others what you want others to do to you."

Like the laws of nature and the universe, principles cannot be questioned, denounced, or otherwise proven. Principle brings with it the intended and unintended rewards for those who respect and live by it, and consequences or punishments for those who do not. Principles are, therefore, often used to guide and evaluate our behaviours.

Understanding and living by the laws of nature and principles empowers, protects and preserves us, because the truth lies in these, and not in personal views. We can neither deny nor ignore the laws of nature and universal principles. In other words, while we have the freedom to behave and express ourselves, we are bounded by the rewards and the consequences of the choices we make. This is also widely known as karma.

On the other hands, when we live a principle-centred life, nature's laws of unity, attraction, intention, fullness, cause and effect work with us, for us, and through us. These laws are always at work, even if we are not. And we live with the rewards and the consequences nature's laws bring, whether we like it or not. Therefore, to get ahead and have a meaningful and joy-filled life, to enjoy the fruits of our labour and attaining wellness and happiness, we must choose to live a life centred around principles.

Living a principle-centred life is an act of "greatness" —-choosing to do what we must for the outcome we want—-because it is how it should be and it's the right thing to do. Choosing greatness is the choice of who we want to become. When we choose to become excellence as a person, and in whatever we do, we do what we must our level best, even when we do not feel like it sometimes. When we choose greatness, we receive the results we want. Greatness, therefore, builds character and earns us the rightful place in the ecosystem of life.

In the book, *The Art of Significance: Achieving the Level Beyond Success*, Dan Clark wrote, "Obedience is the universal first law." People who choose greatness in how they live their lives have become significant to humanity; people who achieved beyond themselves to serve others know that prosperity flows through them to bless the lives of others.

They work hard on becoming obedient by accepting, recognising, and living according to the universal principles and nature's law. Not because they have to, but because they demand themselves to. People of significant do the deeds they sometimes do not like, but which are necessary to realise their desires and dreams.

In my interaction with many people of significance, those who live by their purpose continue to raise the bar to be a better person every day. They focus on becoming proficient at following nature's rules for success. They aim at mastering principled-centred life and develop the right habits with deliberate actions. They build daily routines and behavioural patterns which lead to the desired outcomes. Many people of significance say, "Be an excellent student of the process, and the result will come."

We apply principles in every area of our life; the way we manage our relationships with ourselves, parents, partners, children, friends, acquaintances, and business associates; the way we manage our physical and psychological health, what we consume, what we listen to, the environment we choose to be in, and what we do to our body; and the way we manage our finances, career, business, and investments.

There are rules of consistency of effort, compounding effect, risk and reward, action and reaction which when we understand and work with them, we are leveraging nature's resources to create a healthier relationship, health, and financial standing. There are principles in which we must build our life with the right strategy, structure, system, and tools for achieving our desires and dreams.

In short, the science of success is in obedience to laws of nature and universal principles. There is an old saying; it takes 21 days to create a habit and 90 days to create a lifestyle. Hence, to create habits that produce results we desire for our relationship, health, or financial wellbeing, we must invest a minimum of 90 days of doing the right thing consistently to get there and keep the new habits once we form them. In the third part of this book, we will explore step-by-step ways to apply the laws of nature and universal principles in our daily lives and to form new habits to live victoriously.

3. **THEORY**

Unlike laws of nature and universal principles which are proven and tested over centuries, theories are statements describing how a phenomenon would likely to happen under a pre-existing condition, at a given time and place, with limited evidence, observations, and occurrences.

Theories are tested, hypothesis, or formed beliefs with extensive research and investigation, including careful examinations against those with laws of nature and universal principles.

For the scientific purpose, we hypothesise or make assumptions to idolise a phenomenon to justify and attract further investigations. When a hypothesis is put forth, there will be others who would want to probe and conduct tests to prove for or against the hypothesis. Over a period, when more tests are producing the same results, a hypothesis becomes a theory. But theories are not like nature's laws or universal principles. Theories that have not stood the test of time through the centuries, verified with many by other researchers, in various situations. That is why theory can sometimes be proven wrong over a period.

More than 2,000 years ago, many people assumed and believed the planet Earth was flat. If anyone wandered too far out to sea or land, they would fall off the edge and disappear. Then, in 240 B.C., Eratosthenes of Cyrene, an ancient Greek mathematician, calculated the Earth's circumference by measuring the length of a shadow cast on sticks planted on the ground at noon, at different locations, and theorising that the world is round. Many people mocked him. And, many other mathematicians and scientists used various methods to test Eratosthenes's theory.

It was not until 1969 when humans actually saw the shape of planet Earth with their own eyes on their television through the windows of the space shuttle, Apollo 11, when humans marked another historical event in history with the first flight to the moon. In short, theories need time to go through many tests and be proven over and over again until its truth becomes undeniable.

In a world where we can easily access to communication technologies and marketing platforms, like Tweeter, Instagram, Facebook, LinkedIn, more individuals are propagating their ideas, assumptions, and opinions to push their agenda. It is also normal to encounter newer theories and concepts popping up during times of crisis.

Business plans are also theorised belief with mathematical predictions of desired outcomes by using past data of similar circumstances to inflate an idea. But the plan has not been tested and undergone the stress of many circumstances. It is no wonder, many new businesses and well-known initial public offerings (IPOs) failed, especially in recent years.

Moreover, assumptions and opinions are the lowest forms of human knowledge because they require little to no accountability and no understanding. It is easy to give ideas, but not easy to create results from ideas. That is why many ideas did not take off.

Yet, we should not be too quick to throw away new ideas. As the law of biodiversity teaches us, the more open we are to explore foreign ideas, the newer insights we gain and become more creative in innovating solutions. Striking a balance between these two required experience which takes time. That is why it is said, knowledge comes from learning, but wisdom comes from living.

Someone once said, "The highest form of knowledge is empathy, for it requires us to suspend our egos and live in another's world. It requires a profound purpose, larger-than-the-self sort of understanding."

Coming back to the question, "How do we sift through the tons of information bombarding at us every minute to determine which is worth our careful consideration?" We do this by testing opinions and ideas against the laws of nature, the universal principles.

When we live a principle-centred life, we will become sensitive to ideas that differ from the truth. We are also able to shape our competency to discover new insights, anticipate the future, innovate more, and, get ahead with the ongoing changes better. We can assess the basis of an idea. We can differentiate the ones, purposeful, principled, and solution-oriented, from the others.

Last but not the least, although nature demands we continue to scan, learn, and adapt quickly to changing environments, we do not necessary have to be the pioneer of change. Unless we are in the industry of pioneering, which also required significant resources and reserves, we can get ahead by learning and modelling those who succeed before us. But, we must be obedient to do what we must, and change faster than change itself, and that we are not the last few preys in the herd when the change is like the cheetah who is out hunting for its food.

At some future periods, not distant as measured by centuries,
the civilised races of man will almost certainly exterminate,
and replace the savage races throughout the world.
— Charles Darwin

PART 2

THE HUMAN RACE

4
THE BRAIN
FORMS AND FUNCTIONS

The human brain has a vast memory storage.
It made us curious and very creative.
Those were the characteristics that gave us an advantage.
And that brain did something very special.
It invented an idea called "the future".
—— David Suzuki

THE HUMAN BRAIN is the most extraordinary organ in the entire human body. A small but highly complex structure that regulates millions of bodily functions, movements, speech, thoughts, and memories. The brain also gives shape to the essence of the human mind, human spirit, and soul.

The brain controls spectacular tasks that happen in the body, including synchronising blood flow through 60,000 to 100,000 kilometres of blood vessels, arteries, and veins, with perfect rhythm and pressure. The brain also ensures the food we eat is transported through 7–8 meters of the gastrointestinal tract, extracting nutrients, absorbing energy, and expelling waste as faeces. It also regulates our heartbeat and ensures our respiratory system supplies oxygen to generate sufficient energy based on our physiological needs.

The brain has an enormous capacity to process information. It receives stimuli from the world outside of our body by using the sensory receptors––chemical structures, predominately, protein-molecules, which receive and transduce energy from the outer world into nervous signals and integrate into the biological systems of our body.

Sensory receptors are found throughout our body and in major organs like the eyes, ears, skin, nose, and tongue. Hence, we can see, hear, touch, smell, and taste. Once external stimuli are received, our brains will evaluate and appropriate response to the stimuli.

Additionally, the brain controls the other body's sensors for temperature, body positioning, body balancing, and blood acidity. By that, the brain protects us by gearing the body up for a fight or flight when it senses danger approaching. The brain also puts the body at ease when it senses the environment is safe and favourable to us.

Many operations in the body are governed by the brain, at all times, whether we are awake or asleep. Billions of bits of data from the outer world are received by the sensory receptors and transmute into signals in the billions of neurons, or brain cells. The brain then assigns personalised, meaningful information to us individually, breaks down the data into smaller chunks, compartmentalises, and stores them into short-term and long-term memories at the different parts of the brain, ready to be recalled when needed.

Engineers and neuroscientists have spent many years studying the human brain and creating artificial intelligence that can learn and think like humans. Yet, the smartest machine cannot replace a human a hundred per cent. The deep neural network in artificial intelligence allows neuroscientists to gain further insight into the unique computation and functioning of the brain.

But, despite the advance of smarter and faster superintelligence machines today, we are still a long way from understanding why the humans' brains work the way it does. Even as smart technologies adopt a more human-like intelligence, machines are still miles away from being human, if that would ever happen.

A healthy brain is essential to the foundation of our physical and physiological functions. It directly affects our cognition, emotion, and psychological health, which in turn contributes to our behaviour and the results in our life. By studying the anatomy and physiology of the brain, we can systematically reprogram our brains to move forward in an exciting smart new world.

Once we have a considerable understanding of our brains, we can go deeper into our phycological being in Chapter 5 to understand how the data received from our body sensory receptors generate meaning, feelings, and behaviours through our experiences, beliefs, values, worldviews, and internal representations.

When we appreciate how our brains and minds function independently and co-dependently, we can reprogram our physiology and psychology to our advantage. Then we can remove barriers that prevent us from moving faster in the fast-changing world. Ultimately, a healthy brain increases the capacity of a healthier mind; a healthy mind grows a healthier brain.

BRAIN ANATOMY AND PHYSIOLOGY

The physical brain is a delicate, soft, squishy mass of spidery nerve cells. It is primary fats that could be easily deformed with the touch of a finger. It is a complex organ consisting of specialised nerves and enveloped in supportive tissue. The brain is made up of hormones, the chemical massagers, which trigger cellular reactions to control bodily functions. It also contains enzymes, the catalyst that regulates the biochemical reaction rate. Both hormones and enzymes consist predominantly of amino acids and proteins.

An average adult brain looks like a giant walnut and is about the size of two clenched fists, weighing about 1,500 grams. The size of a brain is relatively small compared to the rest of the body, yet it dominates the entire body. The brain is the energy source and the "software" of our body. Without the brain, our body would be like a robot without a power source and software. When the brain is dead, the body is dead.

The brain is located at the top of the spine and is connected to the spinal cord through the brainstem. There are three major parts in a brain: cerebrum, cerebellum, and brainstem.

1. **CEREBRUM**

   80% of the whole brain is in the cerebrum. The largest part of the brain. The cerebrum is the part that performs higher human functions like learning, thinking, reasoning, interpreting, feeling, having a sense of space, time, direction, recognition of colours, form, size, and speech. It also controls fine muscle movements, small actions like buttoning our shirt, tying our shoelaces, writing, playing musical instruments, or operating tools, and picking up an object between the thumb and the fingers or toes.

   The cerebrum is located in the upper anterior part of the head and consists of two hemispheres. The left hemisphere is responsible for the right half of the bodily functions, and logics like thinking, analysing thoughts, system and process, natural sciences, calculations, and numerical skills.

   Impairment of the left brain leads to weakening or paralysis of the right side of the bodily functions. The severity could cause daily routine and the recognition of objects more problematical. Impairing language, analytical skills, the order of time, cause and effect, and the handling of numbers, including money.

   The right hemisphere is responsible for the left half of the bodily functions, and the artistic, and creative side of things like imagination, insight, intuition, holistic thought, musical awareness and spatial abilities.

An impairment of the right brain weakens or paralyses the left side of the body. It can also reduce the ability to assess depth, shape, colour and size, and consequently be lost in time and space. It can also decrease the proficiency to understand social norms, emotions, and underlying messages, causing the ability to interact with others more challenging, thereby reducing interpersonal ability, consideration for others, and self-regulation.

Figure 4.1: Three Major Parts of the Brain

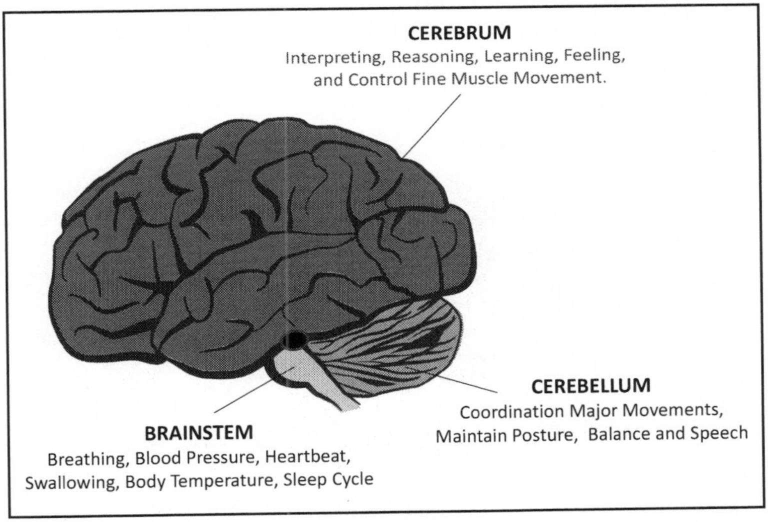

CEREBRUM
Interpreting, Reasoning, Learning, Feeling, and Control Fine Muscle Movement.

CEREBELLUM
Coordination Major Movements, Maintain Posture, Balance and Speech

BRAINSTEM
Breathing, Blood Pressure, Heartbeat, Swallowing, Body Temperature, Sleep Cycle

CopyrRght©Shu-TzeTan

The corpus callosum, a thick band of nerve fibres in the centre of the brain about 10 cm long and shaped like the letter C, connects the two hemispheres of the brain and enables the communication between the left and right hemispheres. If the corpus callosum is underdeveloped, deformed, or damaged, the disability can range from mild to severe, including, falling behind peers in development, never learning to walk or speak, or even blindness, deafness, autism, seizures, and spasticity.

The cerebrum consists of four lobes with distinct functionalities:

- **FRONTAL LOBE**

   The frontal lobe is located at the front and top of the brain. It is responsible for the highest level of human thought and behaviour, enabling us to form complete sentences, and solve complex problems. It is also responsible for our emotional impulses and personalities, which lead to a specific behavioural tendency.

Image 4.2: Four Lobes in the Cerebrum

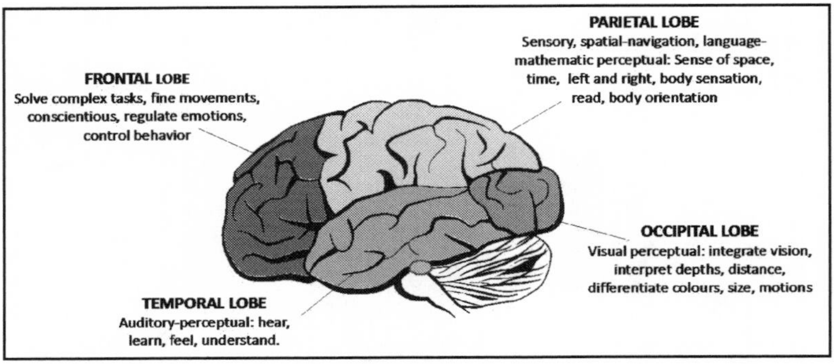

CopyRight©ShuTzeTan

The frontal lobe contains the prefrontal cortex, which is responsible for higher-level cognitive functions, activities that include problem-solving, decision-making, judgment, recognition, social skills, morality, regulation, impulse, and attention. The frontal lobe also comprises the motor cortex, which plans, controls, and executes voluntary movements and fine motor skills in the wrists, hands, fingers, feet, and toes.

   Whenever we engage in intense discussion and solve mentally challenging problems, we tend to place our hands on the forehead. That is the physical language of our body, indicating that our frontal lobe is busy at work.

- **PARIETAL LOBE**

   The parietal lobe is the sensory, spatial navigation, and linguistic perception of our body. It is located behind the frontal lobe and

84

above the temporal lobe. The parietal lobe is responsible for our sensational feelings, including touch, temperature, pressure, and physical pain. It protects us by scanning our surrounding continuingly and preparing for any response when required. When we accidentally touch a hot stove and quickly retrieve our hands, the parietal lobe has prevented us from getting burnt further.

As a processing system for space navigation, the parietal lobe is also responsible for our experiences of space and time, left and right. When we climb a ladder or stand on the edge of a building on the roof-top, our consciousness and awareness are heightened, we become more cautious than usual, thanks to the parietal lobe.

The parietal lobe also interprets language and mathematics by consolidating knowledge through improved neural connectivity, thus enabling us to read, reflect, and develop intelligence. We might catch ourselves leaning back in our chair and putting our hands on the back of our heads after learning a new subject or receiving a piece of fascinating news. That is the body's physical expression of the parietal lobe part of the brain at work.

- **OCCIPITAL LOBE**
The occipital lobe is the visual perception of our body. It is located at the back of the head. The occipital lobe is responsible for the processing of visual-spatial aspects, the interpretation of depth, distance, and location, the differentiation of colours, the specification of movements, the recognition of objects, and the reconstruction of memories.

One of the most critical parts of the occipital lobe is the primary visual cortex, the region of the brain which receives external stimuli directly from the retina of the eye. Our eyes transmit the highest rate of data compared to other sensors—about

10 million bits of data per second, ten times more than our skin, which transmits the second-highest amount of data every second.

This is precisely the reason companies spend billions of dollars on marketing and advertising, using multiple colours, shapes, sizes, to build billboards, banners, and websites to tell stories that wow us. Triggers interest in us by causing us to "fall in love at first sight".

When we fall in love at first sight with something, a living organism, an event, or nature, that state represents a desire we have had through our experience or observation, even if we are not aware of this desire. That split-second moment of craziness, overwhelming feelings of love projects a memory already deeply embedded in our hearts, which, is in our minds, caused by our brains.

▪ TEMPORAL LOBE

The temporal lobe is the auditory-perceptible part of the brain. It is located at the lower brain front, below the frontal lobe, behind the ears, and extends to both sides of the brain. The temporal lobe receives information through sound from our ears and processes the information in a way we can understand by comparing to the information we have in our memories.

The temporal lobe is critical for the function of hearing, differentiation of language, and formation of emotions. It is strongly linked to our visual memory, emotions, language, and understanding.

Shopping malls all around the world make every effort to create the right ambience with the right lighting, the exact colours, styles, smells, music, and story-lines of lifestyles to create stimuli to trigger consumers "buying behaviour." In this way, the malls' owners activate the consumers' temporal lobe to generate feelings of yearning to fulfil their desires.

Music and lights play an essential role in our lives, which is why we love the Christmas season at the end of the year. The scent of Christmas trees, glittering lights, colourful ornaments, aromas of gingerbread, cinnamon, hot chocolate, burning birch wood, roasted chestnuts, watching the snow falling delicately from the sky, and Christmas tunes serenading us at the background—a perfect setting to end the year and fall in love.

The temporal lobe also performs other functions like the forming long-term memories, processing new information, generating visual and verbal memories, and interpreting smells and sounds.

Whenever we feel threatened, mistreated, down or depressed, the tendency to curl up in a corner and cover our ears with both hands is the physical representation of the need for isolation and protection ourselves from being harmed further. Our body will always find a way to tell us what is going on inside us.

While these four lobes in the cerebrum have distinct functions and perform a majority of specific tasks, they work together with other parts of the brain all the time.

2. CEREBELLUM

The cerebellum is located below the cerebrum, at the back of the brain, and positioned directly above the brainstem where the brain and spinal cord code converge. The cerebellum is essential for broad motor skills. It orchestrates voluntary movements, including coordination, movement, balance, posture, and speech, leading to equalising muscle activity.

The cerebellum ensures our whole body is upright in a balanced position while we are standing, walking, climbing the stairs, running, or swimming, by coordinating and controlling large muscles in the arms, legs, and torso.

The cerebellum accounts for about 10% of the total weight of the brain but contains almost half of the total amount of neurons in the entire brain. When the cerebellum receives external stimuli via the sensory receptors, the brain will cause motor movement to respond appropriately to the stimuli. Damage to the cerebellum can lead to balancing problems, slower movements, tremors or shaking, and cause complex physical tasks like sports activities difficult or impossible.

3. **BRAINSTEM**
    The brainstem is the part of the brain that connects the cerebrum to the spinal cord and the rest of the body by transmitting neuronal signals. The brainstem consists of three parts: the midbrain, the pons, and the medulla oblongata.

    The midbrain, which sits on top of the brainstem, controls essential bodily functions, including our eyes and facial expression. The pons, which connects the midbrain to the medulla oblongata, autonomously maintains vital bodily functions including regulating breathing, heart rate, and blood pressure, regardless of whether we think about it or not. The medulla oblongata connected to the spinal cord is responsible for motor control, sensory analysis like hunger, thirst, temperature, consciousness, even when we are awake or asleep.

    The brainstem could be compressed by swelling, blood pressure, or ruptured blood vessels. This can lead to bleeding and strokes with speech impairment, breathing difficulty, or sleep apnoea. In acute cases, a compressed brainstem can affect movement, cause personality changes, or memory loss. Therefore, optimal health––the ideal fat percentage and optimal muscle mass level––is of paramount importance. Every extra fat and weight we have on our body will strain our brain and physical body, and affecting our mind.

Most of the time, these three different parts of the brain; cerebrum, cerebellum, and brainstem, and four lobes in the cerebrum; frontal, parietal, occipital, and temporal lobes, work together simultaneously.

When we suddenly stumble over a stone, our body will quickly rebalance itself before we fall over. This is because when the cerebellum detects the imbalance in the body, the frontal lobe tells the body it is in danger of falling over. The occipital lobe quickly interprets the depth, distance, and location of our body. The temporal lobe reaches into our muscle memory and quickly recalls the muscles used in response to similar situations before. The cerebellum then instructs our main muscles in our hands, legs, and torso to bring our body back into an upright position.

While all these are happening, the hormones and enzymes play a significant role to help send messages quickly from the brain through the brainstem and the spinal cord. Our heartbeat and breathing rate rise, to increase oxygen supply to the brain and muscles; to stimulate respond quickly.

The brain has the ability to grow and reorganise itself to adapt to lost functions. And it can also adapt itself so it no longer needs the part it cannot have. The different parts of the brain have a unique way of complementing and compensating each other. If one part of the brain is affected by developmental disorders, injuries, strokes, or attacks by bacteria or viruses, the other parts of the brain will rewire and find new ways to supplement and offset for the impaired part by forming new neural pathways to develop new abilities. That is the power and beauty if our human brain.

NEURONS

Now that we have understood the brain structure and functioning of each part, we will probe deeper into the world of neurons, the brain cells, also known as the nerve cells. We want to understand how neurons operate in the brain and bodily functions, even when we are unconscious. The deeper we go into our brains, the more leverage we have to tap into our natural resources given by our creator to get ahead in a future that is unknown and uncertain.

The neuron is the basic working unit of the brain. It is designed to convey messages to other nerve cells, or to muscles to perform a task, or to gland cells to synthesise substances, including hormones, for the release into the bloodstream or cavities in the body or outside the body. According to many estimates, there are about 86 billion to 100 billion neurons in our central nervous system (CNS), including the brain and the spinal cord.

Neurons transmit massive signals from the brain to every part of our body, including our limbs, fingers and toes, and through every system down to the tiniest microbes in the human body. That is how our brains control all bodily functions. When the brain receives information from the world outside via our sensory receptors, the neurons generate electrochemical signals in the brain and relay these signals to the rest of the body to cause a response to the external stimuli.

Neurons are like other cells in several ways, but different as they specialise in generating and transmitting messages in electrochemical signals throughout the body with some cells don't. Neurons control the things we do, like walking, talking, and the activities the body performs automatically, like breathing, feeling, and digesting food.

In addition to neurons, there is about three times more neuroglia, also known as the glial cells, than neurons in the brain. A neuroglia is a non-neural cell and does not produce electrical impulses, therefore, does not communicate with other cells. Neuroglia's job is to protect the neurons by enveloping them and provide them with structural support and food.

Image 4.3: Makeup of a Cell Body

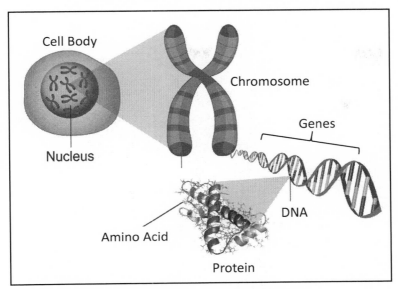

Adapted from www.123rf.com images

Most neurons have a cell body, axon, and dendrites. The cell body is the central part that contains a nucleus which houses the chromosomes. Chromosomes consist of strands of deoxyribonucleic acid (DNA)––the blueprint of life, which can be found in every living thing.

DNA is the stuff that determines nearly everything about us, from our appearance to our personality traits. DNA also contains the genetic code which provides the instructions to make proteins and molecules for growth, function, and health of our body. It allows for long-term information storage memory.

DNA is essentially the protein structure formed by long chains of amino acids. Amino acids are one of the first biomolecules, organic molecules or biopolymers in life, which form protein structures and give shape to tissues, blood, enzymes, skin, and bones. They are the most basic structure of most living organisms.

Amino acids and protein blocks are the precursor compounds, or the originators of chemical reactions to produce other compounds to generate metabolic pathways which lead to physiological processes. In other words, amino acids and protein structures are said to be the essence of all life forms and linked to almost every life process. That said, we are fundamental constructs of amino acids and proteins.

Moreover, there are billions of cells dying and being replaced with new ones every day. Some cells in our body, like the blood neutrophils, a form of white blood cell which leads the immunity system's response, are renewed every 1 to 2 days. Some cells like the fats in our body take 8 years to be renewed. 10% of our skeleton renewed every year.

But, some cells last an entire lifetime and cannot be replaced when they die, like the neurons in the cerebral cortex and the cells in the central nervous system which controls most of the functions in our body and mind. That is why, our daily food intakes must contain a superior source of protein, proportionate to our body size, as the primary macronutrients, for the regeneration of our cells to maintain a healthy body, brain, and mind.

Neurons have the unique ability to receive, generate, and transmit electrochemical signals. When our sensory receptors receive external stimuli, neurons generate electrochemical signals, also known as electrical impulses or nerve impulses, in electrical potentials that travel from the neurons via axons down to the dendrites.

The axon is a long, cord-like extension of a neuron, and is insulated like an electrical wire with a thick layer of neuroglia or myelin sheaths——which are essentially fat and protein——to accelerate the electrochemical signal to transmit to the end of the neuron, the postsynaptic dendrites. The length of the axons varies between 0.1 to 1,000 millimetres!

The dendrites are branched extensions of neurons and connect with other neurons or cells through synapses, a neuronal junction or gaps between two neurons which allow electrochemical signals to be released and received. Transmission happens in synapses when the "electros" in the electrochemical signals release specific "chemicals", or the signal molecules, the neurotransmitters, at the end of the neuron through reuptake pumps. The neurotransmitters will then attach to a type of protein molecule embedded in the membrane, or the receptor at the receiving neuron, and cause several other biochemical events.

After the neurotransmitters have been released and received, a process of inactivation will kick in by an enzyme to stop the transmitting process. The receiving neuron will continue to pass the electrochemical signals to the other neurons the similar way. That is how billions of neurons transmit messages throughout the brain, through our spinal cord to the rest of our body.

Image 4.4: Neuron and Synapses

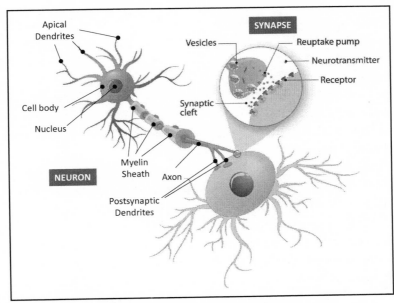

Adapted from www.123rf.com images

Every neuron has a minimal electrochemical charge at a voltage which depends on the neuron's transmitting speed. When we are in a calm, relaxed, or meditative mode, neuronal activity slows down. When we engage in an adrenaline-rushing activity like running, dancing, speeding, or skydiving, the electrochemical signals need to release more neurotransmitters much faster. The myelin sheaths which envelop the axon will accelerate the electrical impulse conduction to increase the speed of electrochemical signals being transmitted to the end of the neuron.

The average distribution speed in healthy neurons and synapses is between 0.5 to 150 metres per second or 1.5 to 540 kilometres per hour! At the highest speed level, it is faster than the Shanghai Transrapid's fastest high-speed bullet train available in the world when this book was written. These are the primary working processes of how our astounding brain operates and controls all bodily functions.

Each of the estimated 86 to 100 billion neurons is connected directly to about 10,000 other neurons, creating well over 100 trillion synapses. It is like a gigantic network of billions of interconnected computers. When a hundred trillion synapses happen simultaneously, our brains light up like the "Milky Way in the Galaxy". However, not every neuron connects with 10,000 other neurons all simultaneously, or else we will become mad. A more conservative estimate, about 10 billion synapses happen at any one time.

The brain is indeed an electrical transmitter. A full functioning brain can generate as much as 10 watts of electrical power. If we hooked a brain with enough scalps, we could light up a bulb.

The study of neurons and genetic elements, including the DNA in the neurons, is still at an early stage of discovery in the world of neuroscience. While records of neurology and neurosurgery studies can be found dating back to prehistoric times, the dictation of neurons and the word "neuron" did not emerge until the end of the 19th century when the first brain scanner with neuroimaging technology was developed.

Scientists today have discovered how neurons, nucleus, chromosomes, genetics, DNA, protein structures, and amino acids come together. However, many scientists vouch we have only found 1% to 2% of the functions of DNA in its role in determining characteristics. There are still 98.8% of the brain cells we have yet to discover and understand. The chimpanzees, for example, are regarded as the closest evolutionary relatives to us because they share 96% of the human DNA. But how can that be when the chimpanzees appear and behave so different from us?

That said, there is still much of the universe inside us waiting to be unlocked and could fundamentally change our understanding of human and life in the future with the acceleration and help of superintelligence machines. Furthermore, we have yet to figure out why humans' intuition, spirit, morality, faith, hope, and love exist and drive our behaviour the way it does.

BRAIN GROWTH AND PROTECTION

The brain is a living being. It continuously grows through the regeneration of new neurons, or neurogenesis, and organises itself through the formation of new neuronal connections, or neuroplasticity. In the course of our lives, neurons grow and die, while the electrochemical signals and synapses can be strengthened or weakened.

Neuroplasticity optimises neuronal networks according to our environment. When we experience new events in life, neuroplasticity happens. For this reason, people who continue to learn new skills, play new games, meet new people, read, solve complex problems frequently, increase neuroplasticity, and are mentally more active and sharper.

For this reason also, it is more important to hire people with the right attitude of learning than to hire them for their technical ability. Because it is much easier to acquire new skills, which is essentially a process of causing our neurons to form new neuronal networks, than characteristically changing them at the mind and emotional level—— an effort which is more complicated than working with the brain.

Neurogenesis and neuroplasticity are also the key components in the brain to become more agile, resilient, and adaptable in the light-speed-changing world. During the pandemic, when we were forced to adapt quickly to the new way of life and work, neurogenesis and neuroplasticity are at work. And after 60 days, we began to form new habits and accustomed to the new ways of working, including, working from home.

The brain and spinal cord have three protective layers: the bone structures in the skull and spine; the meninges, a layered unit of membranous connective tissue that covers the brain and spinal cord; and the cerebrospinal fluid (CSF), a clear, water-like liquid which cushions the brain and spinal cord. To ensure we have a healthy brain structure, brain physics, and strong protective layers, we must have the adequate and appropriate amount of nutrients, clean air, clean water, wholesome environment, and sufficient sleep.

It is not surprising then, people who live in a healthy environment; consume the fitting diet according to the needs of our body; have good quality clean air and pure drinking water; actively participating social and physical activities, tend to get ahead better. Additionally, by keeping our body fat percentage in the bay, we reduce the barriers to neuron-synaptic transmissions.

For similar reasons, depression, dementia, Parkinson's, and Alzheimer's can be delayed or minimised through activities like social interactions, learning new skills, reading foreign ideas, and solving complex problems. These actions stimulate synaptic transmission activities that keep the brain active.

BRAINWAVES FREQUENCY

There is an enormous amount of electrochemical activity going on in our brains as neurons transmitting messages continuingly, even while we are sleeping. Every neuron maintains a voltage gradient according to the types of activity we are engaging in. The difference in the electrical potential in a space across its membrane generates different frequencies and is known as the electrical wave. Different waves and electrochemical charges are generated by the metabolic differences in the ions of sodium, potassium, chloride, and calcium.

When the voltage changes significantly, electrochemical signals or nerve impulses are generated. These electrochemical impulses can be measured and represented in waveforms, like electricity. These waves in the brain are called the brainwaves.

In 1942, scientists found a way to observe and study the electrical activities and brainwaves with an electroencephalogram (EEG). Using an electrophysiological method, the electrical activity of the brain can be recorded by attaching small metal discs, so-called electrodes, to our scalp.

Like electricity, brainwaves are measured in cycles per second (Hertz or Hz). The speed and harmonic or incoherent frequency (wavelength) dramatically affect our consciousness and mood. Slower brainwaves are present when we feel relaxed, meditative, dreamy, enhanced intuition, and creativity. Higher frequencies generate feelings of excitement, speed, and strength. However, an excessively high frequency over an extended time can lead to stress, anxiety disorder, burnout, and depression.

That said, brainwaves change according to what we do and how we feel. Some of us wait for the right feelings or "motivation" before we take action. But highly successful people choose to get into action despite how they feel because they know the right feelings will follow actions and results. While most people tend to believe that motivation causes motion, but motivation can also cause by motion.

As we can measure and understand the power of brainwaves now, we can bring about the desired state of consciousness and become masters of our biological being, instead of being dominated by it. Simply put, we can choose to act despite our feelings towards the surrounding circumstances, rather than permitting our emotions to govern our actions and the results in our life.

There are five levels of brainwave frequency which dominates brain activity differently. Each frequency happens its characteristics and operates at the different states of our consciousness. They are the gamma, beta, alpha, theta, and delta brainwaves:

1. **GAMMA brainwaves (31 to 100Hz)**

   Gamma brainwaves are the fastest and most vibrating waves. It is the subtlest frequency of brainwaves. Gamma brainwaves simultaneously process information from different parts of the brain and pass the information on quickly and quietly. It heightens perceptions, learning, memory, and processing information.

   Our brains produce gamma brainwaves when we are intensely focused, actively engaged in solving a problem, and at a peak state, feeling in the zone. When we experience an unexplainable universal love; a deep empathetic-altruism desire to help people who are suffering; or the bravery to stand out to protect others, even in the face of a death threat, the brain is producing gamma waves, the "higher virtues" brainwaves.

Image 4.5: Five Levels of Brainwave Frequency

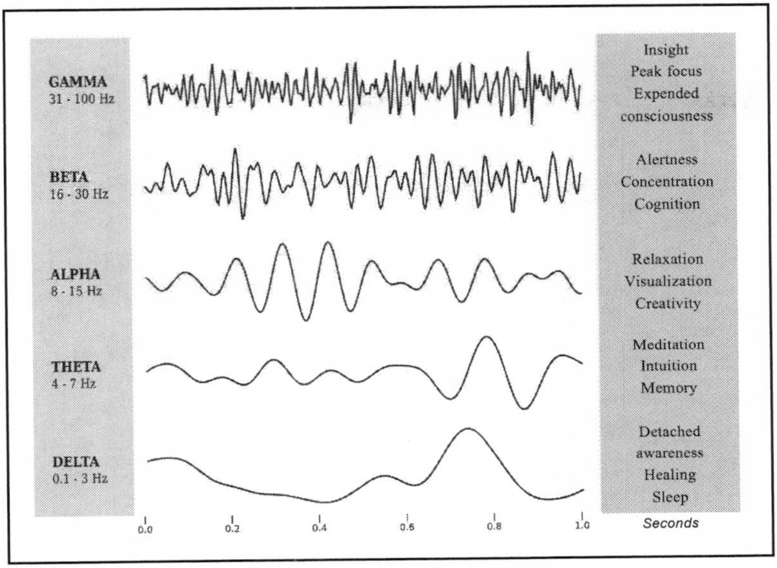

Adapted from www.123rf.com image

The way gamma brainwaves are generated remains a mystery as the gamma frequency is above the neuronal firing frequency. It is speculated that gamma rhythms regulate perception and consciousness. Gamma brainwaves can be boosted through mediation, and by focusing our attention on our breathing, blocking out other senses. Research has also shown that gamma waves are helpful to reduce stress, anxiety, and depression.

A significant gamma wave is also referred to as expanded consciousness and spiritual emergence, a sense of more profound connection with other people, nature, and the universe. However, excessive amounts of gamma waves could lead to hyperactivity, insomnia, schizophrenia, delusions, and hallucinations. It is the fine line where genius and insanity meet.

2. **BETA brainwaves (12 to 30Hz)**

   Beta brainwaves are associated with a highly attentive mind. It is activated during most of our normal waking state of consciousness. When we are actively engaged in cognitive tasks like delivering a speech, solving highly complicated problems, making complex decisions, learning new subjects, or any mental activity with the world outside of us, we are accessing beta brainwaves.

   When we are at work, we trigger beta brainwaves most of the time. However, an extended period of continual engagement in beta wave related activity drains a vast amount of energy which leads to exhaustion, restlessness, or burnout in the long run.

3. **ALPHA brainwaves (7.5 to 14Hz)**

   Alpha brainwaves are the resting state of the brain. Alpha frequency is usually prompted when we are in a deep state of relaxation. Alpha waves significantly boost beta-endorphin, norepinephrine, and dopamine, which reduce pain and increases mental clarity and intuition. Alpha brainwaves also enable us to have a better sense of humour and be more composed.

   Alpha brainwaves are beneficial to our wellbeing in many ways. It supports general mental coordination, vigilance, mind-body integration, and learning. It also boosts relaxation, imagination, visualisation, mindfulness, increases awareness, and presence. However, an abundance of alpha-wave activity in the left frontal areas of the brain can make an individual more biologically susceptible to depression.

   When we slow down our physical activity to a meditative or relaxation state, we can access the alpha brain waves and let thoughts flow quietly. Alpha brainwaves also reduce stress and depression, relieve anxiety, raise resistance to stress, and increase pain tolerance. Some hospitals and operating theatres play alpha-wave music to calm their patients and reduce their pain.

Generally, we feel a sense of peace when we are out trailing in nature, seating by the waterfall or on the beach, far from the noise and buzz of the city, because the earth is like a gigantic circuit. The planet Earth surrounds and protects all living beings with its electromagnetic field, which, like the brainwaves at rest, generates an average natural frequency of 7.83 Hz. Ultimately, alpha waves increase emotional stability, productivity, relationships, happiness, and more.

4. **THETA brainwaves (4 to 7.5Hz)**

Theta brainwaves are present when we are in a state of reduced consciousness, a twilight state, the moment when we are just waking up or drifting off to sleep, or drowning in a light sleep mode. Theta waves increase receptivity, vision, and inspiration. Flashes of dreamlike images and splashes of memories occur during this state. Theta is our gateway to our intuition and creating memories.

In the theta state, we might feel tipsy or experience the sensation of floating beyond our physical body. Our senses are withdrawn from the outer world and focused on impulses originating inside us. When we are in a dreamy state, the brainwaves are at the theta level—space where vivid imagery, intuition, and information beyond our conscious awareness lodge. It is also a space that hosts our fears, troubled history, and nightmares.

Some believe that the theta wave is a state of connecting to spirituality. A transcendence or a meditative state outside of our conscious awareness level. A condition that increases creativity, enhances learning, reduces stress, awakens intuitions, gains insights, and heightens extrasensory perceptive skill. Hence, it is an optimal stage for inducing beliefs or affirmations.

5. **DELTA brainwaves (0.5 to 4Hz)**

Delta brainwaves are the brain's slowest frequency cycle. They are activated when we are in a deep, dreamless sleep. Delta waves are associated with complete loss of consciousness. People with a high amount of delta brainwaves, have longer hours of deep sleep and are more intuitive. They also have a higher level of empathy and, therefore, are more compassionate.

Our neurons and other cells' regeneration is accelerated in this state. Deep recuperative sleep is, therefore, critical for natural restoration and healing of our body. For this reason, when we are feeling down, sad, depressed, hurt, or injured, we have the natural urge of wanting to sleep more.

Now that we know the different brainwaves and how they contribute to the state of our mind and wellbeing, we can begin to be more aware of our surroundings and reprogram our life better. Neuroscience helps unlock the greater natural potential in us.

REPROGRAMMING BRAINWAVES

Different brainwaves control different levels of our focus, motivation, mood, and wellbeing. Just as the law of polarity, everything that exists has the same and exact opposite; we must balance the different brainwave activities. An excessive amount of high-frequency waves can cause delusions, hallucinations, or schizophrenia. An excess of low-frequency waves can increase passivism, sadness, anxiety, and depression. But a balance between the two gives us a sound mind.

It is not surprising at after the build-up towards an adrenaline rush event like hosting a huge conference, Christmas party, or major exams, only to find ourselves feeling exhausted and melancholic the next day. Our body regulates itself like the pendulum swing, balancing a high-brainwave day when we were highly engaged physically and mentally, with a low-brainwaves period, to rest and recuperate. This swing should not be simply concluded as bipolar disorder.

The of the few reasons why depression and poor mental health are on the rise, despite technological advances, is the increase in screening time and many thoughtless hours spent on social media. Spending more than four hours a day on screen without active participation, lower brainwave frequency and increased disillusionment, self-doubt, isolation, which lowers self-esteem, self-identity, inactivity, and thus, depression, aggression, or even suicidal thoughts.

Most of the poor mental health challenges we are facing today can be treated through counselling, coaching, neurofeedback, or biofeedback. Neurofeedback therapists use EEG to monitor brain activity with acoustic or visual signals and attempt to teach their patients to self-regulate their brain functions. The therapists systematically guide their patients to learn new ways of responding to negative triggers by rewarding actions that provoke desired brain signals.

Hypnotherapy can also reverse disempowering mental states like anger, doubt, guilt, sadness, and depression, by creating psychologically safe spaces where the brainwaves are lowered to a trance-like subconscious theta state. This state will lower defences, heighten intuition, perception, imagination, and learning. The therapists will then safely elicit the past "painful" experiences from their patients and guide their patients to let go of the past and capture lessons from that painful experience. By using verbal repetitions and mental images, patients are guided subsequently, through a process of acknowledging and letting go of their pain by forgiving their cause of the pain and replacing disempowering beliefs with empowering ones to regain control over their life.

Therapists also help patients create vivid imaginations of their desires in their mind by painting a picture of how their desired state looks, sounds, smells, feels, and tastes like in their mind-eyes. By tapping into as many sensory organs as possible in their mind, patients create new neuronal pathways which heightened their possibilities.

Since energy cannot be generated or destroyed, but can only be transferred or altered from one form to another, brainwave energy can be transferred from one person to the other and vice versa. That is why, the mood and spirit of humans are contagious. We influence and are influenced by the events and people we spend the most time with. They shape our thoughts, feelings, perceptions, self-esteem, decisions, and actions.

According to Jim Rohn, we are the average of the five people we spend most of our time with. Their enthusiasm, optimism, and approach to issues and life will also have an impact on us. We could not soar like the eagles if we hung out with chickens.

For this reason also, when we expend our learning beyond our area of expertise to a combination of science, art, philosophy, and spiritual knowledge, it enhances our ability to overcome the challenges we face in life as we begin to tap into multiple intelligence which produces different brainwaves. When we armed ourselves with the understanding of what we could do, the abundant resources available to us, and the people we are with, we begin to take our lives in our hands and create the reality we desire. That is one of the most powerful ways to start reprogramming ourselves to get ahead in the new world order.

5

THE MIND
SCIENCE OF HUMANS

Things are not always what they seem;
the first appearance deceives many;
the intelligence of a few perceives what has been carefully hidden.
— Phaedrus

CARL JUNG, a famous Swiss psychoanalyst, once said, "Everything that irritates us can lead us to an understanding of ourselves. The feeling of being irritated is a psychological projection of our self-defence mechanism; to avoid confronting specific characteristics that are in us."

There are systematic patterns in the way we receive and process information. Our minds are creative in finding shortcuts to direct our emotions, decisions, and behaviours, depending on how we shape it. The way we shape our mind's internal representation of the outer world is called metaprogramming—how the brain pays attention to what we have pre-programmed it to pay attention to. Changing the metaprogrammes in our minds is another key to transforming our lives.

In Chapter 3, we have learned that when our sensory receptors receive stimuli from the outer world, billions of neurons transduce external physical energy into neuronal signals internally. Trillions of synaptic activities happen in the brain and throughout the body's central nervous system (CNS), transmitting these neuronal signals to give instructions to our bodily functions.

Our brains go through a process of digesting, interpreting, and filtrating stimuli from the outer world, converting them into messages in electrochemical signals that is "meaningful" to us before absorbing and assimilating to our existing worldviews, forming new "meanings" for us. That process happens in fractions of a second. That is also how we, the humans, acquire new knowledge and why we "change our minds" when we received more information from the outer world. These meanings are the values and beliefs we hold, and they generate emotional forces which move our physiology being into action.

The brain has a unique ability to interpret and reorganise information vital to us before storing into our memories for later use. The brain also sends commands to our body muscles to respond to the external stimuli. The different speed at which electrochemical signals transmit these messages generates different energy waves. These waves penetrate our whole body and back to the outer world to create our reality.

Our brains also have the unique ability to decode and store information in our memory by breaking it down into pieces and distributing it in different parts of the brain. When we need to recall a memory, the brain pulls together the relevant chunks from the different parts of the brain in a split-second, depending on the circumstances in which we need to recall the memory.

During the recall, the brain undergoes a process of "creative reinvention" to retrieve chunks of information mixed with an awareness of the current state surrounding us at the time of recalling and reinterpreting the information. In other words, our brains do not record an event like a written book or recorded video, which can be played back exactly as an event was recorded. When our brains try to remember an event, the information is distorted to some degree.

For this reason, crime witnesses could not remember exactly what they had seen at the crime scene. It is common for witnesses to doubt themselves or become confused when they are feeling stressed and pressured to testify in front of the juries, lawyers, and judges in court. The recollection of the memory of an event largely depends on the emotional state when we need to do so. This also means, no matter how objective we want to be, we are largely, subjective beings. This is why a group view is always better than a single view.

Neuroscientists, psychiatrists, and psychologists generally agree neurons have no emotional properties by themselves and are not aware of their surroundings and unaware of its physical manifestations. Our minds, however, decide which information we would absorb and which we would throw away. Therefore, two people might interpret the same event differently.

In the law of perpetual transmutation energy, energy cannot be created or destroyed, but can be transformed from one form to another. Similarly, the neurons in our brains convert energy from external stimuli into electrochemical signals and instruct our body to respond to the stimuli, and transform electrochemical signals to other forms of energy in the outer world, and hence, create our new reality.

The energy goes through a process in our inner world as new thoughts, feelings, memories, and cause our philology to rise into action and transduce the energy into physical form in the outer world, thus causing consequences or rewards. Hence, the result in our lives is a direct result of the way we process and respond to an event; the way we respond to an event has a lot to do with our belief systems. In summary, our inner world creates our outer world. That is the science of the law of attraction.

Viktor Frankl once said, "Between stimulus and response, there is a space. In that space is our power to choose our response. In our response lies our growth and our freedom." This can be explained in Image 5:1 below. Some people tend to believe an event directly causes the results of their life, the consequence. They do not have any control over what happened to them.

However, there is a space between what happened in our lives, like the unprecedented COVI-19, and what happens in us, how we choose to respond, which produces the results in our lives subsequently. When we can control what happens within us, we can control what happens outside of us. We can reprogram our minds and attitudes to determine how we respond to the event and find new ways to get ahead. When we take ownership, become accountable and responsible, we become a victor, not a victim of the circumstances.

Image 5.1: Inner World Influences Consequence

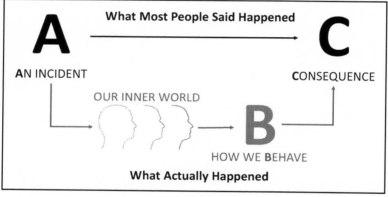

In this chapter, we learn how our minds process thoughts and how we can tap into the different brainwaves to create our reality to realise our desires and dreams. With this understanding, we can reprogram the way we learn, think, feel, and behave to achieve a different outcome in life.

This is where we begin to understand the famous quote from Lao-Tze and Mahatma Gandhi, "Our beliefs become our thoughts. Our thoughts become our words. Our words become our actions.

Our actions become our habits. Our habits become our character. Our character becomes our destiny." First of all, we do that by increasing our awareness of the operating systems in our minds.

LEVELS OF CONSCIOUSNESS

In the early 1900s, Sigmund Freud, the famous Austrian psychologist, developed an iceberg analogy to describe the three levels of our minds and how they work. A model that fits his idea of the id, the ego, and the superego. Freud was not the one who invented the concept of the conscious, the subconscious or the preconscious mind, and the unconscious mind. However, he was responsible for popularising it to mainstream society and subsequently inspired much research.

Image 5.2: Three Levels of Human Consciousness

10% **Conscious Mind**	Rational and analytical Conscious Decisions Short-term memory Beta Brainwaves
50% - 60% **Subconscious Mind**	Feelings and Emotions Background, Filters Long-term memory Alpha or Theta Brainwave
30% - 40% **Unconscious Mind**	Perception, Worldviews Immune Systems Automatic functions Theta or Delta Brainwaves

CopyRight@ShuTzeTan

There are three levels of consciousness in our minds: conscious, subconscious, and unconscious.

1. **CONSCIOUS MIND**

   The conscious mind consists of all mental processes we are aware and think about. Human consciousness accounts for about 10% of our brain's capacity, merely the tip of the iceberg. The conscious mind contains all the activities like sensations, perceptions, memories, fantasies, and feelings which are inside of our current awareness. A level at when the brain generates beta brainwaves when we are engaged in thoughts dealing with logic, facts and figures, analyse numbers and data, process cause and effect, identify and solve problems.

2. **SUBCONSCIOUS MIND**

   The subconscious mind clings to our beliefs, feelings and emotions that we are not aware of unless it is elicited to our awareness level. When we perform a task without being aware of the action, it is a learned respond stored in our subconscious mind

   The time when we stepped on the emergency brake in the car when we saw a dog suddenly dashing across the road, that reflex is a learned reaction, the muscle memory stored in our subconscious mind. Memories in the subconscious mind can be recalled to the conscious level when the situation calls for it without much effort.

   Non-extreme emotional experiences can also be stored in our subconscious. Our subconscious also speaks to us in dreams, intuition, fantasy and physical symptoms like sweaty palms, racing hearts and many more.

   50% to 60% of our minds are on the subconscious level. When our awareness level is heightened, mindful of our present, aware of where we are, what we are doing, and not being overwhelmed by what is happening around us, we begin to gain more control over our thoughts, feelings, and behaviours.

   Research has also found when we train ourselves to be more mindful, we remodel the physical structure of our brains. We increase our mental, emotional, and physical capability. That is, how mindfulness brings a subconscious mind to the conscious level, which increases creativity, intuition, and productivity.

3. **UNCONSCIOUS MIND**

The unconscious mind controls many of our bodily functions automatically, even when someone is in a coma. The unconscious mind is also a reservoir of beliefs, values, feelings, urges, and memories that lie outside of our conscious stratum. These forgotten or suppressed memories drastically influence our thoughts, feelings, judgments, and behaviour.

According to Freud, the unconscious mind is the primary source of human behaviour. It ensures we react precisely as we are pre-programmed. It ensures everything we say and do fit into our self-image and our worldviews. It makes sure our behavioural patterns are consistent with the values and beliefs we hold.

Trauma and abuse are sometimes suppressed into our memory at the unconscious level. It is a form of neural defence mechanism to protect ourselves. Our neurons store unbearable pain or sudden unexpected stimuli, like a severe accident which could incapacitate us if that stimulus is noticed in our conscious mind.

When a person cannot recall what happened after an accident, the memories of that accident were pushed into the unconscious mind. That is nature's way of protecting us from intense experiences that cause extreme pain, anger, guilt, self-doubt, or grief.

Memories hidden in our subconscious and unconscious mind are outside of our awareness level, and hence, we cannot change them. If the memories were painful and are not elicited, they could cripple mental health and cause anxiety, depression, or post-traumatic stress disorder (PTSD) like eating disorder, substance abuse, obsessive-compulsive-disorder (OCD), intense rage, or self-inflicted pain.

It can also cause chronic illness. 60% to 80% of illnesses are stress-related illness unknown to us. But nature has a way of telling us if a hidden memory is there. It will show up in our dreams or manifest itself through our irritation to a particular person, event, or words.

The rising numbers of poor mental health like anxiety, depression, dissociation, loneliness, or public display of anger like destroying public properties, homicides, or suicides today is a clear indication of many unresolved emotional pains.

The good news is, once we can bring to our awareness level of the pain, and let go of the painful memory, we begin to regain control of our minds. This can be done with the help of neurotherapists to elicit the hidden painful memories and reassign new meanings to it so that those events in the past can serve us better. This must be accompanied by new ways and new skills of responding to the same triggers that used irritate us.

That is how we master our past to move forward instead of letting our past command our life. This is also why miracle healing does happen. A chronic illness could cure suddenly without scientific explanation when our minds reassigned a new meaning to a painful event it endured.

Now that we know the different levels of consciousness in our minds, we can increase our success to get ahead by raising our level of consciousness. Many people to that today through meditation, mindfulness, and physical exercise that brings them to the conscious level and peak state.

FILTERS AND INTERNAL REPRESENTATIONS

Massive stimuli from the outer world continuously bombard at the trillions of sensory receptors found in all over our body, beneath our skins, and sensory motors—sounds of buzzing traffic, the screaming children in the background. The smell of coffee from the pantry, taste of sweetness from the doughnut, texture of the clothes on our skin, colours and shapes on our computer screen.

Whenever our body receives external stimuli, our minds automatically filter out information not important to us. Otherwise, we will become insanely mad if all our sensory receptors simultaneously receive and process trillion bits of stimuli all the time.

Interestingly, there is a fine line between "madness" and "genius". The level of filtration by our minds determine the level of "reasonability" and "madness" in us. Aristotle once said, "There is no great genius without some touch of madness." It is believed the mind of geniuses absorbs and processes more information from external stimuli than the average person, and therefore, geniuses are more creative. But, they are also prone to psychological disorders.

John Forbes Nash Jr, a mathematician and an American 1994 Nobel Prize of Economic Science who contributed to game theory and partial differential equations, was one scientist who struggled with paranoid schizophrenia for many years. Vincent Van Gogh, who was regarded as one of the most creative artistic geniuses of his time, suffered from psychotic episodes and delusions. He neglected his physical health by not eating properly and drinking heavily. He was depressed to the point of madness and said to have cut off his own ear and killed himself.

So the next question is, how do our minds filter information? How do our minds determine which information is important, meaningful, and would serve our needs, and which is not?

When our sensory receptors are triggered, our brains use the pre-programmed filters and internal representations in our subconscious and unconscious mind to decide which information to keep, and which to discard.

The filters consist of metaprogrammes, beliefs, values, and memories, which develop through the accumulation of life experiences, exposure, learning, and the environment we are associating ourselves with. These filters also form our personalities, interests, preferences, attitudes, and current states and play a significant role in our cognitive-perception preferences.

For example, some of us are motivated to work towards pursuing a desire, while some of us are driven to achieve because we are fearful of getting into the situation we do not want, and we want to get away from it. Some of us measure success by getting external feedback, while others measure growth through internal self-evaluation, no matter what others say. Some of us love reptiles and keep them as pets, and some of us cannot even stand the sight of snakes and iguanas. Some of us become enraged when we see an animal being abused and will do whatever we can to stop that, but it might not the same effect on others. It is the way we are wired inside, and the world has a different meaning to every one of us.

Image 5.3: Filters and Internal Representation in Our Minds

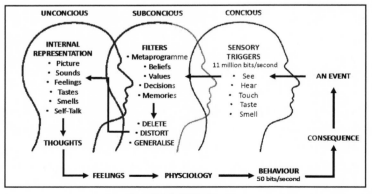

114

As information passes through the filters in our minds, through our metaprogramming, beliefs, values, past decisions, and memories, the process of deletion, distortion, and generalisation happens.

1. **DELETION**

The deletion occurs when we overlook, omit, or tune out. As our minds cannot receive all the information firing at us from the outside world all the time, our minds will delete a significant part of the external stimuli.

That allows our minds to focus on what is important and meaningful to us at any given time and leaves out irrelevant and unimportant ones. As we enter a park in the city, we may notice the freshness of the cool air on our face. But we may not notice the variety of trees or animals in the park. We may notice a bird chirping on a nearby tree, but unaware of the quiet, buzzing traffic far behind us.

Selective attention is, therefore, nature's will. We can minimise selective attention by raising the awareness level of our perceptions and feelings, and being aware of the information we would usually dismiss. When we raise our awareness, we increase our attention to things we tend to disregard. When we do that, we are "opening up" our minds to receive and process more foreign information than we usually would in the past.

Deletion also occurs in incomplete sentences, leaving readers or listeners to fill in the gaps. For example, when someone said, "They know what to do." Would the listener know who they are exactly? What is the thing that they know what to do and not do? How do they know what to do?

Although details are crucial, and detailed statements force us to assume the responsibility behind the words we say, most of the time, we do not do that. Sometimes, this happens when the speaker is unclear about the details or does not want to be held responsible, hence, leaving listeners to form assumptions of the details.

2. DISTORTION

Distortion is a process of having something presented in a way that makes it appear different from the original intent or the truth, and hence, twisting perceptions. Due to our preference, assumptions, biases, and prejudices, our minds distort information we receive to reinforce or diminish specific experiences to fit us.

We distort information according to the level of adoption and assimilation our minds do. We distort information automatically whenever we use assumptions to justify our beliefs, even if we are unaware of it. It is a process of the mind adopting new information received to existing beliefs, values, and decisions we hang on to. Distortion forges new information obtained suitable for us by selectively and integrating with the information we already have in our memory.

People with a growth-mindset are more open to foreign ideas because they distort new information less and allow their mind to understand and absorb foreign information faster. Whereas, closed minded-people are typically more selective in adapting and assimilating the information received. They tend to reject most new ideas to safeguard the existing beliefs, values, decisions, and memories they have and are still serving their purpose well.

For this reason, when we ask more open questions and allow people to share more, we gain more insights into their assumptions, beliefs, values, and decisions. This is why we perceive a similar event differently, and collective insights give us a more holistic view.

Fearful of an adverse event, being hurt, procrastination, or misinterpreting of what others might say are often symptoms of distortion too. Similarly, creativity or innovation, imagining, and visualising, are also forms of distortion, which leads to the reconstructed new ideas.

3. GENERALISATION

Generalisation occurs when we reach global conclusions from one or two experience as a representation to every other experience or everyone else, without paying attention to exceptions. When we extend one single event and generalise it to all other events to achieve an objective, we are generalising. We do that to avoid getting into the details or to simplify a matter.

Generalisation happens most frequently when someone justifies themselves by effecting their experience common to all others. Keywords like "never", "always", "every" is used in generalisation statements. For example, "I can never be competent in this", "No one understands me", "You are always not around" generalise every event or action, without referring to a specific occurrence.

Our minds receive about 11 billion bits of data per second, but only reproduces 50 bits per second to the external world. We only pay attention to a small part of the information received and throw away most of it through our filters. This is why a specific event triggers certain emotions in some people, but not in others.

When we are not aware of the filters in our minds and rely on filtered information, assumptions, and conclusions, we are limiting our beliefs or creating imaginary barriers that may not exist. It is, therefore, imperative that we are aware of these filters to expand our minds. We do this by training our minds to listen to different viewpoints, seek more information and understanding on foreign ideas that challenge our thoughts and feelings.

Once the information has gone through the filters, it goes through a matching process with our internal representation. The internal representation is our model of the world or our worldview. When we were conceived in our mother's womb, our minds have begun to curate inner representation, assigning meanings and values to the stimuli we receive and shape our beliefs.

Our minds confirm what we see, hear, feel, taste, and smell with the experiences we have and stored in our memories. If the matching is favourable to us, it will generate a pleasurable feeling and positive physiological responses. If the information is against our internal representation of the world, our minds will generate negative emotions and responses.

For example, we are attracted to a particular smell because it reminds us of the pleasant smell of our mother. Perhaps we are afraid of spiders because we had witnessed how our mother jumped out of their skin when they sighted a spider crawling across the hallway. We store many life experiences which have deep meaning and impact on us in our long-term memory, in the unconscious mind.

Our internal representation takes shape at a very early age. Babies started life by demanding to have their needs to be met. Because they can only eat, poop, and sleep with the help of adults. Life began by focusing on fulfilling their own needs and was, therefore, self-centred for the sole purpose of survival. But babies will soon realise there are other people around them, and these other people have needs too. Kids as young as 18 months of age have been encouraged to share themselves, their attention, and their toys with others. The way they realise and learn of these can be pleasant or traumatic and create internal representation in their inner world.

From the age of 3, the expectation of sharing becomes frequent and formal. From the age of 4 onwards, some begin to realise that sharing is a good thing. Children's moral reasoning starts to form from the age of 6 years old. Between the ages of 7 to 8 years of age, they become more receptive to social norms, fairness, and justice.

During these tender years, people around young children play crucial roles in communicating and shaping their values, beliefs, and worldviews. Children learn and adapt to the values and beliefs of people who are important to their lives. People they look up to, admire, and respect, including their parents, grandparents, older siblings, aunts, uncles, older cousins, nannies, and school teachers.

The filters and internal representations are also formed from people they do not like— people who hurt them or cause harm to their loved ones. They might decide not to become like the people they do not like.

Internal representations continue to build up and evolve as they guide our interactions with the world. Our beliefs, values, and worldviews continue to intensify as more evidence agree or dispute existing representations. The information that does not match with our internal representation it would generate negative emotions. If the information is congruent and serves our purpose, it will be further strengthened and intensifying our internal representation.

We become more agile and adaptive when we are more open to exploring foreign inputs that challenge our existing perceptions, emotions, and behaviours. When we are open to new inputs, our neurons will form new synapses throughout our body to cause a new physiological reaction, and hence, produce different results.

By changing the filters and internal representations in our minds, we begin to have different beliefs, different ways of thinking, and thus different behaviours and outcomes. The more open, receptive, and agile we are to foreign inputs, the faster we can bring about change in ourselves and the world. That is how we reprogram our minds to get ahead into the unknown, yet an exciting era.

REPROGRAMMING THE MIND

Now that we know our minds have the power to process information and make it meaningful to us, we can rewire our minds physically and psychologically to be more agile and adaptable to the new world.

The three most important actions we can take are: protecting the mind, reprogramming belief systems, and optimising health.

1. **PROTECTING THE MINDS**

   As the mind is the most powerful system in the world, we get to protect it and provide it with the input it needs to continue to serve us better. Since the visual and auditory sensory receptors receive most of the information from the external world, we also need to select what we see, hear and read carefully.

   We could spend hours watching dramas, fantasy films, listening to critics without finding solutions, or reading negative posts and lamenting depressing news on social media. Or we could spend hours watching a documentary or autobiography shows, listening to Ted Talks, reading well-researched books, and spending time with the people we want to become. The environment to which our minds are exposed over an extended period will promote or prohibit our growth.

   The information we continuously receive from the activities we engage in will shape the filters and internal representation of our thinking. As our thoughts, beliefs, values, and worldviews change with new experiences, our attitudes, and behaviours will change. So are the results in our lives. Protecting what goes into our minds is, therefore, one of the first keys to getting ahead.

   Our parents are right when they tell us to "choose your friends wisely." Collin Powell, a well-respected General of the United State Army and the Secretary of State to George W. Bush once said, "Never receive counsel from unproductive people. Never discuss your problems with someone incapable of contributing to the solution. Not everyone has a right to speak into your life. Hence, we should never ask for advice from someone we do not want to swap places with, and we need to choose our associate wisely."

   We become like those we are closely connected to, for better or for worse. That is because the energy from our enthusiasm, beliefs, values, worldviews and attitudes to life will penetrate through the transmission of energy vibrations through our neuronal signals.

That also explains why we feel exhausted when we spend time with the wrong people and in the wrong environment. When we radiate more energy than we receive, our energy is sapped. But when we spend time in a positive and reciprocal environment, our energy levels rise. Great leaders who achieve significant results are eager readers and are part of the inner circle of other leaders with common goals. They share and give input together. Just as our body needs to eat regularly, so do our minds. The first step in reprogramming our minds is to shield it from negativity and feed it with positive matters.

Since our minds could not distinguish between what is real and what is not, the hours we spend watching make-believe video clips and carefully selected blissful posts on social media make us feel, "I am not good enough because I am not like them." When we face the real world, which is different from the make-believe world, we begin to experience alienation, isolation, depression, anger, and develop aggression. These feelings generate negative frequencies or aura in our minds.

Consequently, people who went through social media fasting" for a few days suffered withdrawal syndrome, like other addicts. And as they began to replace the hours spent on social media with activities like personal communication with others, exercising together, reading books, learning new skills, and other empowering activities, they began to think and feel differently and become a different person. When we replace our habits, we change.

Ultimately, we have a responsibility to ourselves and our loved ones to protect our minds. We work with the laws of nature to do our best. As nature is not biased and does not judge, it does not play favouritism. In areas we spend most of our time with, the energy frequency will impress our brainwaves, which influence our thoughts, feelings, and actions to create our reality.

2. REPROGRAMMING BELIEF SYSTEMS

Our belief systems come from our worldview and assumptions of how the world works. One of the biggest obstacles to get ahead is our beliefs. There are many missed opportunities due to self-limiting beliefs, which create emotional barriers and prevent us from achieving what we are capable of. That is why anyone can be who they want, but not everyone will.

It is unimaginable how many self-sabotaging conversations and behaviours destroy opportunities. Yet many people are unaware of their self-limiting beliefs, which prevent them from reaching their fullest potential. If we have recorded what we tell ourselves every minute of the day, we will be shocked at how unkind we are to ourselves. We often sabotage our success.

The most common self-sabotaging behaviours are projected through self-talk. Words like "I can't" "I am not good enough" "I am shy" "I am a procrastinator" "I do not have the money or the time," and even, "I am not that courageous or not that smart" reflect the assumptions and beliefs we hold internally.

Saying, "I will try" instead of saying, "I will," and "If God's willing" instead of saying "I will do it with the power and faith God has granted me" is another subtle, self-sabotaging word. When we say, "I will try," or "If God's willing," we create a psychologically backdoor for us to escape, just in case if we cannot achieve what we have set out to do.

That also means, "I do not want to be held responsible for any results." On the contrary, saying "I will" does not mean that we will not fail, it what we do after each fall that matters. When we take the results of our lives into our own hands, we will gather ourselves after each fall and find new ways to reach our desires.

Use of the word "but" is another subtle projection of self-sabotaging behaviours. "But" makes the justification permissible, and as human beings, we have learned to forge excuses from the day we find ways to truancy at an early age. We simply use "but" to escape the brutal truth in our lives.

Since our minds do not know what is real and what is not, and nature's law does not choose between the good and the bad, when we say, "I want to lose weight, but I have inherited my parents' genetics" or, "I want to achieve my goal, but I am a procrastinator", nature will respond to the two opposites with one idea cancels out the other. For this reason, we do not see any progress, even if we have a strong desire. So, in our conversations, we get to be aware of the "but."

Nature creates whatever we believe. Our words generate the neural signals and influence the brainwave frequency that permeates inside and outside of us, aligning our feelings and behaviour so that everything we say becomes true. The results further reinforce our limiting beliefs. It is a downward spiral vicious circle.

That is a socio-psychological phenomenon, a self-fulfilling prophecy. A prediction or expectation fulfilled simply because our beliefs lead to a behavioural adaptation to meet the belief. It is a unique way in which our body aligns and sabotages itself to satisfy what we believe and expect.

Self-limiting thoughts also provide psychological safety, sympathy, and forgiveness if we are not able to live up to an expectation, whether the expectation is legitimate or not. To make matters worse, if our self-limiting conversations and behaviours are accepted and compensated by others, it will fuel our thoughts, "It's okay if I don't fulfil my desires."

A self-limiting belief is a form of avoidance. We use self-limiting conversations and behaviours to avoid facing the brutal truth in our lives. Instead of entering the uncomfortable space of confronting the problems behind our feelings of envy, denial, doubt, anger, guilt, and sadness, we are moving further away from reality through self-limitation.

Self-limiting beliefs protect us from facing the brutal truth by increasing our inability to face challenges. With self-limitation, we allow the circumstances around us and others to control our lives. We become victims of circumstances and others. We justify our inaction with excuses and blame. A self-imposed disorder we often do without realising it.

Aggression behaviours towards others is also a form of projection of self-limiting beliefs. Verbally or physically belittling others is a form of a psychological need to elevate oneself to be better than others. That is why people who are hurting, hurt people. And the person who is hurting avoids confronting issues they have with themselves internally.

We must stop degrading ourselves with self-limiting beliefs and behaviours. It is inappropriate and dishonouring our parents and our creator. Timidity has nothing to do with humility. Diminishing ourselves is not an act of humility, and it is not attractive at all. We overcome our self-limiting beliefs by reprogramming our belief systems. As earlier discussed, our minds continue to evolve with whatever we expose it to over an extended period. We change our belief systems by changing what we see, hear and read over time.

One powerful way to change our belief systems is by minding our language. Language is a powerful aspect of the human mind and creativity. Our brain forms countless structures, ideas, and meanings with word combinations from the language when we learn to speak, understand, read, and write. These structures influence our moral judgments and construct our thoughts, beliefs, and behavioural patterns.

There is an old English expression that says, "mind your Ps and Qs" which means, "mind your language, mind your manner, and be on your best behaviours." Religious teachers will tell us to watch what we say and not to use damnation words. When we "watch what we are doing," we control what comes in and out of our thoughts, words, and behaviours. That is why, when we change the words coming out from our mouth, our world changes.

A simple change, like replacing "but" with "and" immediately changes the state of our minds. "But" stops us from thinking about possible solutions. "And" opens our minds to find solutions to reach our goals. For example, when we say, "I want to lose 10 kilos by January 2020, <u>and</u> I tend to hesitate," we recognise both our desire and a problem we have without being judged, then our brain starts to generate possible solutions.

We can also change our words by replacing phrases like "I do not know how" with "There is someone I can learn from." Replacing "I am not good at it" with "I can learn to get good at it" change our outlooks. When we use empowering statements and ask the right questions, our minds begin to think of possible solutions. Hence, empowering words serve our purpose.

Neurolinguistic therapists help their clients similarly change belief systems by asking a series of reflective questions, to give new meaning to a painful event that forms behavioural patterns that no longer serves them. When we are in a psychologically safe space, we can face up to the old beliefs, acknowledge how the old beliefs have served and protected us all these years, but no longer so. Once we can face up to what is going on inside us and make the change with new meanings, we can move forward to achieve the desired results.

That is why influencing others takes time. While we provide information to our stakeholders, we get to give them time to reflect old beliefs with new information and assign meaning to them. Once they have a psychologically safe space to re-evaluate and change their beliefs and values, their thoughts and decisions change.

Being grateful is another powerful way to change our belief systems to fight self-limiting beliefs. When we acknowledge and are thankful for the good things that have happened in our lives, even if we sometimes feel unworthy, we begin to be grateful for what we have rather than focusing on what we lack.

The more grateful we are, the more appreciative we are of life and the people around us. When we acknowledge what we already have, instead of having to protect ourselves from further hurts with limiting beliefs, we will have more courage to move forward. Recognition of what we have received even from people we did not expect humiliates us and helps us to be aware of the love, care, and resources around us.

Being grateful also means being able to say thank you when we receive compliments from others. In saying, thank you, we accept the feedback from others that we are on the right track. We acknowledge our growth, and we commit ourselves to move forward. When we say "thank you" to pay compliments, we also pay tribute to the person who is grateful for his encouragement, grace and ability to spot goodness. When we reciprocate by appreciating them, we grow.

Gratitude encourages us to become a better person, to take more ownership of our lives. Once we have acknowledged the abundant resources that help us move forward, our thoughts are more likely to be open to constructive feedback, we begin to see more opportunities and realise more resources available to us, and therefore, move forward better. When this happens, positive emotions begin to flow, and our brain waves start to generate energy that forms the desired result. It also prepares us to take on more significant responsibility and make a difference for others. And our needs for actualization are also met.

3. OPTIMISING HEALTH

Health is the most crucial asset in life. It is the primary source of happiness in life. Poor health limits our ability to connect, work, live, and play. Poor health reduces economic opportunity and can lead to medical debt and even bankruptcy. It robs those affected and those around them of quality of life and joy of life.

Poverty is both the cause and the consequence of poor health as is poverty in terms of relationships and financial resources. When we become a good steward of our health, we would learn to manage our relationships and finances well. Therefore, it is essential to optimise our health to be ahead of the change.

Our minds are like our bodies. It needs to eat, sleep, poop, and repeat. Our body consists of cells that also regenerate themselves. Some cells regenerate within a few days, like the white blood cells, which are the leading players in fighting infections; others, like the red blood cells, within a few months. Some of our cells, like bones in our bodies, regenerate about every 7 to 10 years! So if we do not do the right thing for our health today, we may not immediately notice the adverse effects. The effect could occur in ten years.

We have 37 trillion cells to feed correctly so that our body has the right ingredients to regenerate bones, muscles, cerebrospinal fluid, and membrane to protect our brains and minds. Optimum health is, therefore, closely linked to flexibility and adaptability in the new world.

SCIENCE OF OPTIMAL HEALTH

In this chapter, we learned that when we are physically weak, our neurons trigger certain emotions which will affect our brainwaves, behaviour, and energy, with adverse consequences that, in turn, cause further downward feelings. Therefore, a healthy mind requires a healthy brain and body.

Four primary aspects of life that contribute to health: food, sleep, physical activity, and the environment:

1. **FOOD**

   We are what we eat. In addition to having culinary experiences, we also have a primary purpose of providing our body with the appropriate food it needs for efficient regeneration and bodily functions.

   In the last chapter, we learned that every cell in our body is made up of long chains of amino acids, which essentially form protein structures. These protein structures form the cells, tissues, organs, muscles, blood, hormones, and enzymes.

   We have also learned that chemical reactions and neuronal activity rates in our brains are a function of the quality of hormones and enzymes in our bodies. Hence, feeding our body to ensure the trillions of cells has the required materials, and the appropriate amount of nutrients to grow is vital.

   Nutrients in the food we consume can be divided into two main categories: macronutrients and micronutrients.

   Macronutrients are nutrients that our body needs in vast quantities. Macronutrients consist of protein, fats, carbohydrates, and water. Besides water, macronutrients are energy suppliers and indispensable for the body to grow, repair, and develop new tissues, guide nerve impulses, and regulate the life process.

   Micronutrients are nutrients our body needs in a lesser amount. Vitamins, minerals, and phytonutrients are forms of micronutrients. They are crucial for metabolism or chemical reactions in the body and the maintenance of all tissue functions. The primary purpose of micronutrients is to enable the chemical reactions in our bodily functions like synaptic activity in our brain.

   80% of our health is due to what we eat and fail to eat every day. A healthy adult human body should consist of 60% fluid, 18%

protein, 16% fat and 8% fat. However, most of us are out of that ideal proportion. Meanwhile, while more people are learning to eat healthier nowadays, unfortunately, the foods we have today are mostly processed, added with artificially flavoured, coloured, preservatives, and sodium.

Typically, an adult would need 0.8 grams of protein per kilogram of body weight. That is about 56 grams a day for an average sedentary adult weighing about 70 kilograms. Foods including dairy products, cheese, meat, poultry, fish, eggs, soy, mushrooms, lima beans, bean sprouts, Brussels sprouts, green peas, spinach, asparagus, artichokes, and broccoli contain protein and amino acids that our cells need.

In addition to protein, our body needs carbohydrates to fuel energy. The finest source of carbohydrates is complex carbohydrates from fruits and vegetables. Fruits and vegetables are best consumed whole, not in puree or juice form. That allows our body to work its way through to break down, digest, and absorb the nutrients naturally. When we blend vegetables and fruits into juices, we remove the work our body needs to consume energy from the food we eat, and to stay healthy. Moreover, when we consume juices or purees, we take in more fructose than we would normally require compared to eating whole fruits or vegetables.

Unfortunately, most of the food we consume is produced with simple carbohydrates. A significant portion of the food we take consists of like rice, including brown rice, multigrain rice, flour products including pasta, cakes, doughnuts, pau (Chinese buns), and flatbread, which are simple carbohydrates.

Simple carbohydrates are not ideal for our body because most micronutrients, vitamins, minerals, phytonutrients and fibre have been removed. Thus, when we eat simple carbohydrates, we are consuming sugar. And sugar is the root of all evil to our health.

According to the American Heart Association (AHA), men need an average of only 50 to 90 grams of carbohydrates per day and women an average of 50 to 80 grams of carbohydrates per day, depending on the level of physical activity. Excess carbohydrates that are not used or burned per day are stored as fats in our body, which becomes a problem. If we eat carbohydrates more than our body needs on any given day, the carbohydrates are converted into fats in our body.

Fats are also a source of nutrients that our body needs. On top of keeping us warm, fats also provide our bodies with energy, help our bodies absorb nutrients, and produce essential hormones. Fats are crucial for the formation of the cell membrane and the envelopes around the nerves, forming clots and fighting inflammation.

There are three types of fat: saturated fat, unsaturated fat, and omega-3. Saturated fats do not have double bonds in their chemical structure. Saturated fats are "saturated" with hydrogen molecules and contain only single bonds between carbon molecules, and therefore, have a solid consistency at room temperature. Due to its chemical structure, saturated fat causes cholesterol to build up in our blood vessels, increasing the risk of heart disease and stroke.

Many of our foods today contain saturated fat, which is harmful to our body. Saturated fats are found in animal meat, ready-to-eat snacks like crackers, crisps, biscuits, pastries, processed foods like hot dogs, sausages, bacon, dairy products including cheese, butter, milk, and certain oils like kernel and coconut oil.

Unsaturated fats contain one or more double bonds in their chemical structure and are therefore liquid at room temperature. The appropriate amount of unsaturated fats intake is pleasant for our body. We should include both monounsaturated and polyunsaturated fats found in nuts, olives, rapeseed, sunflower seeds, corn oil and avocados in our diet.

The third type of fat, which is crucial for our body, is omega-3 fatty acids. Research has shown that, while our body can produce most of the fats from other fats or raw materials, it cannot produce omega-3 fats. We can only feed our body with omega-3 fats with a genuine source of food, in fish, seaweeds, walnuts, flaxseeds, edamame, soybeans, and chia seeds.

Omega-3 fats are essential to creating a healthy membrane to protect each of the estimated 37 trillion cells in our bodies. A healthy membrane allows nutrient molecules from the food we eat to be absorbed into the cell. It also allows waste and toxins to be purged out from the cell.

If the membrane is unhealthy, the cell will starve because nutrients cannot get into the cell, and the cell becomes constipated when waste cannot be expelled from the cell through the membrane. A weak membrane causes cells to become weary, stressed, lethargic, decrepit, deformed or intoxicated, leading to heart disease, depression, dementia, arthritis and other health conditions.

While fats are vital for our body, the access fats are stored under the skin, behind the muscles, around the vital organs, in the blood and fluids in our body. Excess fats cause our organs to work harder than they should, limit synapses, and weaken electrochemical signal transmission activities. That, in turn, drastically increases the risks of hypertension, type-2 diabetes, Alzheimer's disease, Parkinson, sleep apnea, heartburn, joint pain, and difficulty in movement.

In addition to macronutrients, micronutrients are needed to ensure the wellbeing of cells. Most cells in the body consist of DNA, which contains genetic codes for the regeneration of new cells. Unhealthy or deformed cells carry genetic defect code and therefore regenerate defect cells, hence, cause various health risks, including cancer.

Micronutrients consist of vitamins, minerals, and phytonutrients which are essential groups of a nutrient our cells need. Vitamins are essential for energy production, immune function, blood clotting and many other functions. Minerals play a crucial role in growth, bone health, fluid balance and fine body processes.

Phytonutrients are extracted from plants that protect them from germs, fungi, bugs, bacteria and other threats, and therefore a significant source of antioxidants for our bodies.

Many people believe we can obtain sufficient minerals and vitamins by increasing fruit and vegetable intakes. Some will go vegan in hope to become healthier. More people are consuming more fruit and vegetables for health purposes. Many of us believe we do not need supplements if we consume a significant amount of fruit and vegetables.

However, according to the World Health Organisation (WHO), our body needs one serving of the five colours each from fruits and vegetables in every meal to obtain the required minerals and vitamins. A serving is about the size of our fist. Five portions of fruit and vegetables in five different colours per meal would leave a dent in our pocket over an extended period.

Furthermore, what confidence do we have on the amount of nutrients that remain in fruit and vegetables we buy on the market? Nutritional values in fruits and vegetables begin to deteriorate the moment they are being picked from the tree.

Moreover, according to a report in the International Journal of Science and Technology Research, water-soluble vitamins like vitamin C can be easily being destroyed during food processing and storage, and even exposed to temperatures as low as 30 degrees Celsius.

On top of that, extensive commercialised agriculture, agricultural activities, pollution, floods and climate change are causing soil quality to deteriorate. The quality of the physical, chemical and biological soil is declining worldwide, and the ability to produce high-quality, nutrients, fruits and vegetables is decreasing compared to centuries ago. Therefore, we have no choice but to add to our diet with supplements to fill the nutritional gaps in the food we take today.

Natural food supplements produced with fruits and vegetable extracts are more expensive compared to supplements produced by fruits and vegetable essence. But, cheaper compared to numbers of whole fruits and vegetables we should be consuming every day.

Some doctors advise against taking supplements, but not all doctors are the same. They are as good as the latest updates they know about humans and life. *"What the doctor doesn't know about nutritional medicine may be killing you"* according to a medical doctor, Dr Ray D. Strand, who is the author of that book.

Dr Ray also wrote, "Extensive studies have revealed the 'triage nurses in our bodies recognise damaged cell parts and then repair them. The body breaks down the damaged cells completely and then rebuilds them from scratch." Hence, our body needs the right nutrients to repair itself.

Many types of dietary supplements are available in the market today. But like anything else, everything appears similar, but they are not the same. Many dietary supplement companies do not have certified bioscience efficacy tests because the Food and Drug Associations (FDA) do not require that from them.

Unlike the regulation FDA imposes on drug manufacturers, all drug companies must conduct extensive laboratory, animal, and human clinical trials before submitting their data to the FDA. The FDA will then conduct independent tests and will only approve the drug for sale if the benefits of the drug are significantly more than the risks of its intended use. The process of getting every drug that is tested and approved for sale is a lengthy, complex, and costly process.

The FDA does not have the same authority to test and review supplement companies. The agency only audits the manufacturers and distributors of dietary supplements to ensure that they do not market products that are adulterated or mislabelled. In other words, dietary supplement manufacturers are responsible for proving that their products are safe, and the information on the label is truthful and not misleading.

For that reason, we need to be prudent consumers in choosing the appropriate dietary supplements which conduct biomonitoring and bioassessment to determine the effect and effectiveness. Choose dietary supplements consists of ingredients from certified organic farmers at the highest level.

Today, many consumer advocates are pressing the FDA to include dietary supplement products in its jurisdiction to review and approve the effectiveness and efficacy of what is claimed. Meanwhile, independent scientists are working together to test dietary supplements that claim to do what they do and publish the results on www.consumerlab.com.

Beyond the food we consume, water is another crucial component of our body's diet. About 60 to 70% of the human body consists of water in many forms, including blood, saliva, urine, semen, enzymes, hormones, and more. Most of the water in a human body is in the cells, tissues, muscles, brain, organs, blood, bones, and enzymes. 80% of our brain consists of water. Maintaining hydrated is, therefore, crucial for our brain and body.

The water has three critical roles; transporter, regulator, and stabiliser. Water provides oxygen and nutrients throughout the body and eliminates waste from the body. Water also regulates our body temperature. When we are feeling too warm, our body emits heat by excreting water.

Water also stabilises the internal environment of our body to maintain effective metabolism. It also keeps the mucous membranes moist, allowing body cells, hormones, and neurotransmitters to grow. Water also acts as a shock absorber for the brain and spinal cord. That is why we need to drink at least 2.5 to 3 litres of water daily for our body to function optimally.

It is vital to ensure that we consume sufficient clean water without contaminating chemicals like benzene, which often leaks underground and enters into water pipes, it is crucial to have a good water filter. We also want to choose water filters that can filter and kill water-borne diseases like germs, bacteria, and viruses including hepatitis, E-coli, corona and many more.

2. **SLEEP**

Sleep is also vital to our physical and mental health. Sleep relaxes our muscles, slows the frequency of our brainwaves down, lowers cortisol or the stress hormone level down, and strengthens the immune system. Since our brain has a way of regenerating itself, our body needs sufficient sleep for our brain to do its work of restoring, rejuvenating, building muscle, repairing tissues, and synthesising hormones.

Sleep helps our body and brain cells recover, detoxify, and heal. That is why, when we are sick or injured, our body would want to sleep more to fight inflammation, infection, and trauma. That is another reason why insufficient sleep increases the risk of health problems.

Sleep deprivation also reduces the clarity of our thoughts. There is extensive research on the effects of inadequate sleep on our health, cognitive abilities, and memory. Research has shown that sleep deprivation causes a condition like drunkenness. When we do not sleep for 17 hours straight up, our alertness is like those under the influence of alcohol with a blood alcohol concentration of 0.05%. A level considered "impaired" on the scale of legal alcohol consumption—a state where we will not concentrate well and are more accident-prone.

According to neuroscientist Dr Matthew Walker, who is also the author of the book, *Why We Sleep*, an overtired brain and body make us vulnerable to cancer. Alzheimer's disease, depression, anxiety, obesity, stroke, chronic pain, diabetes, and heart attacks, among other medical conditions.

Dr Matthew Walker also explained sleep helps with our brain activity in the hippocampus area. The hippocampus plays a vital role in receiving information, associating learning with emotions, and forming new memories.

In other words, sleep is closely linked to our learning ability. When we have a full 8 hours of sleep, we improve and restore the quality of our memory and learning. Sleeps also enable our brains to sort and process the information of the day, and this is crucial for creating long-term memories.

People with a full sleep of 8 to 9 hours have significant healthy learning activities in the brain. Meanwhile, there is no significant neural signal detected in people with sleep deprivation in the region. Sleep deprivation seems to turn off our information field and block incoming files, preventing our brain from storing new information in the memory file, consequently, impairing learning.

During the deepest stages of our sleep, low-frequency brain waves cause bursts of electrical activity that act as a file transfer mechanism. This brain activity transforms memories from short-term temporary memory into long-term permanent memory, protecting, and preserving them in our memory. It is, therefore, beneficial to take a short nap whenever our minds are exhausted. We often get new insights and ideas after a good sleep.

Most of us find it a challenge to have sufficient sleeps. However, we can re-prioritise our daily routine. Sleep is an activity that most of us love and should be the easy way to reprogram ourselves and our minds. Since sleeping is not a luxury, but a biological necessity, we can sleep 7 to 8 hours every day without feeling guilty.

3. **PHYSICAL ACTIVITY**

Most of us associate health with regular exercise. But that is because of people's urban lifestyles today. If we were physically active, hunting, fishing, farming, and harvesting food, instead of sitting in front of our computers for hours; if we mop the floor, clean the toilet, wipe the windows of the house, wash all our towels by hand daily, instead of having the maids or the robots to do the household chores, we would not need to schedule a time for exercise.

But due to the modern lifestyle, we spent more than 8 hours at work. We do not have time to do many of the above activities, so we resulted in finding ways to move our bodies. One of the easiest physical activities is to walk 10,000 steps every day to achieve health benefits. Performing high-intensity interval training (HITT), or with yoga, we can exercise the main muscle groups on in our body in the comfort of our home.

4. **ENVIRONMENT**

The brain cells take signals from our environment and convert them into electrochemical signals that vibrate through our bodies and transmute them into our reality. Spending time with the right people, reading the right books, listening to the right material, and being in the right environment for an extended period will promote or hinder our growth.

We are what we watch, listen, and read reading well-researched books, and biographic books influence us. Listening to recordings or reading books relating to setting and achieving a goal gives us the courage to pursue our dreams. Materials relating to dealing with people help us grow in our relationship with others. Subjects on how individuals and organisations overcome challenges increase our solution orientation. We begin to feel different and experience different results in our life by reading 15 to 30 minutes per day.

Another way to achieve optimal health is to put ourselves in an environment that allows our brains to relax and grow. Alpha-wave music from 8 to 12 Hz helps our minds relax, which increases concentration. That is the best state of mind to read, learn and think.

Theta wave music from 3 to 8 Hz puts us in deep meditation, a "dreamlike" state that promotes imagination, intuition, insight, immunity, and healing properties. Spending time outdoors with nature's average frequency of 7.83Hz, by the sea, or in the woods; hike, picnic, meditate, read a book, or take a nap, allow our body to reorganise information in our minds, relax our brains, and recuperate our bodies.

With a broad and profound understanding of how our brains and minds work and what we could do to improve, we now arm ourselves to become an optimal self, physically and psychologically.

PART 3

THE RACE OF
BEING HUMAN

6
HUMAN POWER
PURPOSE AND MEANING

····——————————————————————····

The ones who walk in purpose do not have
to chase people or opportunities.
Their light causes people and opportunity to pursue them.
—— Anonymous

····——————————————————————····

"WHAT DO YOU WANT TO BE when you grow up?" This is one
of the most famous questions toddlers get asked at the age as young
as 4 to 5 years old. That is where the dream of becoming whoever
we want to begin. The dream of becoming an astronaut, scientist,
firefighter, merchant, doctor, or whoever we can imagine. Nothing
could stop us from our imagination then. Children love to play out
the role of their imaginary professions for hours till the day ends and
to continue the next day again.

My dream was to become a doctor, to get rid of pain, heal the sick,
and help people to live a better life. Although I am not a medical
doctor, I hold on the belief that every human, no matter what state
of life we are at, can grow to have a better life than we already
have today, and continuingly live our fullest potentials, living a
meaningful and joy-filled life, while helping others to do so too.

Somehow God has guided me through a career and a business
that allow me to work with many great individuals to help fulfil their
dreams, for them and their family. I believe many of us still have

childhood dreams to be whoever we dream of becoming. Those dreams have never left us. Some of us are blessed to be living that dream today. But some of us have not yet become the person we dreamt of becoming.

Another popular question children get asked often is, "What would you like to do if you have a million dollars?" I can still recall vividly on that specific morning more than 3 decades ago when my favourite teacher asked my classmate and me to share our wishes if we have a million dollars. Many of us said we would give our parents some money so that they do not suffer so much from work stress and might not have to work anymore. We also wish our parents could spend more time with us.

Also, we would buy our favourite toys, get our fast cars, build our dream house, and take many vacations with our parents and loved ones. Those who were wiser suggested we should put aside some money for investment to extend what we have.

Most of us also discussed how we could use some windfall to help the disadvantaged and make the world a better place for all. I remember the laughter and joy we had that afternoon, listening to the many ideas, desires, and dreams what life could be if we have the resources to do whatever we want.

Although one million dollars today may not be much for everything we dream of having that day, those two famous questions have encouraged and taught us to dream big, without limitation. We were given a chance to envisage our future without being constrained by our abilities and resources, including time and money.

We were excited about sharing our dreams and believed we could be whoever we desired to be. We build models of our dream house, fancy toys, holidays and spent hours play-acting our imaginary life and the person we want to become.

But as time goes by, we grew up. Many of us have pushed our dreams aside. The world systems have institutionalised us to fulfil our bosses' and clients' dreams instead. Those who have the most intense burning desire influence others to help achieve their dreams. They institutionalise social systems and structure others must follow to get ahead. Formal education structures, ivy leagues, qualification papers, appointment criteria are examples of the system.

Most of us grew up with our parents telling us to study hard, to get good grades, to get a better job, to have a better life. However, many people who have an exemplary character with excellent track records, but do not have the necessary qualifications required by the world system are side-lined, and pass over for a job and promotion.

It seems like there is nothing wrong with the social structure and system we grew up with because those who complied were lavishly rewarded. On top of that, over the past few decades, the world has created a "credit system" that encourages us to live a life on our income level, not our net assets. We begin to live by "borrowed wealth" and "borrowed glory". Many financial institutions encourage their clients to pursue a lifestyle. Little did we realise most jobs do not pay wages that commensurate with our efforts and on par with inflation. Furthermore, with more technological advancement, business models are evolving, profit margins are shrinking even as productivity and efficiency increases.

At some point over the years, our childhood dreams slowly recede into the background as we pursue what the world defines as "success". However, this world is changing. The new world order is emerging. The social system, which once dominated the world, is less serving today than it used to be. Increasingly, more people are asking, "Is this the only way?" And especially after the pandemic took many jobs and businesses away from hundreds of millions of people.

It is vital, then, for us to rethink, what matters to us most. If we did not have a clear vision of what we must have for ourselves and our family, we would not have set ourselves goals and engaged in deliberate actions to achieve our desires. Others will ultimately continue to get us to work harder for them to achieve their dreams and goals. And because most people around us are doing so, it seems appropriate and is often outside of our awareness level.

I remember one of my associates once told me about an encounter and realisation she had. One day, she received a call from her private banker, who said to her that she had not maximised the credit facility offered by the bank based on her high-income pay. The banker suggested that she could use that credit facility for investment and offered a lower than the market interest rate for her to do so. She admitted she was flattered as the banker had stroked her ego by offering her more money. But taking up more credit facility is not in line with her plan.

She has a life plan that is meaningful and important for her and her family written before that call. That plan detailed out her family's ambitions, desired lifestyle, emergency needs, and financial standing she wanted to pass on to her children to sustain their education needs if she died suddenly. In her life plan, she also developed a clear roadmap and milestones for each of the net asset and net liquid asset she wants to achieve. So she turned down the banker's offer.

She said, if she had not had that written plan, she would likely to have accepted the offer and increased the liabilities and risks to her family. And she also said, she would become the bank's asset rather than creating more assets by leveraging on the bank without asset backing.

Having spoken to many business owners and chiefs, I found out many people wished to do something else apart from the position or business they are in now. While their current profession or business offers a comfortable life, childhood dreams have never ceased. However, people feel trapped in their current role because their career or business currently is providing them with the financial means to the obligations they carry, as well as the recognition in the community they serve.

Some eventually made a career change on their own accord. They planned and prepared themselves financially before leaving their profession to pursue their dreams. But some were laid-off from their jobs before they were ready. Especially when there was a change of guard at the top or when the market badly hit their business. Many of us eventually asked, "What do all these mean?" at some point in our lives.

The 2020 pandemic was an example of one of the most significant recessions that have led to the millions of business and job losses across all industries worldwide. The decline in business activities is astonishing. Many feared the pandemic would prolong global recession as mass unemployment and foreclosure continue, with no returning to what it used to be in sight.

The weekly unemployment insurance claim in the United States alone shot up from an average of 350,000 since the last recessions to the high of almost 7 million in April 2020. By July, nearly 53 million jobless claims have been filed alone as the pandemic continues to devastate the country and halt businesses. The unemployment rate shot up from below 4% in March to a high of 14% in September. While the unemployment rate has dropped in October 2020 to 6.9%, the road to recovery is still uncertain as the infected cases continue to surge.

The World Economic Forum (WEF) estimated the world would lose a total of 180 to 200 million jobs by 2022. On top of that, WEF also estimated 800 million jobs would be replaced by automation, smart technologies, and smart robots while new jobs will emerge, but more than 60% of the skill-sets we have now will no longer be relevant.

On top of that, according to a report by IBM in early May 2020, more than 54% of Americans surveyed would maintain remote work as the primary form of work after the pandemic ends. More than 70% would welcome that as an option. The time saved by commuting has allowed them to work more, spend time with family, pursue various hobbies and sleep more. And, due to the challenges of the education faced by their children, more women are volunteering to leave their job to home school their children. And younger people today are finding difficulty coping with the sudden change the pandemic has brought.

It is not surprising that at some point in our lives, we would ask, "What is the purpose, after all?" Moreover, Fyodor Dostoyevsky, a Russian philosopher and journalist, once said, "The mystery of human existence lies not in merely staying alive. But in finding something to live for."

PURPOSE

Having a clear purpose is like having a lifeline to hang on to as we journey through tough times. Our purpose keeps us focus on activities that are important and meaningful to us. Living life with a clear purpose in mind has a direct influence on the state of our minds. We wake up every morning, feeling more excited to start the day. Without that, one will begin to wonder the worth of their life. As many people are living in isolation now, due to the pandemic lock-down and working from home, we must have a purpose for our life beyond work.

Purpose gives us clarity and propels us to engage in meaningful activities to achieve what we set out to create. Purpose helps us to put events in our lives into perspective. It motivates us to move forward and to cherish life despite the adversity we face. It makes life more exciting and fulfilling. It brings true happiness and joy when goals are achieved, and dreams come true.

Without purpose, we would go through the motion in life meaninglessly. When we feel meaningless, we will feel down, depress, disassociate ourselves with the world outside, and may result in suicidal thoughts. Without purpose, we would be vulnerable to mood swings. We would feel like we were on top of the world one moment and the edge of a cliff the next. Our emotions would depend significantly on the event and circumstances, and not on growth, achievements which increase self-confidence, self-esteem, and self-pride. Life would become random and haphazard.

Without purpose, we could indulge in hours of mindless activities, browsing through social media, video clips, or watching movies for hours on end. Without a clear purpose, we could cling to mindless activities, the toxic relationship, or harmful environment. We could surround ourselves with people who complain, criticise, condemn, abuse, or blame the government, the circumstances, and others without proactively participating in changing what they do not like.

Without purpose, we may find life hectic, but we may also sense something that is missing. We may feel a void in our life and unfulfilled even if we are busy in life and have many material possessions. Over time, we would not enjoy the things we do, especially the activities we do over and over again. Though the repetition is a function of discipline and the right, repetitive action builds habits that lead to success. Repetitions without purpose lead to boredom and eventually burnout. The sense of "aimlessness", a symptom of a midlife crisis. This is where one begins to ask, "What is life after all?"

Purpose gives life. When we live our lives purposefully, we choose to become accountable and responsible for our lives. We live life intentionally and take deliberate actions while focusing on what we want to achieve in the end.

When we know our purpose, we are better at regulating our mood and emotion. We can identify the root causes of our feelings, find practical solutions, and get back on our feet quickly. In other words, when we have a clarity of purpose, we are more resilient. We bounced back quickly. That is why living a purposeful-life with deliberate actions is the key to get ahead in times of rapid change and uncertainty.

In Chapter 5, we have discussed how the mind is so robust and can trigger a vicious cycle of a downward spiral if we do not control it.

Similarly, we will drown in the busyness of life unless we have a deep sense of purpose on every task we perform. Conversely, we experience an upward spiral of success when we live purposefully and intentionally grape every opportunity to grow. That is why the likes beget the likes. True happiness is found when goals are reached.

PURPOSE AS HUMANS

"What is the purpose of life?" "What is my purpose of existence?" These are common questions that people, young or old, successful veterans or someone who just started in life would ask more than once in life. If these questions remain unanswered, we will wander through the wilderness of life, uncertain about our existence, especially amidst the smarter and faster machines that are quickly replacing many humans jobs and functions.

Regardless of how successful we are in our career or business, how wealthy or well-known we are in our field of expertise, we will experience the feeling of loss at some point in our lives if we do not continuingly renew our purpose. We could be living and exemplary life of what the society defined as "success", but if we do not have a personal reason, we will begin to question our own existence. Over time, we would begin to feel exhausted, empty, indifference, apathy, and tune out.

However, if we have a clear life purpose, no matter how insignificant whatever we do seems to others, that purpose will evoke in us an inner drive to live and grow while pursuing our desires and dreams. In a smart world where innovations and smarter machines are quickly replacing human functions, we need to revisit the purpose of "humans".

The biggest myth of purpose is this; for years, we have been told to "find our purpose". Some of us went for annual retreats, engaged in meditates, escaped the hustle and bustle of life once a while to review our purpose. But some people do not know what their purpose is and hope to "find" that "purpose" special to them one day.

The truth is, we do not have to climb the highest mountain or swim through the deepest sea to find our purpose. Because we do not "find" our purpose. We "create" our purpose.

Purpose grows in us when we begin to do what we are supposed to do. We create our purpose because:

1. We already have a predestined purpose that comes with our birthright,
2. We fulfil our purpose by the agreements we choose to make in our lives, and
3. We expend our purpose by responding to a cause or a calling.

In Chapter 3, we have considered the ultimate purpose of every living organism according to which nature's will is "to go forth and multiply". And, we have also learned that we have the instinctive need to protect, provide, belong, acknowledge, grow, and contribute. For these reasons, the three most purposes of humanity are:

1. **TO LIVE UP TO OUR BIRTHRIGHT**

In the circle of life, every one of us has a role to play. The moment we are conceived in our mother's womb, there is a predestined purpose in our life by the One who has given us life. This purpose lies with the family, the environment, and the community we are born into. It is our birthright.

Our birthright is not a position to be won. It comes with it the privilege and possession, also the formidable expectations and responsibilities, regardless of how we feel and our worldviews. We are presumed to live our part and the purpose that comes with our birthright as a member of the community and society we are in.

Every one of us has the birthright and the duty as the son or daughter of our parents, as brother and sister to our siblings, as adults to our nieces and nephews, and to the other members of the community. We also have different responsibilities according to our birth order.

As the firstborn in the family, we are usually expected to be a good example for our siblings to follow, and to guide and protect them, especially when our parents are not around. Similarly, as the firstborn to a ruler of a kingdom, that child is the apparent heir ordained to succeeding the king or queen. That child will be groomed and prepared in earnest for the throne which will be thrust upon him or her, and undergo intensive training to be ready to assume the weight and responsibilities as the head of the kingdom.

Our primary purpose of life is to protect and preserve our family. We get to become the right person to extend the good name of our family, our family's legacy and bloodline. We do this by protecting, providing, and preserving our family members, living right for each other. As members of a clan, community, constituency, and government, we take pride in being an honourable and a trusted member of society, to live harmoniously with others. That is the primary purpose of our lives.

Every religion teaches us the golden rule, "Do to others what you want from others." Some are formulated positively, "Treat others as you want to be treated by others." Some come from a prohibitive angle, "Do not treat others as you do not want to be treated." Ultimately, the message is the same. Every one of us has a role to play in the way we treat each other. We are instructed to live virtuously for one another.

In his inaugural address, John F. Kennedy said, "Ask not what the country can do for you, but what you can do for the country." Therefore, ask not what others can do for you, but what you can do for others.

We owe it to our parents and our Creator to live our life purposefully and intentionally to honour them. We do that by continually expanding and improving every aspect of our lives: our self, our relationships, our physical and mental health, and by being a prudent steward of the resources at our disposal. These are what we can do for our family, others, and the country.

That said, we also get to be the trusted guardian to the abundance resources nature has given us——planet Earth. Planet Earth is the primary source of life, providing us with clean air, pure water, nutritious food, and shelters.

The Earth also protects us with its energy frequency of 7.83Hz, the Alpha wave, which contains natural energy——a source of energy for our mental health. It calms our body, relaxes our minds, and lifts our spirits. That vibration regulates our physiology, emotion, immune systems, thoughts, and creativity. In other words, planet Earth is the fundamental source of life which provides and protects our physical and psychological needs.

We are responsible for using the resources planet Earth provides sustainably, so it continues to provide for our needs for generations to come. When we plough the land according to its timing for planting, harvesting, and resting, the Earth will continue to feed us. When we hunt and fish responsibly, taking only what we need and letting the rest to breed and multiply, we will have a continuous flow of supplies from nature.

When we use the natural regeneration process to restore degraded land, crops can begin to grow on the once barren land and provide us with food again. We must reduce the large-scale deforestation, commercialisation, chemical-intensified soil, genetically-modified seeds, monocultural agriculture practice, and mining that are hurting planet Earth.

Moreover, planet Earth ultimately generates the world economy. All the ecosystems of the economy are put in place to grow, produce, distribute, and conserve what produces Planet Earth gives us. So, when we take care of the planet first, people second, according to nature's laws and universal principles, profit will flow.

That said, the most fundamental purpose in life is to protect the sources of life, the planet Earth, and essentially, our life. When we fulfil our purpose predestined by our birth and do what we must according to nature's law, we will be blessed with beautiful relationships, optimal health, and abundant resources available to us.

Imagine the positive impact on the country, community, society, and economy when everyone takes full ownership to live up to our predetermined purpose. We are becoming a better person, a better community, a better culture, and a better government. It starts with us.

2. TO HONOUR THE AGREEMENTS WE MADE

The second most important purpose of being human is honouring the agreements we made. When we establish an agreement with ourselves or with another person, we give our word to do our part to achieve an outcome together. These agreements come with a purpose, the duties and responsibilities, and what we are committed to delivering.

When we apply and accept a position in the company we work for in exchange for a salary or commission; when we offer our customers our products or services in exchange for payment; when we choose to enter into a partnership in business or marriage and agree to create a desirable future together, we make agreements. When we pledge our allegiance to a country, we made an agreement in exchange for protection, provision, and opportunity.

Often the agreements we have made are intended to benefit 's efforts mutually and to fulfil each other's needs. The benefits can include shelter over our family and our heads, food on the table, education for our children, a safe place to belong, respected, celebrated together. The opportunity to grow and create When we live purposefully and honour our agreements, we begin to experience a sense of quiet confidence, pride, and achievement for our effort.

Every agreement and relationship we have entered has a specific purpose, expectation, and desired outcomes. More often than not, the expected desired outcomes to fulfil our psychological needs are stronger than our physical needs, even if we are not aware of that. The emotional pain of a broken agreement is often greater than the physical pains, and the impact could last a lifetime. It is, therefore, an honour to do our part well, fulfil our responsibilities for ourselves and the other parties.

It is normal to expect profits for our effort following the agreements we made. When we choose to work for an employer, we are hired to achieve the company's goal for profit, in exchange for an income. Businesses profit from delivering products or services that meet their clients' needs. We use the income to pay for our living expenses and the lifestyle we desire. That is the circle of life. Profits are the measurable outcomes or results which come in many forms; payment, return, protection, respect, recognition, growth, actualisation, multiplication, happiness, and love. The ones who failed to play their parts right and deliver profits will face the consequences of breaching an agreement.

There will be times when we need to break an agreement. Sometimes we could have reached an agreement, and over a period, that agreement no longer serves a common purpose because the needs of either party have changed. Either party might come to a point seeking to break away from an agreement.

Breaking away from an agreement is a common process, some come with consequences and financial losses, and often, it might not be an easy process to go through. Yet, we should cut loss amiably. That is why, every agreement should comply with regulations, and underwriting mechanism for either party to exit, and an efficient neutral intermediator who promote peaceful separation.

In a rapidly changing environment, we will grow beyond our current needs and capability faster than the past. The ability to break away from an agreement and minimise losses require us to collaborate and negotiate respectfully even during tough times, and to seek a mutually benefiting understanding with others. It requires us to listen more and respect other people's needs, concerns, and resources, preserve the relationship and long-term wellbeing of everyone.

When we can to cut loss agreeably, that allows us to move on quickly. It also forces us to be more responsible for the choices we make, defines our purpose better, and become more considerate towards the needs of others. If we ignore the strain in the relationships rising in an agreement, we will face the worst consequence subsequently. Hence, honouring an agreement we made and objectively handled an expiration goal, strength our ownership and responsibility towards the decisions we make with others.

3. **TO RESPOND TO A CALLING**

Beyond the purpose that comes with our birthright and agreements we have made, there is a third purpose into which we grow into, commonly known as the "calling". Many of us find it hard to answer the question, "What is my purpose?" Because we do not know what our calling is. We may even feel inadequate for not knowing our calling.

But we do not have to feel that way, because many people do not know what their "calling" is throughout their life. Some of us only began to realised later in life what we have been doing and are great at is perhaps the "calling". We could even fulfil our "calling" without knowing it. There are only a handful of people who have heard the voice of God, calling them to take on a specific role in society, even if the "calling" might not appear like one at first. For that reason, we do not necessarily have to "wait for our calling" to "find our purpose" to commit to a cause.

"Calling" can be associated with the accumulation of life experiences and wisdom through many years of practice in the field we are excellent and known in. "Calling" takes time to grow from what we are good at and is passionate about to respond to a cause. When we are being invited to take up a role to make a difference in an organisation or community, we are given a choice to respond to a cause. We can choose to accept or reject that invitation. Even for those who have heard God's "calling", they can decide to respond or not.

Every one of us has the propensity to expand and grow. So if we decide not to respond to a particular cause, the seed will germinate in us, to a point hard to ignore. It might grow to the point of affecting our self-worth and self-trust. We might start to feel frustrated, disappointed, useless, unfulfilled, and unhappy over time. We might even become indifferent, resentful, or bitter because we know deep inside, we could have responded to a cause, but decide not to. That is why Abraham Maslow said, "If you deliberately plan on being less than you are capable of being, then I warn you that you will be unhappy for the rest of your life."

Living a purposeful-life by responding to a cause does not mean that we are spared the disappointments in life. But we still choose to respond to the cause by using our life experiences, skills, and available resources.

Mother Teresa, a legendary Albanian nun in Ireland, did not start with an enchanting beginning. She heard the voice of God, calling her to emigrate to India to teach in a monastic school in Calcutta, and she did. The widespread poverty in Calcutta left a deep mark in her heart.

Subsequently, Mother Teresa left the monastery in Calcutta when she heard a second call from God to help the poor and the needy. She began to build schools, shelters, homes, and hospitals for the poor, homeless, war refugees, and abandoned infants. Eventually, she founded the Missionaries of Charity in various parts of the world to serve the poor and destitute.

Despite the significant contribution and influence she had, Mother Teresa said, "I have never had the clarity of my' calling'. What I always had is trusting." She decided to respond to the "calls" and did what she could and grew along the way.

Many leaders who have contributed significantly to the world responded similarly. They know deep within them the opportunity presented to them is not for self-preservation but has a bigger purpose for humanity. They begin with a simple act of doing what they could in response to a cause and eventually left behind a path others inspired to follow.

Two years ago, I had the privilege of meeting Sir Andrew Philip Witty, the former president of a global pharmaceutical company in a leadership institute with which I once associated with. He shared his leadership journey, which humbled many of us in a conference. When he was first appointed as the Chief Executive Officer (CEO) of the company, he went to a restroom, looked back to the man in the mirror and asked, "What is my purpose in this role?"

According to Sir Andrew Witty, that appointment to lead the world's largest pharmaceutical company carries with it a huge responsibility. He believes that the role comes with a higher purpose he must fulfil—a purpose beyond the job itself. He believes the appointment at the age of 44 must be beyond meeting the company's quarterly results and shareholder expectations. He knew he was called to make a difference in for the entire world.

Sir Andrew Philip Witty said, he believes and is grateful that God has prepared him over the years, since the early years of his career life when his first joint the company as a management trainee. He was given the privilege of working under many prominent leaders and mentors over the years, who prepared him for the role as the chief. He honoured the role entrusted to him, and eventually transformed the company and the entire pharmaceutical and healthcare industry.

Sir Andrew Philip Witty has been recognised for many of his contributions, including his effort in persuading the industry to produce critical drugs affordable for more patients. He was knighted in the 2012 New Year Honours for services to the economy and the United Kingdom pharmaceutical industry. In 2018, he was awarded the Warren Bennis Award for Excellence in Leadership at the Linkage Global Institute for Leadership Development (GILD).

Sir Andrew Witty is also the recipient of the Society of Chemical Industry (SCI) 2019 Society Medal—the most prestigious medal established in 1896, to mark the outstanding merit in furthering the connection between science and business. Sir Andrew Philip Witty was also a key member in helping the World Health Organisation develop vaccines for COVID-19 in 2020.

PURPOSE GIVE LIVES

Since the prehistoric period to ancient history; through medieval years, to modern and contemporary age; through evolutions and revolutions, natural disasters, plagues, the rise and fall of civilization, humans have survived the worst kind of disruption and disasters in the past.

In 1347, the world faced with the deadliest pandemic, known as the Black Death. A plague that killed between 75 and 200 million people from an estimated world population of 475 million at that time. That pandemic lasted for 4 years till 1351. That was before the Spanish flu which broke out during World War I in 1918 which infected 500 million people worldwide and caused approximately 50 million deaths.

After the early 1900s pandemic and World War I, the Great Depression of 1930 kicked in. It was the worst financial and economic meltdown in history which lasted almost 10 years. Then came World War II, which killed more than 60 million people, including 6 to 7 million Jews who were systematically exterminated by Hitler's Nazi Party during the Holocaust period. Together with that, tens of millions of people arrested and put in concentration camps waited to be massacred and disposed of systematically.

During the Holocaust genocide years, Viktor E. Frankl, a world-renown psychologist, was transported in between four Nazis' camps, including the Auschwitz in Poland where his parents and brother were killed. Frankl made many observations during that horrendous period on how humans survived one of the darkest times in history.

He witnessed hundreds of thousands of starving and sick prisoners of war, locked in rows of unliveable barracks with horrid living conditions, sleeping side by side with dead bodies, denied of proper food and health care.

Upon arrival at the extermination camp, men and women were separated through a selection process which took place immediately as they disembarked from the train that transported them to the camp. The ones who were deemed as able-body were used as forced-labours to generate an economy for the political party or given the task of genocide until they no longer had the stamina to work. The ones who were weak and elderly were sent to the gas chambers as fast as the facility can do what it was purposed to do.

Frankl also noticed the prisoners who survived had a much long-lasting will and endurance to stay alive. Despite the brutal conditions, they clung on to the hope of reuniting with their family members again after the war. They live each day with the sole purpose to stay alive long enough until the end of the war, even though they did not know when the war would end.

Some war prisoners were scientists, artists, writers, musicians, and people known for their work, which were burned and destroyed by the Nazi. They determined to stay alive so that they could reproduce their work and pass on their research to the next generation. As a psychologist and psychiatrist, Frankl was determined to rewrite many of his research manuscripts. On top of that, the hope of reuniting with his wife had kept Frankl alive.

Many of them did not know if their family were still living, and they did not even know if they could survive the war long enough till the end of the war. But, Frankl wrote in his book, *Man's Search for Meaning*, "Love transcends the physical person of the lover. Love finds its deepest meaning in their inner self, in their spiritual being. Whether their wife, children, parents and loved one is still alive or not somehow ceases to be of importance. When someone has that deep meaning within them, nothing could touch the strength of their love, their thought, and the image of fulfilling their purpose—to stay alive for them."

Set me like a seal upon thy heart; love is as strong as death.
— Viktor E. Frankl

7

HUMAN EDGE
VIRTUE AND CHARACTER

If I have an hour to solve a problem and my life depended on it,
I would use the first 55 minutes,
determining the proper question to ask.
For once, I know the proper question,
I could solve the problem in less than five minutes.
— Albert Einstein

IN SEPTEMBER 2019, the global financial market was shocked by the collapse of a company with a much-anticipated initial public offering (IPO) at a staggering valuation of $47 billion. Before the launch date, the company presented itself as the next up-and-coming technology mega unicorn.

However, when the company's book was opened to the public what the Wall Street saw was merely a real estate firm offering co-working office space, no different from their competitors. With 280 sites, 86 cities in 32 countries, the investment in high-end technology has escalated the company's cost significantly, compared to its competitors of a similar size.

That company had been pitched as a "technology company" instead of a "realty company", by emphasising their "high-tech" environment like face-recognition for sign-ins, bookings, and interaction with tenants globally. The founder of that company said they were not simply another co-working space company, but what they were doing will "change the world". But many economists challenged the initial valuation.

One of the company's biggest investors, a Japanese conglomerate, eventually bought into that company. The CEO of that conglomerate defended their initial valuation by saying, "What we saw was something completely new by using technology to build a network of communities." He eventually admitted his judgment was wrong and said he was "foolish" to have invested an $ 18.5 billion to that company.

The subsequent revaluation fell by more than 85% in December 2019 and depreciated to $2.9 billion by March 2020. The COVID-19 pandemic further devastated this company. They have laid off more than 8,000 people since January 2020 while the board faced with millions of square feet office-space problems, deserted by both its financial backers and tenants during the pandemic.

The founder of that co-share office space company went further to trademark the brand privately. He sold the trademark rights back to the company for a $5.9 million in 2019 but later agreed to return the money after the deal was criticised. He also bought few real estate on his own accord to lease back to the company. A brilliant strategy, but crossed the ethical line in many ways.

This case has drawn international attention to the true values of start-ups and business ethics today. The amplified "potential growth" has boosted business valuations in recent years before the 2020 pandemic outbreak. Many technology-related companies have inflated their investors' hopes in the race to become the next unicorn company––start-ups company with a value of over $1 billion.

But the investors' sentiment is shifting, especially after the pandemic caused a monumental impact on the global economy. Financiers are more rigorous and cautious in supporting new business ideas.

CB Insights published an article titled *The Top 20 Reasons Startups Failed* in November 2019 after 101 autopsies of failed-start-ups were conducted. The top reason, 42%, of start-ups fail because they offer products or services that are "nice to have" but without "market needs." The second and third reasons why start-ups failed were: "money ran out" and "not the right team."

After a 5-years of work with 21 researchers, Jim Collins and Jerry Porras, the author of *Good to Great* found, "maximising the wealth, profit, or growth of shareholders" was not the driving force behind great companies. Great companies accepted that profitability is essential for business sustainability. But, the deliberate choice to "commit to a cause" is what keeps them going. These are companies that have been around for more than 50, 100, and some, almost 200 years.

Their solemn commitment towards a cause has a compelling reason for becoming their best. Great companies have understood the role they play and how they create value for others. This purpose becomes a code of conduct on how to serve the cause and achieve financial goals. Purpose-centeredness drives the culture of success.

"BORROWED" LIFE

On December 2, 2001, Enron Corporation rocked the market with a bankruptcy declaration when regulators discovered the truth. They managed to deceive Wall Street with bogus holdings and off-record accounting by using a special-purpose vehicle to hide its mountain of debt and toxic assets for an extended period.

The worst economic catastrophe jolted the world again in December 2008 since the Great Depression of 1929. It began with the banks giving out too many housing-loans and sub-prime mortgages to homeowners with questionable credit. Some allowed their customers to borrow 100% or more of the value of the mortgage-mortgaged property.

Millions of consumers found themselves flooded with "free money" in "borrowed wealth"––money seating on top of piles of loans, not on a paid-up capital or assets. These sub-prime mortgages were created to feed the financial industry's appetite for mortgage-backed securities sold through the secondary market, and the consumers' greed to chew more than they can afford.

The impact of the entire market collapse was immense: 8.8 million jobs were lost, 8 million homes were foreclosed, and home prices fell by an average of 30-40% during the downturn. Simultaneously, debtors found themselves having oversized loans beyond their capacity.

That has led to the evaporation of an enormous household wealth amounting to $19.2 trillion-dollar. Since the dive of the financial crisis in March 2009, the market had recovered by more than 300% by August 2019. New empires have emerged, and Wall Street bounced back with more sparkles than before. But many of those affected by the subprime crisis have not recovered and may never do so.

The U.S. government eventually had to throw in the lifelines to stop government-backed institutions from drowning in the swirl of irresponsible debt they helped create. Some banks responsible for the fall have been bailed out, and none of the bankers has been charged with any crimes. Wall Street is said to have been spared any serious legal, economic, or political consequences for its irresponsible behaviour.

Meanwhile, oversized ethical agencies, councils, institutions, and academies sprouted like mushrooms overnight. Governments and corporations pumped billions of dollars annually into policymaking, auditing, monitoring, and retraining businesses and employees to ensure that they practice "business ethics". Some organisations include ethical behaviour performance in their employee's performance evaluation process. But has workplace and business ethics improved over the last decade?

While the business cycle continues, new "borrowed" wealth emerged through start-ups, with trillion dollars investment poured in with the hope to discover the next billion dollar value company. Governments, businesses, and private debts continued to soar, eventually blew up in 2020.

Global debts surged to a record $272 trillion-dollar by September 2020 and are expected to reach $277 trillion-dollar or 365% of global gross domestic product (GDP) by the end of the year, according to the Institute of International Finance (IIF). By the third quarter of 2020, the developed market debt-to-GDP has hit a record of 432%, nearly 250% in the emerging market, and 335% in China.

The United States debts were estimated to jump from $71 trillion-dollar in 2019 to $80 trillion-dollar in 2020. That is four times the cost of the Great Rescission, according to David Cutler, the former U.S. Treasury Secretary Lawrence Summers and fellow Harvard University economist.

European Union (EU) leaders agreed to an $860 billion-dollar COVID-19 recovery fund in grants and low-interest loans for countries severely affected by the pandemic outbreak on 21 July 2020, on top of a pending historic seven-year $2 trillion-dollar budget deal to rebuild Europe's economy with the green and digital transformation initiatives from 2021 to 2027. That would push Europe into a total debt of $53 trillion-dollar.

We are drowning in the ocean of debts even after we have won the war with the pandemic. IIF said, "There is significant uncertainty about how the global economy can deleverage in the future without significant adverse implications for economic activity."

Governments around the world have been trying to prop up the economy with multi-trillion dollar economy stimulus packages. These government-aided funds temporarily transferred financial responsibility from corporations, businesses, and households to the federal government. Consequently, allowing governments to gain some capitalism power to influence future business decisions.

We barely survive in an economy that ripped off the wealth of our future generations. On top of that, smart technology and industrial revolution 4.0 will increase productivity and efficiency faster and cheaper, but not promoting income growth. How do we solve this trillion-dollar trap when debt is growing faster than the economy? The COVID-19 pandemic is, perhaps, the black swan; the final grain of sand that brought down the mountain of global debt and pushed us into a new world order.

In financial planning 101, we learned the key to financial success comprised of living within our means, paying off debts quickly, and putting aside savings for times of emergency. For years, the IIF has been urging more people to be financially literate to reduce household debt and be prepared to survive through a life crisis. When we do the opposite, we will be obliged to those who lend us the money. That is why the rich––the ones who accumulated more in assets during the good time––will become richer and the poor poorer.

However, many people have done just the opposite. We have accumulated massive debts that are so complex; we do not know how to get out of it. We have allowed and tolerated the elevation of debt for far too long. It is not surprising; poor mental health is escalating. When incomes stop, when there is no buffer left to cushion the crisis, anxieties soar. Because we have not been responsible in the way, we manage our life and finances when times are good.

That reminds me of a story my parents used to tell us when we were young: The Ant and the Grasshopper. The Grasshopper spent its better days of summer playing and singing while the Ant worked industriously to store up food for winter. When winter arrives, the Grasshopper finds itself dying of hunger and begging the ant for food. Similarly, we could have worked harder to store up more before the winter came.

BUSINESS ETHICS

We might ask, where is the business ethic in all those that have happened? "There's no such thing as business ethics. How can that be?! Because a single standard applies to both your business and personal life." John C. Maxwell stressed when someone suggested he to write a book on business ethics. Maxwell emphasised that there should be no distinction between business ethics and personal ethics. "If you want to be ethical, you live by a standard across the board."

He also pointed out that we get to live by the unyielding ethical principle that governs our lives, shape our character and conduct. Those who live ethically permeate values in every aspect of their life. They will stand the test of time. They will not yield to pressure and will continue to make decisions on ethical principle, even in the face of death.

Maxwell also believes those who behave unethically are driven by convenience and hunger to win at all costs. In his view, people who act unethically justify their actions with relativism. They choose their ethical standards to rationalise their behaviour, rather than behave according to ethically. We have seen much of these happening today, including amongst the heads of business and country. People in positions of power with questionable behaviour confuse the public by justifying their behaviour while undermining our human moral code.

The questions we should think through are, "What does it take to be an honourable and trusted leader?" "How do we expect our children to pledge allegiance to those who do not live ethically?" "What role models do we have for our future leaders today?" Unless we stop tolerating unethical behaviour, the future will be unsafe as smarter technologies are easily accessible to everyone, including unconscionable humans.

Maxwell goes further, suggesting the one universal ethical rule everyone should follow the golden rule—do to others as you would wish them to do. Because the golden rule is deeply rooted in many cultures and religions, this should be the integrity guideline for our lives. The golden rule is the essential moral yardstick to promote the ethical character, responsibility and competence. It requires we be virtuous, honest, just, fair, and respectful as we fulfil our duty to one another.

Every one of us should not have difficulty following the golden rule, as no one wants to be treated worse than others. If I may extend it further, treat others in the way we would like others to treat our children, our parents, our siblings, and our partner—people matter most to us, because we are less tolerant of people who treat our loved ones badly.

So if we can get back to where we are today, why has ethics deteriorated so much in some governments, businesses, and individuals? Do we have no shame in spending billions of dollars to ensure we behave when we expect our children to well-behave? Did we not hope younger workers would behave better?

What did our ancestors do in the past to maintain high ethical standards in society? How did our ancestors instil virtue at home, in the community, in an organisation and the country? What are the most important virtues? We have to travel back a long way to the original purpose of education.

ORIGIN OF EDUCATION

The history of education can be traced back to the last 150,000 to 200,000 years when archaeologists found drawings on cave walls. Before livestock farming, agriculture, and domestication began, humans lived a nomadic lifestyle in small groups. They were hunters and gatherers of food from the wild.

Education was informal but practical, then and served two primary purposes. Firstly, to satisfy the basic needs of protecting and providing for the family. Male adults would train their sons in physical abilities and build stamina. Young boys were taught how to manipulate tools for hunting, fishing from the wild and how to build shelters for their families. Secondly, to be a person of value so that he can fit into the community. Female adults would teach their daughters to collect food, nurture relationships, and to maintain harmony within the family.

As the tribe grew, hunting, gathering, and agriculture began to be more organised and structured. Education became a formalised process of enculturation. Young people were taught the dynamics of their environment so that they could recognise and learn the expected behaviours, boundaries, norms, values, and cultures. They are expected to have the ability to fulfil specific roles and responsibilities within the tribe.

Adults in the community are role models who teach and demonstrate practical skills throughout their lives. The tribe often regards the elders as the wisest; having advanced through many challenges, and is respected for their wisdom.

As soon as the boys reach puberty and capable of reproduction, the community will perform a ceremony to symbolise the transition from childhood to adulthood. It is a form of social recognition for reaching the age of responsibility, fertility, and productivity within the community. As soon as the boys and girls reached puberty, they could start their own family within the tribe or in another tribe.

Beyond that, education after puberty went beyond the limitation and protection of the family, and often outside the tribe in the wild. Over time, education becomes standardised and regulated.

The ways of life are passed down from one generation to the next through observation, imitation, role-play, games, participation, and the assumption of responsibility in the community. Repeated exercises and skill evaluation are common. The education process back then was more comprehensive than modern education today, as it integrates everyone to their community.

Today, social integration in education takes place outside the classroom. It is not surprisingly, students who are actively involved in clubs, associations, and community service are better prepared socially in addition to their academic achievements. The extracurricular activities help build trust, communication, people, skills and pave the way to better leaders in society.

Historically, education was much more extensive and comprehensive. Learning took place naturally outside the classroom, with no restrictions, and continued throughout life. Education has been designed to cultivate young people into adulthood and to shape their behaviour so that they can fulfil their ethnic, religious, social, and economic duties.

One notable example is ancient Chinese formal education, which was distinguished by its outstanding secular and moral character. The fundamental purpose was to develop a sense of moral sensitivity and duty towards the state and its people.

For the Egyptians, the purpose of education was to secure the political loyalty and culture of their time. The priests taught subjects like humanities, social sciences, natural sciences, medicine, mathematics, and geometry in formal schools. Professional skills like architecture, engineering, accounting, or becoming an artisan are generally carried out outside of the formal education system through apprenticeships with craftsmen over an extended period.

Among the Mayans, character building was one of the most noticeable aspects of their upbringing. The cultivation of self-restraint, collaboration, and moderation was highly emphasised throughout the different stages of socialisation. The highly educated were known for their extensive knowledge of literature, history, writing, divination, medicine, calendar system, religion, and moral leadership. They served the rulers and the nobility as the most influential advisors.

The original purpose of education——to prepare an individual for life——has not changed much. Today, however, the focus of education is on securing a job. Educational institutions have developed more technical related programs in areas including design thinking, agile, data analytics, coding, programming, human resources, logistics, and even organising skills like event management.

We are deviating from the original purpose of education and narrowly focused aspects of vocational training. Not precisely what education was supposed to be. This narrow approach has created an enormous gap in what we need to move forward in the new world.

Samuel Smile, a well-known Victorian Scottish writer and social reformer, wrote in his book *Self-Help*, "The best practical training is active participation in life and collaboration with others. Schools, academies, and colleges are only the beginning of educating. However, what we do daily at home, in the street, at the workplace, in the field, through the rise and fall we learn to be a worthy member of the society."

Friedrich Schiller, a German philosopher, wrote, "The education of the human race, must include action, conduct, self-culture, self-control; all that tends to discipline a man truly and fit him for the proper performance of the duties and business of life. A sort of education not to be learnt from books or acquired by any amount of mere literary training."

Jim Rohn also said, "Successful people believe formal education will earn you a living. People of significance know self-educating will make you a fortune." Lifelong self-learning is a necessity for us to stay ahead in this volatile, uncertain, complex, and ambiguous world. Moreover, to be excellence, a master, a person of wisdom in the field we choose, we get to pursue excellence, and that takes time to grow.

So whenever we assess someone, instead of asking about the certificates they have accumulated, seek to understand the many challenges they have overcome, the wisdom and insight they have gained, through the application of the knowledge attested to them. Ask them who inspires them and who they inspire. We are the "guru" only when others say we are. Putting a title to our name does not make us so. It takes 10,000 hours or more of deliberate action to become excellence and exceptional.

VIRTUOUSNESS

Studies have shown that people with greater mental health, exemplary performance, and better leadership skills have high emotional intelligence. A skill that is of paramount importance in the 21st century. According to Peter Salovey and John Mayer, the psychologists who developed the emotional intelligence (EI) model said, the ability to sense the feeling of one's own and others, identify different emotions, and use emotional information to guide one's thinking and behaviour is a critical skill in dealing with people.

Way back in the 5th century BCE, Socrates, the famous ancient Greek philosopher said, to be aware of our owns and others' emotions so that we behave appropriately in responding to the various human emotions, we must be virtuous.

Virtue, or arete in ancient Greek, means "excellence of any kind". Hence, being virtuous is about being excellence. Being virtuous is the primary quality of wellbeing, happiness, and living with diverse backgrounds and perspectives of others. It is also about being in control of oneself and upholding one's ethical behaviour for all.

Being virtuous goes much deeper than having a good character or emotional intelligence. To be virtuous is a personal conviction, a decision to form the habits deliberately in our minds and our conducts, to be in harmony with the order of nature, including all living beings and the humans in it.

Sadly, virtuousness is often an after-thoughts discussion. When was the last time we begin business discussion or performance review by focusing on the virtuous character we want to advocate? Have we talked enough with the younger ones about virtue? We rarely ask, "Who do I want to become?" We often focus on "What do I want to do or have?"

Virtuousness is universal to all cultures and traditions. According to Socrates, too, to create a harmonious and functional society, society should instil four primary, virtuous characters in everyone. The four primary virtues are; prudence, justice, fortitude, and temperance.

1. **PRUDENCE**

Prudence is also known as wisdom. Prudence is the first of the four primary virtues. It is the ability to take appropriate action, and that requires wisdom. Unlike knowledge, the accumulation of facts and information, prudent people have the knowledge and experience to make the right move, use the proper tools, at the right time.

Knowledge is a tool, while wisdom is the craft of using the right knowledge at the right time. A person with wisdom is wise to understand the relationship between knowledge and wisdom, and how knowledge impacts different people, different situations, differently. Therefore, wisdom is acquired only through many hours of practice, and that requires a long time.

Wisdom cannot be taught in the classroom. It can only be acquired through consistent action over an extended period with accountability partners or mentors. We gain the feedbacks required to make improvements and become better over time with efforts. It is no wonder people well-known for their expertise spent many years of apprenticeships with masters of the field. That is how masters and craftsmen groom young artists, philosophers, scientists, merchants, accountants, and other professions.

Graduating from three to four years of the ivy league, universities, acquiring a degree, getting certified, verifies the knowledge and skills we have acquired. But wisdom and mastery are achieved through many hours of practice and experience, which requires intense focus, determination, perseverance, and persistence. This is done until the ability to respond appropriately to a specific situation has become our muscle memory, becoming a part of who we are.

Malcolm Gladwell in his book, *Outlier: The Story of Success*, wrote, "Looking at all cognitively complex activities, from chess to musical instruments to neurosurgery, there is an incredible "consistent pattern" that we would not master if we had not done the same thing for ten years." Specialists who are first-class in their field manage to improve their arts more than others by working many hours in the same field over an extended period.

In other words, if we have acquired new knowledge and skills and expect to be the expert overnight, that may be too dull-witted. It is commendable to invest in education throughout our life, and we should do so because it improves us. But mastering our game takes time.

A notable example is that of the famous painter, Leonardo Da Vinci. When he spent years observing nature and studying the autonomy of humans, animals, and birds, his paintings improved substantially. The anatomical studies helped him understand what is beneath the nuke skin, the muscle, and bone structure that gave form to his subjects. That required many more years of careful observation in addition to the initial years of schooling and apprenticeship with his master.

In essence, mastery, or prudence, is the result of 10,000 hours or more of cumulative deliberate actions combined with various insights from diverse areas.

2. JUSTICE

Justice or fairness is the second primary virtue. That is a crucial pillar that forms the foundation of every society. Fairness or to be "just" means to grant equal rights by adhering to moral excellence and ethical principle. It is about being honest, principled, true, noble to ourselves and others, even when no one else is watching. It is an act of respecting the interest, property, and safety of others.

Fairness must not be mistaken for equality. Those who cannot distinguish between the two may feel they have been unfairly treated. Equality is the condition of being equal in status, quantity, and value. If we make the same effort, we would expect the same reward, provided all other factors are the same. However, since we have many differences: family background, upbringing, exposure, personality, cognitive abilities, and life experiences, two people cannot be the same, and therefore, to achieve 100% equality is highly impossible.

Fairness also means keeping the vows we make in the hope and to achieve and preserve harmonious relationships. Efforts and achievements are created to be shared in a fair and a just manner. When we swear our oath to our fellow countrymen or take a vow with someone, we solemnly commit ourselves to fulfil our duty to preserve the relationship. We promise to be a person responsible for behaving, caring, and serving the person we have promised. Let us not forget our duty before asking what our country or our partner is doing for us.

Legally, an oath or a vow is an agreement we committed to fulfilling and are liable to forfeiture in the event of failure. A vow is a solemn promise to be loyal, faithful, devoted, and steadfast; to protect, provide, love, and care. It is honourable and of noble character.

Fulfilling the promises we have made increases our self-confidence and self-esteem. When we can do what we say we will do, we feel useful and good for achieving. Our self-worth increases when our actions to our words produce results—our sense of self-control and personal power increases. Psychologically, when we feel more secure, we can express and regulate ourselves better, we are more willing to accept the diverse perspectives and differences in others.

Fairness requires us to first, take ownership and acknowledge the results in our lives as the consequences of the decisions and actions we took or did not take. When we fulfil our part on the promises we made and do what is required, the universe will respond accordingly. Actions also cause the neural electrochemical energy within us to generate brainwave frequencies and transmute to physical form, our outer reality. In short, justice and fairness in life come from us. When we are fair, the world is fair.

3. **FORTITUDE**

Fortitude is commonly referred to as grit or mental toughness. It is the third primary virtue. Fortitude is defined as the firmness of character, a kingly trait. It starts with a decision and the willingness to commit to a cause for the long term. People with fortitude are tenacious, steadfast, and have unwavering beliefs, hope, and faith. They are brave, courageous, and do what they know they must do, despite fear, anger, pain, or intimidation. They with grit hold on to the end in mind.

Grit is a significant predictor of success. It is the willingness to persevere long before their heart's desire comes to life. Grit is more than doing what we like, what we are passionate about, or what we are good at. People with grit respect nature's law and push themselves to obey the process of success. They do what is necessary to achieve what they want. They have the personal conviction that the results will eventually come if they do everything required to get there.

People with grit are solution-oriented. They work tirelessly for days, months, and even years, and eventually, come up with the ultimate solutions that produce the best result. They are determined, persistent, patient, and persistent. They know that the agony of not fulfilling the heart's desire is much greater than the pain of failure, rejection, loss of face, and even risk whatever that may be.

According to Angela Lee Duckworth, a psychologist who wrote the book, *Grit: The Power of Passion and Perseverance,* people who commit to long-term goals are willing to work hard. They are intentional, and because they do that over an extended period, they become a person of excellence and produce excellent results.

Most people do not change, not because they do not want to, but because they lack consistent effort. Conversely, grit can only be developed over a more extended period through daily deliberate action, consistently. As consistency comes from prioritising what we need to do to get the results we want daily, grit is intentional. That is why, written goals, vision boards, and daily action journals or checklists to help us stay focus on what is critical.

Fortitude also comes from the ability to bounce back from rejections or failures repeatedly. That is resilient. Resilience grows in us when we are prepared to move forward despite our circumstances. Resilience requires mental strength––the ability to keep going on while holding on to faith, hope, and optimism amid disappointment and fear.

Moreover, the more we bounce back from each failure, the "pain of failing" loses its effect on us. We can, therefore, move faster, stronger and closer to our goals through time, while our resilience and mental strength grow. When we are willing to face the brutal truth and acknowledge defeat when we fall, putting our ego aside, and relooking at what we can do differently to move forward, we will grow. Failures humble us and put us in a state of vulnerability. But failing also strengthens us, when we pick ourselves up to move forward after each fall.

4. **TEMPERANCE**

Temperance is the ability to abstain or withhold oneself. The ability to refrain from doing something that is not right, unjust, lawless, or overindulging in a particular desire. Temperance requires self-regulation. Submitting to a moderate attraction and desire for pleasure means we can control ourselves. It requires us to watch our actions, words, thoughts, and what we use or consume. It also requires us to delay the need for instant gratification.

Sir Thomas More, the chancellor to King of England Henry VII's in the 1500s, described temperance as "the disposition of the mind which binds the passion". Frances Elizabeth Caroline Willard, who was famous for lobbying for women's right in the 1800s, said, "Temperance is moderation in the things that are good and total abstinence from the things that are foul."

In the hype of human rights, freedom of speech, and movements today, we rarely discuss the need to moderate between our urges and the wellbeing of others. Social problems like substance abuse, bullying, harassment, infidelity, violence, or the unlawful display of anger are due to the lack of abstinence or self-regulation——the spur to express or gratify one's needs is greater than the effect of one's action to others.

In a famous social science marshmallow test, social scientists found children who were able to reframe from eating a marshmallow put in front of them for 15 minutes to be incentivised with a second one, having more willpower to control their impulse. They could delay the need to gratify their craving instantly for a better reward later. The researchers also found many of the children who passed the experiment, performed better at school and later in life.

In a world where we have a wealth of information and entertainment on the go, it is difficult to do without many distractions in life. We could easily surf the internet, play games, or watch movies for an hour or more without realising how the time has flown by. Our ability to limit or refrain from futile activities and to use our time wisely has become a rare commodity. Those who control their time and use it wisely to cultivate better relationships, health, and wealth will have better outcomes, more meaningful, and happier life.

Insufficient emphasis on virtuous behaviour has contributed to a high level of questionable practices and vices in our society today, costing billions of dollars in the efforts to ensure we behave fittingly. That must change if we want to reset in the new world order with a better version of the human race.

Over the years, I have received many enquiries from my clients on how to create a virtuous culture. There is no shortcut to building the ideal culture. It takes time. We could have town halls, engagement activities, or any form of communication to raise expectations and reward those who behave appropriately. We could also enforce rules, create performance guidelines, and alienate or punish those who failed to follow. However, this does not mean that the desired culture is created.

Culture is created by people who have the expected character and competence working together towards a common goal. The best way to have the right culture is to create it. First, define what "right culture" is to make sure that only the "right" people are in the company is the utmost importance. That is why it is so crucial to have a clear set of the company's competency guidelines—the expected observable behaviours, skills, and knowledge across different job levels.

Second, making sure the right recruitment and succession process of evaluating and selecting the right people are systematically structured. Third, ensuring learning and leadership development programs are created intentionally to groom specific, requiring competencies across all levels. Upholding the expected behaviours through performance reviews or appraisal, and removing people who do not fit into the culture is equally critical.

Above all, it is vital to appoint the rightful leaders at each level, who are credible and who reflect the desired behaviours. Moreover, culture is groomed through role models and imitations than through instructions and enforcement.

Virtuousness is formed within a person and is best nurtured from an early age. Through instruction and modelling by parents and further reinforced by the adults and elders in the community. At the tender age of two to five, children begin to exhibit behaviours through their moral beliefs. Their moral code, which ultimately shapes their conscientiousness, begins to grow.

Children first adopt their parents' rules, often to gain their parents' approval. The instructions of the parents, when internalised by the children, eventually become part of what they are. Sadly, much of the nurturing today is left to nannies, babysitters or teachers. Most parents do not have time to nurture and instruct their children today. There are also ways to develop virtues in adults. When we determine to become virtuous, we can. Chapter 8 will include how we do that systematically.

A man far oftener appears to have a decided character
from persistently following his temperament
than from persistently following his principles.
— Friedrich Nietzsche

VALUE-DRIVEN SOCIETY

In January 2020, I met with the president of an angel investors' network in Malaysia. He shared a deep concern he has with the companies' business plan today. Having gone through nearly 500 business plans over a period of 12 months, the president and his evaluation committee could hardly find a handful of ideas worth investing in. Subsequently, when I met the formal acting group CEO of a Malaysia's early-stage start-up influencer, he said the same too––the lack of a compelling reason for solving societal problems in many business proposals was overwhelming.

The president of the angle investors' network, who has built, listed, and sold a couple of companies before saying, a trustworthy business is purposed on bringing solutions to what the market needs, not what we think the market needs. According to the president, many start-ups today focus on the unique selling points to be profitable, but not on how they want to solve the daily pressing pain of customers.

Business plans should be simple, straightforward, with logical solutions, and back by numbers. Some of the best business plans he came across were conversations over a cup of coffee and a napkin. We should not get into business to create unique products, using the latest technology, or providing the best services. These are expected of any successful businesses. It is also not about having more time and earning more money. But the fundamental purpose of any business is to solve problems the market faces, bringing solutions to society.

So back to our question, "How do we move forward in the new world order and uncertain future?" Perhaps a better question to ask is, "What are the pain consumers are experiencing now?' 'How can I help solve those pains?"

After a catastrophic COVID-19 pandemic, we should first ask, "How has my customers' needs and behaviour changed?" We could get involved in a business that we are passionate about and probably do the things we are good at. But, if the business does not serve the market needs and what they are willing to pay for, our effort would not matter. We will become irrelevant and not profiting from our hard work. Consequently, we will not meet our purpose and needs of providing for our family.

There is a Japanese concept, IKIGAI, which means "a reason for being" or a reason to jump out of bed every morning because we have a life worth living. Ikigai beautifully sums up where we can create value to society. According to Albert Liebermann and Hector Gracia who wrote the book, *Ikigai: The Japanese Secret to a Long and Happy Life*, happiness is attained through worthwhile actions which produce meaningful results.

The origin of the word, Ikigai, goes back to the Heian period, 794 to 1185, from an island in Okinawa, Japan, a place with the most centenarians in the world. Many of the people living in this place are leaner, healthier, and age much better than their peers in other parts of the world. The people of Okinawa eat a low-calorie, low-carb diet, and have lower rates of heart disease, diabetes, and cancer.

And, the people living in Okinawa have a stable social network that creates a strong sense of security and belonging. They live a physically active lifestyle and fulfil their social role beyond 90 years of age. They maintain a positive outlook on life, have healthy coping skills, and a deep sense of spirituality, meaning, and purpose.

Ikigai emphasises the importance of purpose to create a life worth living. The feelings of excitement, contentment, gratefulness, fulfilment, and happiness or joy are experienced when there is balance in our actions and what the world needs. True happiness and joy are found in the combination of passion, talent, needs, and values when we do what we love, what we are good at, what the world needs, and how much they are willing to pay for what we do for them.

Image 7.1: Ikigai – A Reason for Being

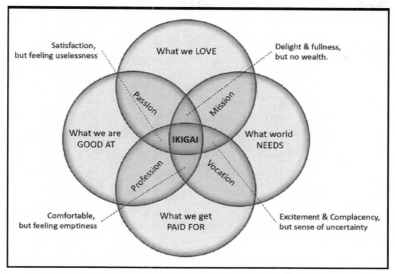

Concept by Akihiro Hasegawa. Image reproduced by ShuTzeTan

Jim Collins shared a similar concept, the hedgehog concept, in his book *Good to Great*. According to Collins, organisations will more likely succeed if they can identify the one thing that they do best. Like the hedgehog, by embracing simplicity has a single clear purpose of protecting itself from the fox. Unlike the fox, which uses multiple strategies to catch the hedgehog, but often goes away defeated, pricked by the hedgehog's spines.

When we focus on getting to the equilibrium between what ignites the fire in our spirit, what we do best, and what makes money, we strike a balance between effort and reward, purpose and profit. Like Newton's third movement theorem, there is an equal and opposite reaction for every action.

Over the years, I have read through many of the company's visions and missions. There are hardly any differences between one and the other. The vision to become the outstanding providers of the products or services they produce, to create the most value, to serve the best customer experience, to be the most innovative, and to make a difference in the world.

Organisations whose vision is to improve humanity, animal, or planet Earth, are similar, and their visions are only worded in different words. It is the same with us. We aim to make a difference in the world, creating a positive impact on the lives of others, and meeting our own needs.

Unfortunately, many of the company's annual strategic planning or performance discussions focus on "what goes wrong" and "what we need to do right" rather than "WHY" we need to do what we need to do. We must balance between "WHY" with "HOW" to bring meaning to our effort.

Vision and action, passion and profit go hand in hand. When we have a compelling reason, that vision will drive us to take necessary action to create the outcome. When we have a deep burning desire, our decision becomes simple. In most cases, we do not need more "HOW" but a bigger "WHY" especially when we are not in motion.

One of the most common questions my clients ask is, "How do we get someone to change?" We can only do so when we know what will compel them to change. A reason that will help them get away from their worries or get closer towards achieving their goals. Not a compelling reason we presume would get them to change. So, to get others to change, we must understand their "WHY" or "WHY NOT".

In this context, two other common questions people asked are, "Should I acquire certification in coding, programming, data analysis, coaching, or peruse MBA?" "What should my children study so that they could get ahead in life?"

While continuous educating improves our knowledge and skills, and it is desirable, but what we have learned does not guarantee us a good job. The principles, concepts, and systems in what we acquire will expand our capability, imagination, and creativity, hence, increase our ability to move forward better. However, additional certificates or degrees do not ensure employability.

With more easily accessible online courses worldwide, acquiring knowledge becomes easier and cheaper. More people are getting online degrees and certifications, especially during the pandemic lockdown period. What sets us apart from others is our experiences, our ability to deliver, and who we are within.

When we are being known as a person of excellence––the quality of being outstanding or excellence––we become attractive and more sought after. Excellence can only be achieved through many hours of work, experience, and delivered results.

The best-seller author, John Maxwell, put it splendidly, "Credibility is a leader's currency. With it, he or she is solvent; without it, he or she is bankrupt." Today, the world prefers to buy from sellers who are considered acceptable by other consumers and stay away from those with poor consumer reviews. In other words, marketing power is shifting to consumers.

That said, being excellence––the quality of excelling––is no longer a choice, but the currency of life. It is a life-long process of growth.

Furthermore, the technical skills we are acquiring can quickly become obsolete with the speed of technological advancement. It is therefore imperative that we focus on becoming excellence in every aspect of our lives, attitudes, and ability to build a healthy relationship, health, and wealth, which are closely linked to our profession. John C. Maxwell sums it brilliantly by saying, "Credibility is a character and competence combined."

CREDIBILITY = CHARACTER + COMPETENCY
— John C. Maxwell

It is inevitable then, to get ahead in the new world order, we must:

1. **UNDERSTAND NEEDS**

   First, to be relevant, we need to decide how we fit in and benefit society. We can only do this if we know the needs of others, and understand which of their needs are being threatened. And, we have the freedom to decide what needs we will create for them intentionally.

   Identifying needs has little to do with creating unique products, providing the best service, or adopting the most advanced technological advantages. It has everything to do with the role we choose to play and the solutions we decide to provide because the market is crying out for it. We, therefore, need to spend more time understanding consumer behaviours and market needs. Ask better questions and listen more, especially with the impact of COVID-19 and global economic shifts that are affecting lives and livelihoods.

   Once we have identified and understood the challenges society faces, we can look for the simplest, most logical, and straightforward solutions. We may not get it right for the first time. But through determination, perseverance, and persistent, we will get to the correct solutions eventually.

   Throughout history, innovations surged as responding to economic, pandemic, resources, and political crisis as compared to continuous improvement efforts. Creativity heightens when we are time-pressed for solutions and is often linked to the complexity and radicalness of solutions.

2. **PURSUE EXCELLENCE**

   Secondly, we choose to become excellence and produce excellent performance. Excellence is not excellent, nor is it about being perfect. Excellence is a character. When we strive for excellence, we always get better than the best we can and produce excellent work. We do that by finding the best solution for our customers as our mission, always. Being excellence has nothing to do with pioneering unique products or services. It has everything to do with who we become in the way we deliver our products and services. It is a continually growing process to become better each day.

If we want to become financial planners, we must strive for excellence and first of all in managing our own finances well. If we are going to be an entrepreneurial mentor, we must get into business and learn to grow a successful business ourselves. If we want to become a business or a life coach like any football coach, wouldn't that be fair to say, we also need to know the rules of the game in business or life and apply them to ourselves first? Excellence means continuingly breaking through our level best.

Being excellence is an attitude. Viktor E. Frankl said, "Everything can be taken from a man but one thing, the last of the human freedoms; to choose one's attitude under all circumstances, to choose one's way." Attitude is a personal choice and a reflection of our character. Our character is a reflection of our habits, which in turn is a reflection of our daily deliberate actions.

The pursuit of excellence in who we become and what we need to do is a will to commit ourselves, to doing something consistently over a prolonged period, and to make improvements daily. As we become a better version of what we can be every day in our lives and work, our confidence, esteem, results and rewards increase. We feel grateful, fulfilled and happy.

In short, being relevant and thriving in the new world order is within our will and our power. We own this to ourselves and our family.

8

HUMAN CHOICE
ACTION AND FREEDOM

Success is neither magical nor mysterious.
It is the natural consequence of consistently
applying fundamentals.
—Jim Rohn

IN THE EARLY 1920s, physicists had a discovery that completely changed our understanding of matter, physics, and mechanics—— quantum physics. Compared to classical physics, which deals with the behaviour of matter and energy that we could "see", quantum physics explains the behaviour of matter and energy under extreme conditions, either on a large or microscopic, invisible scale.

In a physical world, things we can touch and see are molecules formed by combinations of atoms. For example, two hydrogen atoms molecule (H) and one oxygen atom (O) form water, the H_2O. The centre of an atom (the nuclear) contains tiny particles, protons, neutrons, electrons, participles that were previously "invisible". We could not see these particles with our naked eyes nor through any instruments. But quantum physics has enabled us to "see the invisible".

Quantum physics provides us with a microscope image of nuclear reactions. We are now able to understand how atoms lock together the way they do and the forces with which they interact. With this

189

understanding, scientists were able to cause the collision of particles within accelerators and create most of the modern technologies we have today, like transistors, magnetic resonance imaging (MRI), lasers, and nuclear power.

With advancing science and technology, quantum physicists have manipulated various matter by splitting and combining particles at the atomic level in a controlled way to create synthetic or smart and advanced materials.

However, quantum physics also tells us how likely a particle system will behave in a certain way; it will never tell us how every particle that belongs to this system will behave. An object may have a probable chance to be at point A, another probable chance to be at point B, and so on. In other words, the behaviour of particles is random. Objects exist in the haze of probability, and nothing is certain. Therefore, we cannot predict every event accurately. We could only predict the likelihood of an event.

While some physicists suggested the probability that a particle at a certain point is random or accidental, Albert Einstein, a German-born physicist who developed the theory of relativity, argued strongly against it. Einstein rejected the idea that Mother Nature and the universe are random and that events happen purely by chance. He countered, "God does not play dice with the universe" and "God does not create the universe and then leave it to chance." Einstein believes in any quantum randomness and there is a range of outcomes——a limit to randomness. Therefore, all course of events is predetermined.

For example, when we throw a dice, the result is random within the six possible outcomes as the dice have six surfaces and thus six possible numbers. If there is a dice that has 16 surfaces, then there are 16 probable outcomes. The outcomes from the 16-surface dice are more random compared to the 6-surface dice. So if a series of events has a broader range of outcomes, it seems, the more random compared to a narrower range of outcomes. In other words, even if the results of an event appear random, it is not.

Nassim Nicholas Taleb, a statistician, veteran trader and renowned risk expert, explains how we are often fooled by events that seem random. In his book *Fooled by Randomness: The Hidden Role of Chance in Life and the Markets,* he wrote we can't predict with certainty the outcome of a single event. However, through a series of repeated events, say 1,000 events, we can determine the range of results and thus the level of randomness. In other words, the quality of a single decision cannot be judged by its outcome.

IS SUCCESS RANDOM

We can observe the principles of quantum physics in an effort to achieve an outcome. If we presented a business plan to a single or even a few investors and were rejected, it does not mean that our plan does not work. If we make a similar presentation 100 times or more, we can better assess a range of likely outcomes. Repetitive actions, therefore, help improve the quality of our presentation.

And if, after each presentation attempt, we make improvements with the feedbacks collected, we can narrow down the probable results to a single, final act that has ultimately brought us to a huge success. The only problem is we do not know which is the last act, and when will the breakthrough comes, but it will come. For this reason, it appears as if the mega-success occurred overnight, but it is not.

Walt Elias Disney, the first creator of the world of animation, approached many financiers and was turned down 302 times before someone believed in the Disney vision and invested in the project. Disney World became the first-ever entertainment theme park in the world. When Howard Schultz, a Starbucks employee, wanted to buy the brand to bring the Italian cafe to the masses, he presented his proposal to 242 investors, and 217 of them rejected him.

Michael Jordan once said, "I've missed more than 9,000 shots in my career. I've lost almost 300 games. 26 times, I've been trusted to take the game-winning shot and missed. I've failed over and over and over again in my life. And that is why I succeed." Today, Jordan is one of the greatest basketball players of all time.

Thomas Edison went through 10,000 attempts to invent the commercially-viable light bulb, and said, "I have not failed 10,000 times. I have not failed once. I have succeeded in proving that those 10,000 ways will not work. When I have eliminated the ways that will not work, I will find the way that will work."

The point is, we do not know which of these last acts will land us with enormous success. Just like that one last grain of sand which brings down an entire sandhill, one more presentation could land us with the biggest deal in our life.

According to Nassim Nicholas Taleb, humans tend to look for patterns and find out what causes an event, even if there is none. Our tendency to believe in our rationality often leads us to ignore or even overlook the apparent trends. That is common in people who are new to a particular area.

Taleb goes further, saying that because events in life are only coincidental to a certain extent when life brings us one of those unexpected terrible blows, we can deal with it with full control, not forced by chance, but by our reaction. We have 100% freedom to make the right choice and to take full responsibility for the situation. We are in charged and are accountable regardless of what happened.

One of the most significant lessons I have learned about success and mastery is from professional traders. Trading is like life: it appears random, but it is not. Experienced traders who have traded through many economic cycles would say that the market is very dynamic, but it is not random. They become competent traders through many trades executed through the years, and over many economic cycles.

Professional traders have trained themselves to use different trading strategies in different market conditions, using a set of rules systematically. They respect the fundamentals that affect business, including the economy at large, geopolitical relationships, sectoral movements, the value of companies, including the revenues, earnings, margins, growth potential, and the management team.

They also get competent in the technical analytics to understand trends, chart patterns, price movements, volumes and more to capture the dynamics of demand and supply and identify trading opportunities. They painstakingly studied and anticipated major shifts to plan for each trade carefully.

Professional traders, just like any other professional, journal the principles and rules that govern the decision in every trade they perform. That allows them to review and evaluate the quality of their decisions and make improvements over time. They learned to trust and master the process to the point of becoming emotionless to the outcome of each trade, be it a win or lose a trade. Like quantum physics, we cannot judge the quality of every trade, but the quality of many trades.

Ray Dalio, who founded Bridgewater Associates, the world's largest institutional investors' hedge funds company, is one of such examples. Dalio also authored the book, *Principle*. He records every principle and rule behind his investment decisions so that he can review and improve over time. That helped him to shape subsequence decisions with principles and not swayed by market sentiments.

Dalio also brings this practice to his team and applies to his management decisions too. Today, Bridgewater Associates manages approximately $150 billion in investments for some 350 of the world's largest and most demanding institutional clients.

FREEDOM TO CHOOSE

The greatest gift our creator has given to the human race is the freedom to choose. The autonomy to choose our response and perform an action selected from two or more options is not limited by external factors, regardless of the situation we find ourselves in. In addition to our emotions and logical thinking, humans have a higher decision-making capacity than other animals because we have a more comprehensive understanding of possibilities. We understand the advantages of being able to perform both emotional and rational decisions.

By Newton's third law of motion, however, there is an equal and opposite reaction to every decision and every action taken. Zig Ziglar said, "You are free to choose. But the choices you make today will determine what you will be, do, and have in the tomorrows of your life." Each decision comes with its predestined rewards or consequences.

Hence, freedom is not free. Freedom comes at a price. The choice of staying in bed longer or going for a jog every day before work, eating a bagel or eating a healthy protein-packed breakfast will have an impact on our health over a more extended period.

According to Jim Collins in his 4 million best-selling management book, *Good to Great: Why Some Companies Make the Leap and Others Don't*, companies who leap from good to great and grown ten times more than the average choose to be great. "Greatness is not something predetermined, predestined, or carved into your fate by forces beyond your control", Collins said. "Greatness comes with the choices we make every minute, every hour, every day."

Jeff Olson says in his book *The Slight Edge: Turning Simple Discipline into Massive Success and Happiness*, many actions are "so easy to do, and easy not to do". In other words, why some leap from good to great, and many don't, reflecting the choices they made.

Those who we have become today reflect the choices we have made in the past. Who we become in the next 12 months or ten years depends on the decisions we make at every moment. Ultimately, "I am not a product of circumstances. I am a product of my decision", quoting Steven Covey. When we make the right choice every single minute, the result will be rewarding.

That is why, however volatile, uncertain, complex, and ambiguous the world may be, we have the power to determine our future. Furthermore, we all have nature's laws and universal principles that guide us to be a better version of ourselves every day.

Ray Dalio also said there are principles which should guide our actions to achieve results. Our success is the direct result of our unique ability to follow the rules set by the laws of nature and universal principles. If we do not follow these rules, we will be disempowered in the long run. Freedom, success, and getting ahead in the new world are therefore in our hands.

Principles are what allow you to live a life
consistent with those values.
Principles connect your values to your actions.
They provide clear guides on the way we do
things by empowering and sustaining us.
— Ray Dalio, *Principle*

So if we want to achieve the desired results in our lives, if we are going to make our dreams and wishes come true, we must make the right choices––decisions following nature's laws and universal principles. No matter how hard it may seem. Because the regret for not achieving the desired outcomes is more painful than the discipline of action, rejection, and failure.

Moreover, results do not care about our feelings. People of significance demand themselves to be obedient to nature's laws and universal principles, and proven systems of success, even when they do not feel like doing it sometimes.

By learning the principle of quantum physics from people who master their craft, we can meet our innate human needs by taking extreme ownership, prioritise virtuousness, and build habits of greatness:

Image 8.1: Meeting the Human Needs

GROW & CONTRIBUTE ➡	HABITS	Fulfillment Needs
BELONG & ACKNOWLEDGE ➡	VIRTUOUSNESS	Relational Needs
PROTECT & PROVIDE ➡	OWNERSHIP	Basic Needs

Copyright©Shu-TzeTan

1. TAKE EXTREME OWNERSHIP

To get ahead so that we can protect and provide for our family no matter what circumstances we are in, we should take extreme ownership of our lives. Face the brutal truth of the situation and the risk we are confronting. We have often witnessed foreclosures or layoffs that escalate around us, and intuitively we know if our business or our job is also at risk. Still, we hope the worst will not happen to us, yet most people not ready for the rainy days.

But if we could anticipate this risk and design alternative plans before the worst happens, we would be in a much better position to deal with an unknown future. If we could help companies create business continuity plans (BCPs) to mitigate risk, we could apply the same knowledge and skills in our lives. We know, we should dig the well before we need the water.

Taking extreme ownership of our life is also means not waiting for external help. The moment we ask, "What is the government or my boss doing to ensure my business or job is secure?", we have given away our power to others. When we hope for the succeeding bailout, we are not taking charge of the situation we are in. Alternatively, when we take full ownership and become responsible, we have total control by finding alternatives to the manual through the situation we are in to create the results we want.

According to Jocko Willink, a retired U.S. Navy SEAL, taking full ownership means, "Owning everything in the world. No one else to blame." In a book Wilnk and Leif Babin authored, *Extreme Ownership: How U.S. Navy Seal Lead and Win*, they shared how two of the U.S. Navy SEAL officers who led the most highly decorated special operations unit of the Iraq War demonstrated leadership principles in the battlefield, business, and life. Leaders who took extreme ownership did so even when their team committed death threatening mistakes during their absence.

2. PRIORITISE VIRTUOUSNESS

Smart technology has enabled collaboration to happen faster, easier and cheaper. Starting a business or acquiring new knowledge is now available to everyone as long as they are connected to the internet. Anyone can take a new course online, start a business, or use a crowd-sourcing method to solve a problem together. What sets us apart from others is our credibility, who we are, our character and our competence.

Furthermore, as the world is becoming "borderless", "leaderless", and to a certain extent, "lawless", nature's laws and universal principles dominate us. We must live virtuously to fulfil our needs to protect, provide, belong, acknowledge, grow, contribute, and to live harmoniously. Moreover, as users and innovators of smart technologies, we must first maintain virtue within ourselves and among ourselves, so that artificial intelligence and superintelligence robots do not become evil.

3. **BUILD HABITS OF GREATNESS**

The way to move forward in a world full of people with skills and abilities like ours lies within us. When customers buy our products or services, they are buying us. The quality of being great, outstanding and excellence, is larger than our ability, higher than paper qualification, position, and importance. Greatness is not reflected in wealth or popularity. It is leadership, reliability, service, efficiency, and results combined.

Greatness is the deep belief one has despite the surrounding noise. It is a quiet confidence and courage that transcends all normality and naysayers. Self-talks like, "I don't have the time and the money", "I am too busy", "Discipline is too tough", "I am a procrastinator", "I do not know how" are barriers to greatness.

When we choose to be a person of excellence, we take it upon ourself to be responsible for becoming great in every aspect of our life and achieve the results we yearn for in our relationship, health, and wealth. We ensure we first live by nature's laws and universal principles, we walk the talk, and achieve results before we train, coach, or mentor others to do so.

Greatness is developed through consistency by doing what we must over an extended period. Not surprisingly, many great leaders, like Jocko Willink, say that "Discipline, in our thinking and our action, is the path to freedom."

GETTING AHEAD

Lao-Tzu once said, "The journey of a thousand miles begins with the first step." Most complex endeavours usually begin with relatively simple tasks. First of all, we need to know where we stand in the entire ecosystem of life to have a compelling reason and a clear roadmap to do what we must, to move forward.

There are two questions we should continually ask ourselves in a rapidly changing, uncertain world. These are the primary questions the chiefs of countries, companies, and consulting firms get paid in a hefty sum to answer strategically.

The two most important questions are:

1. **WHAT ARE THE MAJOR SHIFTS HAPPENING AROUND ME?**
   To remain relevant and move forward in the uncertain future, we must face up to what is happening around us. Questions like, "How would the new world order look like?" "What is the impact of the COVID-19 pandemic to the world politically, economically and socially?", "What are the ripple effects on businesses, jobs, and humans be in the next 6 to 18 months and beyond?" These are the questions companies asked, to stay ahead, and we should too.

   What we read and where we get our daily news from determines our awareness of the rapid changes taking place around us. Global companies subscribe to research papers, business outlook reports, and expect their decision-makers to interact across disciplines and industries to widen their perspectives and knowledge. Some companies host webinars, town halls, and forums to keep abreast with changes to be prepared before changes happen. As the new world we are in today is interconnected and interdependent, we can learn from those who are moving ahead of us.

One of the most important sources of information we should equip ourselves with is the World Economic Forum (WEF). Founded in 1971, the WEF is a non-profit international organisation dedicated to improving the state of the world. The WEF held an annual meeting that brought together more than 3,000 business leaders, international policymakers, economists, and journalists to discuss global issues and collaborate on several initiatives. The WEF also congregates six regional meetings annually for a similar purpose.

The WEF meeting in Davos, Switzerland, in January 2020 marked the 50th WEF Annual Meeting. World leaders discuss critical issues related to ecology, economics, technology, society, and geopolitical challenges. The WEF also regularly produces a series of reports and updates. That is where we can get an insight into the agenda and programmes that world leaders are working on. Moreover, changes take place where leaders congregate.

Other sources of information to help us stay on top of the rapid shifts are the forecasts and outlooks by organisations like the Bain & Co, Boston Consulting Group (BCG), McKinsey & Co, Gartner, Harvard Business Reviews and many more. These companies work closely with their customers worldwide and continuously conduct surveys to inform world leaders about the impact of change on business, work, and life. Many of these reports are readily accessible to the public. During the COVID-19 lockdowns, there were many such updates shared, and many world leaders pointing out how we can get ahead.

To be aware of the rapid changes around us, we look at changes in the global economy, geopolitical relations, and social contracts. We also examine how consumer behaviour, demographic structures, investment flows, innovation, and the development of new business models are changing.

The world population will grow from 7 billion to 8 billion in 2020, and to 10 billion by 2025. In the next 5 to 10 years, the economies from the Seven Emerging Countries (E7) including China, India, Brazil, Mexico, Russia, Indonesia and Turkey are going to double the economies of the Group of Seven Countries (G7) consisting of Canada, France, Germany, Italy, Japan, the United Kingdom and the United States.

China's Belt and Road Initiatives or also known as One Belt announced in 2013 is positioned to do just that. It is an ambitious programme with six major corridors designed to promote regional integration, trade and economic growth. The One Belt will affect world trade, the economy, investment and the financial landscape.

Moreover, 80% of the middle class and 75% of growth will come from emerging markets. 90% of those under 25 live in emerging markets. These are signs, showing us areas where governments and corporations will be spending more or slowing down, and where opportunities will raise and fall.

Developments in megacorporatioins like Amazon, Alphabet, the parent company of Google and several formal Google subsidiaries, Apple, Alibaba, Facebook, Microsoft, Huawei, Tencent, Walmart, and the like, will continue to change the world. Sectoral shifts, particularly in technology and communications, will affect productivity and other sectors, especially consumer staples and discretionary, healthcare, and finance. The decisions of industry leaders affect trade agreements, investment, innovation, and taxes. They are the driving forces and shakers of the global economy and will affect humans life and livelihoods.

We can also gain valuable insights from the companies' annual report. In particular, annual reports of the company we are working with our customers and our competitors. Annual reports give us a glimpse of a company's winning strategy, and future direction, potential trends, and the strength of the management's decisions on top of their financial performance.

Other organisational reports such the customer service scores, organisation and operations reports, leadership and succession plans, and employee engagement valuations, risk evaluation and mitigation plans help us to learn strategies that would work and would not work in different circumstances.

Companies can appear brilliant with the latest innovations and products offerings but will be of little value they cannot acquire, keep, grow, and be profitable. That is why, some say, ideas are cheap, but the results speak. We need both the ideas and results——purpose and profit.

That sounds like a lot of reading and preparation to do before we even start planning strategically and taking action. That is what global companies do in strategic planning. Greatness requires both patient understandings of the world needs before we determine how we can add value and get ahead.

2. **WHAT DO I WANT TO BE 10 YEARS FROM NOW?**
This second question is like the two popular childhood questions, "What do you want to be when you grow up?" and "What would you like to do if you have one million dollars?"

Questions like these allow us to imagine who we can be if resources, including time, are not a constraint. It is a question of what we want. However, these questions seem more challenging answering as adults. We could have a great career, paying the bill and giving us the lifestyle now. However, if we go through life with whatever job we landed on, we will eventually regret not having lived the dream in our heart, especially when our income ceased.

To answer the question, "What do I want to be ten years from now?" We can start by stating our desired outcome according to our basic needs, relational needs, and fulfilment needs respectively, as examples below:

- **BASIC NEEDS**

  "I have created a minimum of $10 million asset which generate passive annual incomes to provide for my family. I am providing the best for my family and I so that we can indulge in meaningful activities.

  I built an 8,000-square-foot eco-house on the land I purchased by 55, where intelligent robot helpers, human cooks and gardeners take care of us. That allows me to spend almost 50% of my time in different countries, indulging in nature, culture and history, experiencing the local delicacies in the marketplace, reading a well-researched book on the beach or hiking up the Alps in Europe every year. I continue to write many books and speak on many global platforms."

- **RELATIONAL NEEDS**

  "I work with global leaders, influencing and learning together for the betterment of the human race. I am part of the global leadership network and business association. I spend most of my time travelling and connecting with my associates globally, working and impacting lives together. We are playing a bigger game of life to help others live their fullest potential.

  In the new world, there is so much more for us to do: helping people to deal with themselves and the new reality, forgiving and letting go of the past, appreciating lives and cultivating right-thinking, to thrive in the uncertain yet exciting future."

- **FULFILMENT NEEDS**

  "I have a healthy, sexy and dynamic physics, and I live a life beyond 100 years. With the advances in medicine and health care, this is now possible.

In 10 years, I continue to enjoy optimal health, energy, and sharpness to do the things I love and inspire others to do the same. I continue to make positive impacts on the surrounding life. Sow the seeds of greatness, care for more leaders around the world, so we can advance the movement of greatness to make a significant difference to humanity worldwide.

Last but not least, I will look back at the end of my life, knowing that I have lived an extraordinary life."

In Chapter 4, we have learned words have power——whatever we imagine in our minds will generate the electrochemical energy of the 100 trillion synapses in our brains that vibrate and transmute into the physical world, into our reality. So, when we write our desires, we avoid using negative statements. Pessimistic statements generate unfavourable emotions and energy that attract what we do not want.

Wishes, visions, dreams, and goals are best written in affirmative statements, and statements of ours in deeds. So, when we read what we have written every time, they are not in the future, they are current, and we actively participate and move forward towards what we desire.

On top of that, as we do not laugh at our children's dreams and wishes when we ask them, "Who would you like to be?" there is no desire or dream too big or absurd, even if it sounds impossible to achieve. We would not allow constraints to hold us back. Instead, we start with child-like faith and dream big. And to realise our dreams, we systematically break it down to actionable steps with realistic goals.

Moreover, when we summon the power of will and do what is required, we will achieve what we want. Throughout history, humans' desires have invented steam power, electricity, nuclear power and more. We have flown to the moon, created self-driving vehicles, invented unmanned smart machinery, and soon, making space travel the next entertainment. The bigger our desires, the stronger our conviction grows and pushes us to expand our capabilities to create extraordinary results.

Now, we also know that "Pictures paint a thousand words." To increase the chances of realising our desires, we must have a clear, brightly lighted, mental picture of the dream we desire. And we must convert that mental picture into a collage of images. There is a physiological and psychological reason for creating a "dream board" or collage.

Firstly, we receive the most information through our eyes as our eyes transmit most information compared to other sensory systems. When our visual receptors receive about 10 million bits of information per second, these stimuli generate electrochemical energy and send directly to our occipital lobe in the cerebrum region of the brain. Since the cerebrum sphere covers the left and right hemispheres, these stimuli will light up both our logical and emotional memories and reconstruct new ones.

When pictures of visions and desires are carefully selected to represent our desires, we are creating physical stimuli by using our dream board to ignite the positive emotion within us every time we look at it. In conjunction with that, when our brainwaves continually fire up with the vision of our dreams, it generates neural electrochemical energy and positive emotions. That energy will transmute to the physical world and realise our desires, even if we are not aware of the process.

Our dream board keep us focus on what we ultimate want from the efforts and the sacrifices we are willing to make to achieve our desires. For this reason, companies spend millions to create their vision board, corporate video, and communication materials to represent their vision to achieve a similar effect. Lifestyle advertisements do the same too by using bright colours, lifestyle pictures, music, and particular scent to ignite consumers' buying behaviours.

Now, let us not conclude too quickly that we can realise our dreams by daydreaming or meditating on our dreams. These energies generated through our sights must be transmuted to other forms through our daily deliberate action to create results. As many of the holy books say, "faith without work is death."

SYSTEM IN MAKING DREAMS COME TRUE

Ray Dalio, in his book, *Principle* shared how systemise decision-making yield better results than leaving it to the decision-makers. Through his years of experience, he found that when the decision-making process is systematically structured with principles, which is hard to screw up, because, it forces people to face the cause-effect relationship directly. Comparatively, decisions that are dependent on the quality of people and their decision-making do not do so well compared to systemised decisions. Hence, to realise our desires and dreams, and not leaving it to chance, we create systems.

Brian P. Morgan, the co-author of, *The 12-Week Years*, said, "Vision without a plan is a pipe dream." Wishes, visions or dreams are only fantasies or empty wishes without action and execution. Morgan also said, "Knowledge is not power if not acted upon." It is not difficult to dream dreams or acquire knowledge, but few do something about it.

So, to realise our dreams, we plan strategically and create a system we can follow step by step to generate the appropriate emotions within us and to fulfil our desires. The process of developing the plan and the system also allows us to assess how much effort we need to put in, how much risk we could take, and how willing we are to work diligently in achieving what we want.

While the results we want do not care about how our emotions, our emotions have an enormous impact on the way we achieve desired outcomes. Conscientiously, following a systematic process, ensures we move forward despite our feelings. We create a strategic system with the following process.

Image 8.2: System to Realise Dreams

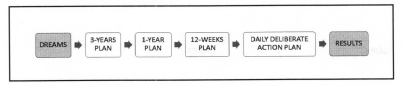

1. **3-YEAR PLAN**

   Firstly, we develop a 3-year plan which forces us to set realistic milestones to realise our desires and dreams. A 3-year plan helps us to be aware of the changes around us and to figure out what we should do to get closer to our desires. A 3-year plan allows us to identify the long-term risks and opportunities. It helps us avoid being caught up with short-term activities and urgent but unimportant tasks.

   In a 3-year plan, we define the critical milestones to achieve by the end of year-1, year-2, and year-3. During the process of developing the 3-year plan, we bring our desires and beliefs in our subconscious mind to our conscious awareness level. We do that by setting realistic and measurable plans, with logic, facts, and numbers. A clear plan minimises disillusionment, confusion, and frustration while bringing dreams to life.

   While developing a 3-year plan, we carefully weigh our passion with the market needs, and what we do well with what customers are willing to pay. So that, our effort is meaningful and profitable––IKIGAI––balancing between work and rewards. The 3-years plan should be holistic to sustain long-term needs, integrating the three fundamental elements of life––relationship, health, and wealth. It should also include the three levels of humans' basic, psychological, and fulfilment needs.

   I have often used the "Wheel of Life" template to help my clients assess "where they are now" and "where they want to be in the next 12 months to 3 years" before developing a 3-years plan. The "Wheel of Life" is a powerful tool which provides a vivid visual representation of our current state of life compared to what we desired.

We do that by first, using the "Wheel of Life" template to assess, "How satisfied I am with my current status" in each of the nine areas of life, with the rating from "1" to "10", "1" is the "least happy", "10" is "the happiest."

Once we have completed the self-assessment, we can develop a solid 3-year plan to increase our happiness. We do that by first, acknowledging the way we think, our attributes, our abilities, then identify the knowledge and skills we need to acquire to achieve what we desire. We discover new areas where we can learn, people who can coach and mentor us, as well as areas we need to eliminate to grow.

By the end of every year, we use the same "Wheel of Life" template to measure our life state again to determine our progress. When we have taken the necessary actions, our happiness will increase. The joy of beholding the glow in my clients when they noticed their own progress is one of the greatest fulfilments of my work.

Image 8.3: Wheel of Life

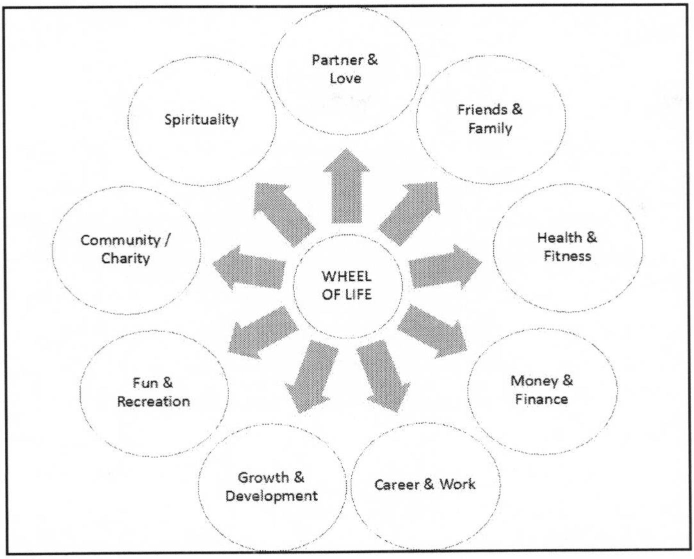

Concept by Paul Meyer. Image reproduced by ShuTzeTan

A well-developed 3-year plan requires correct information and formulation to set specific, measurable goals. For example, to ensure that I can protect and provide for my family, to sustain my family's living expenses, pay the bills, insurance, taxes, and loans, I would need at least an X amount of the annual recession-proof, passive-recurring, asset-based income.

To achieve that, I would need a net liquid asset of the Y amount, the total asset minus all the liabilities, including the property price of the main house in which my family and I live. The net liquid asset of the Y amount must generate investment returns that are equal to the annual passive-recurring income of the X amount I need.

If I needed a $100,000 (X amount) passive-recurring income annually to cover my family's living expenses, I would need $100,000/0.10, which equates to a net liquid asset of $1,000,000 (Y amount), provided I could get a 10% yearly return on my investments. But if my yearly investment return is at 5%, I would need \$100,000/0.05, which equates to a net liquid asset of \$2 million.

And, to guarantee that my net liquid asset can sustain my family and me for the next 50 years or more, I need to calculate the "actual" return on my investment. Assuming inflation is at 8% per year, my actual return on investment is 10% minus 8% inflation. In other words, actual investment return is merely 2% per year. The net liquid asset I must accumulate is \$100,000/(0.10-0.08), or \$5 million, to generate \$100,000 passive-recurring income annually for as long as my family and I live.

Once I know the above figures, I can assess the gap I have: How much net liquid asset do I have now compared to what I need? How can I increase my net liquid asset? Will my saving rate fast enough to get me to the amount I need within the timeline I want? What business model or systems generate the passive-recurring income level I need for the tenure of my family's and my life on Earth?

On top of the above, I would want to calculate the actual inflation rate according to where I stay and my lifestyle to ensure my net liquid asset can sustain my as long as my family and I are still alive.

I would also want to weigh investment vehicles that can deliver the actual return I need without compromising the future value of my net liquid assets and income needs. I want to ensure my net liquid assets continue to generate the passive-recurring income and are willable to my next of kin when I die.

There are many details that we need to work through just for one single goal. That is what planning is all about. That is why the saying, "there is no free lunch."

Apart from the basic living expenses I need, if I want to build my dream house. I would like to know the cost of building the designer-eco-home at the top of a hill, the cost of putting in a marble top modern kitchen with a view extending beyond the patio, with a view overlooking the infinity pool cliff off the hill. The more numbers I have, the more realistic my dream will become, and the close I will be to realise it.

Beyond the house, what would the budget I would want to put aside for equipping this dream house with the latest smart home technology? How much would be the cost of having a few robot helpers, gardeners, nannies, and a master-chef for the family?

If I wanted the best medical care for my family, how much should I put aside for future medical expenses? What would be the price of growing a new heart, kidney, lung, or a limb from my stem cells, for a transplant, or to get my body frozen to be revived again in the unforeseeable future simply because I can?

If travelling is my passion, what would I want my annual travel budget to be? How much do I want to put aside to enjoy comfortable holidays, staying in 5-stars hotels, flying in the first-class and private jets, having my personalised tour-guides and drivers, experiencing the Michelin starred culinary around the world? The lifestyle I dreamt of having will escalate my annual passive-recurring income requirement and therefore my net liquid assets.

In addition to satisfying our basic human needs, we also have the desire to meet the second level of human relational needs to belong and acknowledge. Who am I? Who do I want to be known for? What reputation do I want to have? With whom do I want to be associated? To which inner circle do I want to belong? To whom do I look up and want to emulate? Which values do I bring with me? What type of mindset and attitude do I need to develop to become who I want to be?

Following which, we also have human fulfilment needs to be met. What is my ultimate purpose of existence? Who do I exist for? Who do I give to? Where would I like to make a difference? How can I contribute to the betterment of the human race and planet Earth? What legacy do I want to leave?

Defining a crystal clear 3-year plan will take time and effort. The process of painstakingly drafting the plan is a decision to be excellence in live a life by design. That requires determination and mental discipline. As we go through this process, our sense of responsibility grows. The level of seriousness in realising our dreams lies in the effort we are willing to give, sacrifices we are willing to make, details we are willing to get into, and the brutal truth of our state we are willing to face.

When we first develop a 3-year plan, it may seem vague at first. But as we gather more information and interact with people who are ahead of us, and grow with every action taken, our plans become concrete. A clear plan helps us to verify the price of the prize we desired.

2. **1-YEAR GOAL**

The 1-year plan allows us to draw up a more realistic plan for our dreams, without losing sight of the bigger picture in life; our surrounding, including the environment and economic condition. With a 3-year plan, we break it down further to a 1-year goal.

A 1-year goal gives us the time we need to work on critical milestones to get closer to our dreams. In a 1-year period, we might be using the time to explore or formulate ideas, build prototypes, test our plans, and simultaneously win buy-ins from key stakeholders, including customers, investors, employees, employers, and family members.

A 1-year goal in business could be the time needed to better understand our customers' landscape by testing the acceptance of our products, services, and distribution channels. 1-year give us sufficient time to accumulate feedbacks and continuingly make improvements to our business when we launch our products and services to the market. We would be meeting many potential investors, business partners, vendors, or getting the approval of policymakers, or board members to get to the most fitting ones.

If we are employees, we could be looking for new job opportunities or finding ways to diversify our incomes. We could be attending courses or gaining insights from people who have taken the path before us.

One year gives us the time to adjust our plan to get closer to our dreams. It gives us time to build, test, and familiarise with the new structures, systems, and processes to be successful. It gives us time to grow.

3. **12-WEEKS GOAL**

Jim Rohn once said, "Without a sense of urgency, desire loses its value." While a 1-year goal helps us break down a 3-years plan to a realistic milestone, the 1-year goal, unfortunately, creates an annualised or 52-week thinking and the feeling that "I still have time".

If we do not have shorter-term plans, we would not realise every week, every day, every moment is critical to get closer to our dreams. That is the reason many who have made New Year's resolutions did not achieve much in the first half of the year and only struggled to catch up in the second half of the year. An annualised thinking lacks the sense of urgency we need to spring into action.

Brian P Morgana and Michael Lennington, the authors of *The 12-week year: Get More Done in 12 weeks than Others in 12 months*, say, "The 12-Week Year help us avoid the pitfalls and low productivity of annualised thinking. In 12 weeks, there simply isn't enough time to get complacent, and urgency increases and intensifies. *The 12-weeks* creates focus and clarity on what matters most now. In the end, more of the important stuff gets done, and the impact on results is profound."

In a 12-week goal, we chunk down the year-1 milestones into four quarters or four blocks of 3-month milestones to achieve. The 12-week goal gives us a sense of urgency and forces us to review our progress more regularly with more frequent feedback. As new habits are formed within 21 to 60 days, the 12-week gives us sufficient time to develop new patterns in our thinking process and daily activities to get us closer to our dreams.

4. **DAILY DELIBERATE ACTION (DDA) PLAN**
    John C. Maxwell once said, "I can predict the long-term outcome of your success if you show me your daily habits." Success does not come from what we do "occasionally", but on what we do "consistently", every week, every day, every moment. Once we have a 12-week plan in place, we chunk it down to develop a weekly and daily DDA.

DDA is a daily dashboard that allows us to set and track the tasks we execute every day to get closer to our dream. By completing and ticking off the daily tasks planned in our DDA, we can monitor our progress and make improvements. DDA is unlike a "to-do list." It is a list of tasks we want to execute intentionally and repeatedly every day over time until new habits are formed to get closer to our dreams.

A DDA is like the dashboard football coaches used to keep track of the practices their players engaged in every day, to gauge their progress and identify potential performance problems. That allows the coaches to formulate tactical changes needed to help their players get closer to the desired outcomes.

DDA ensures we engage in activities that are not urgent but are crucial to achieving our desires. It ensures we use our time and invest our resources wisely. When we have a dashboard, we know exactly what we have done or have not done every day to achieve our goals. DDA forces us to face up to our thoughts, beliefs, actions or inaction and be responsible for our results.

DDA is a fantastic tool to help establish new routines to develop new habits of success. When we take intentional action every day for 21 to 60 days, we begin to move in an "auto-cruise" mode without negotiating with the circumstances we are in.

That is, how habits are formed. We begin to do things subconsciously, like going to the bathroom every morning, often with our eyes still closed, brushing our teeth, and taking a shower. When we have developed new habits, we will do our morning run; read our affirmation; read a few pages of a book; or meditate for 30 minutes, regardless of the weather or the circumstances around, just as we would go to work every Monday to Friday, sunshine, rain, or snow.

Furthermore, when we focus on doing the activities required to achieve our goals, we would not have the time and the mental space to stay with disempowering, negative thoughts, procrastinate, or engage in activities that pull us away from our goals. When we take action, we begin to replace disempowering thoughts and behaviours with empowering ones. In the next section, we will work on developing a personalised DDA to realise our dreams systematically.

As Rome was not built in a day, we need time to draw up a concrete ten-year plan. On an annual basis, companies spend months developing strategic plans with more comprehensive frameworks, models, and templates. The key is, use the ones most relevant to our current state, starting with the simplest process first to get to the action quickly.

In my experience of working with multi-national companies, annual planning would typically start 5 to 6 months or more before the new financial year. It involves going through many types of research and reading to scan the global economic landscape, studying the shift in consumers' behaviours, technology, business models, regulatory, and monitory systems, and anticipate what could happen in the coming 12 to 24 months before we get down to annual strategic planning.

The planning starts with a review of our current state, our strengths and gaps in our finance, operation, talent, and customers to ascertain the desired goals we want to achieve realistically. Planning involves weeks of discussions with the board and key stakeholders across all business units to agree on the key result areas we would work towards together before the final annual plan is completed.

Then comes the cascading of the plan to the other members of the organisation, as departments and teams begin to develop quarterly, weekly, daily actionable plans to achieve the business goals. We would record, report, and review progresses on a daily and weekly basis and make improvements along the way. On a monthly and quarterly basis, at the end of every "12-week", we would review and adjust the goals and plans to get close to the desired outcomes.

Many people might not realise this, while we spend a significant amount of time preparing before putting our annual plan together with as much information and analytics as possible, most of the important decisions are made distinctly and intuitively. A point in time when we know it in our guts, a specific goal we must achieve. The amount of effort poured into preparations and analytics will ensure we do not go too far off from reality.

Albert Einstein once said, "If I had an hour to solve a problem, and my life depended on it, I would use the first 55 minutes to ask the right question. Once I knew the right question, I could solve the problem in less than five minutes." To redesign a life we want and achieve our purpose and dreams in the new world and a new reality, careful planning is inevitable and does require time and effort.

Clarity of what the future would look like with detailed execution plans helped build the fastest train, the tallest tower, and longest bridge. Beijing Daxing International Airport in China is one such notable example. It was first proposed in 2008. Construction work only started six years later in December 2014 and took five years to complete. The entire airport area is more than half the size of Hong Kong, 47 square kilometres, with the main terminal occupying 695,000 square metres. At full capacity, the airport could handle 100 million passengers and 880,000 flights a year.

Careful planning with artificial intelligence and years of preparation has enabled China to build a 1,000-bed hospital in Wuhan in 10 days during the Coronavirus pandemic at the end of January 2020. A breathtaking pace that has awakened the whole world and opened up new possibilities in this new normal. All this starts with detailed planning. And opportunity comes to those who are prepared.

DAILY DELIBERATE ACTION (DDA)

Jeff Olson wrote in his book, *Slight Edge: Turning Simple Disciplines Into Massive Success and Happiness,* "Success is a matter of many simple actions that are easy to do and easy not to do." Jim Rohn says, "What is simple to do is also simple not to do." The secret to success is not complexity, but simple tasks repeated over an extended period to ignite the miracle of the compounding effect. It is the double-a-penny-a-day principle. We create that compounding effect by using DDA to track our daily activities.

Benjamin Franklin, or widely known as Uncle Ben, was a writer, scientist, political philosopher in the 1700s, and eventually, became one of the founding fathers of the United States. He is also known for developing a self-tracking system to monitor his behaviour and daily actions to become a better person and be more productive.

That systems eventually became the dairy, scheduler, check-list, to-do list, and journaling template many leaders use today.

At the age of 20, Benjamin Franklin drew up a list of 13 characters he wanted to develop to live virtuously. He designed a tracking system to do that (Image 8:4). The 13 virtuous characters are:

i. **TEMPERANCE** (T). Eat not to dullness. Drink not to elevation.

ii. **SILENCE** (S). Speak not, but what may benefit others or yourself. Avoid trifling conversation.

iii. **ORDER** (O). Let all your things have their places. Let each part of your business have its time.

iv. **RESOLUTION** (R). Resolve to perform what you ought. Perform without fail what you resolve.

v. **FRUGALITY** (F). Make no expense but to do good to others or yourself—waste nothing.

vi. **INDUSTRY** (I). Lose no time. Be always employed in something useful. Cut off all unnecessary actions.

vii. **SINCERITY** (S). Use no hurtful deceit. Think innocently and justly. If you speak, speak accordingly.

viii. **JUSTICE** (J). Wrong none by doing injuries or omitting the benefits that are your duty.

ix. **MODERATION** (M). Avoid extremes. Forbear resenting injuries so much as you think they deserve.

x. **CLEANLINESS** (CL). Tolerate no uncleanliness in body, clothes, or habitation.

xi. **TRANQUILLITY** (T). Be not disturbed at trifles or accidents common or unavoidable.

xii. **CHASTITY** (CH). Rarely use venery but for health or offspring; never to dullness, weakness, or the injury of your own or another's peace or reputation.

xiii. **HUMILITY** (H). Imitate Jesus and Socrates.

On top of the 13 virtuous characters check-list, Benjamin Franklin also developed a journal (Image 8:4) to track his daily productivity. In that journal, he starts the morning by writing down, "What good shall I do today?" and by evening, he would reflect and record, "What good have I done today?". By using these two journals, Franklin intentionally developed the right-thinking, the right attitude, the right character, and fitting habits.

Image 8.4: Benjamin Franklin's 13 Virtual Daily Journal

TEMPERANCE							
	Sun	Mon	Tue	Wed	Thu	Fri	Sat
Temperance (T)							
Silence (S)	**	*		*		*	
Order (O)	*	*	*		*	*	*
Resolution (R)			*			*	
Frugality (F)		*			*		
Industry (I)			*				
Sincerity (S)							
Justice (J)							
Moderation (M)							
Cleanliness (CL)							
Tranquillity (T)							
Chastity (CH)							
Humility (H)							

Template by Benjamin Franklin. Image reproduced by ShuTzeTan

As the secret to success lies in our daily habits, a check-list, schedule, or diary helps us build routines consistently. It keeps us focused and ensures we act intentionally every day to achieve our desires. The results in our lives have little to do with the circumstances we are in, but our ability to be consistent and repeat the same daily actions over an extended period is the key to success. Moreover, in a world tempted with so many exciting possibilities and potential opportunities, the ability to stay focus on one thing and be consistent until results come has become a rare commodity.

Image 8.5: Benjamin Franklin's Daily Journal

The morning question: What good shall I do this day?	5	Rise, wash, address *Powerful Goodness*: contrive day's business and take the resolution of the day: prosecute the present study: and breakfast.
	6	
	7	
	8	Work.
	9	
	10	
	11	
	12	Read or overlook my accounts and dine.
	1	
	2	Work.
	3	
	4	
	5	
	6	Put things in their place, supper, music, or diversion, or conversation; examination of the day.
Evening question: What good have I done today?	7	
	8	
	9	
	10	Sleep.
	11	
	12	
	1	
	2	
	3	
	4	

Template by Benjamin Franklin. Image reproduced by ShuTzeTan

Our DDA is the most significant success predictor. When we create our own DDA and apply a similar system in our business and investment, we will begin to notice of our actions and inaction, we become more conscious with our time, energy, resources, investments, and grow more intentionally and deliberately.

We can develop a DDA according to the daily and weekly actions we want to take to get closer to our goals. We can personalise our DDA to include areas like relationships, health, and wealth to meet our basic, relational, and fulfilment needs. DDA can be categorised in ways to achieve our short-term and long-term goals. It brings our action or inaction towards our conscious level. When we designed our personalised DDA, it becomes meaningful.

Following are some examples personalised DDA:

Growth DDA
- Read a book for 30 minutes every day before I start working.
- Listen to at least 1 to 2 podcasts of leaders I want to emulate every day when I am exercising in the morning and doing household chores.
- Have a weekly check-in with my team members every Saturday at 11:00 am.
- Seek weekly counsel with my mentor on Thursday at 4:00 pm.

Relationship DDA
- Have dinner with my parents and sister every Sunday.
- Go for a date night with my core team members once a week.
- Check-in with 2 associates every day.
- Connect with my key leaders once a week.

Health DDA
- Swim for 30 minutes before taking a shower every morning.
- Meditate 15 minutes every morning after exercise and shower.
- Drink 3 litres of water and take my supplement every day.
- Keep my carbohydrate intake between 50g and 80g per day.
- Have a carbohydrate-fast day once a week.

Wealth DDA
- Read global market updates, international news, business, technology and consumer outlooks for 2 hours every day.
- Meet or follow-up with 5 clients every day.
- Review my daily activity, business, and finance performance every week.

Contribution DDA

- Mentor 2 persons voluntarily every week, 1 hour each.
- Volunteer in the coaching bureau once a week.

A personalised DDA template could look like one in Image 8.6. We can use numeric to fill the columns in the DDA to keep track of our daily activities. For the tasks we have not completed, we also fill them with "0". When we do, psychologically, after a few days or weeks of many "0" on the DDA, that "0" becomes intolerable to the point of pushing us to act.

When we fill up the DDA consistently every day over 21 to 60 days, new habits begin to form. Just like the many new empowering and disempowering habits that have formed in our lives during the pandemic lockdowns. Some of us watch more movies, play more games, others begin to read more books, exercise more, cook and bake more, or even start an edible garden.

Image 8.6: Daily Deliberate Action (DDA) Journal

	Mon	Tues	Wed	Thurs	Fri	Sat	Sun	Weekly Reflection
DEVELOPMENT								
Read Market Updates - 1 hour	1	1	1	1	1	1	1	
Read a book - 30 minutes	1	0	0	1	1	1	0	
Listen to 2 podcasts p. day	0	0	0	0	0	1	0	Focus on this next week
Speak to coach 1 p. week	0	0	0	1	0	0	0	
HEALTH								
Meditate 30 minutes	0	0	0	0	1	1	0	
Walk 10,000 steps	1	0	1	0	1	0	1	
HIIT 15 minutes	0	0	0	0	0	0	0	Start doing this next week
Drink 3L of water	1	1	1	1	1	1	1	
Take my supplement	1	1	1	1	1	1	1	
BUSINESS GOALS								
Read my goals & affirmation	1	1	1	0	0	0	1	Aim for consistency: every day
Prospecting 5 p. day	3	4	4	3	1	2	3	Aim for consistency: 3 or more
Invitation 3 p. day	15	10	5	5	5	5	5	
Present solution to 4 p. day	2	3	2	1	3	3	3	Aim for consistency: 3 or more
Follow-Up 6 p. day	3	2	1	1	0	0	0	
Team check ins 3 p. day	1	1	1	1	1	1	1	

Gary W. Keller, the co-founder of the world's largest real estate franchise technology company, said that each of us has "ONE THING" we can do to make everything else easier or unnecessary. In his book *The ONE Thing: The Surprisingly Simple Truth Behind Extraordinary Results,* Gary noted, behind every successful person, is the ONE THING that must be achieved first.

That is what we will do. Once we have identified the one area of our life, we must get good at; we can develop a personalised DDA to monitor our tasks and progress. When our DDA is personalised to the ONE THING we must get done in our lives, then everything else will become easier or unnecessary.

Now that we have established the action required to realise our dream on top of the burning desire to realise our dreams, why more than 80% strategic plans and the annual resolutions failed? In the final chapter, we will look into the other factors of success, beyond logic, analytics, and planning.

Excellence is never an accident.
It is always the result of high intention, sincere
effort, and intelligent execution;
it represents the wise choice of many alternatives—
choice, not chance, determines your destiny.
— Aristotle

9
HUMAN SPIRIT
FAITH, HOPE, AND LOVE

There is a powerful driving force every human being that,
once unleashed, can make any vision, dream, or desire a reality.
— Tony Robbins

PETER DUCKER, one of the most influential thinkers of management, once said, "Culture eats strategy for breakfast." No matter how solid a strategic plan is, it is only as good as the people execute it. Similarly, no matter how strong our desires and dreams are, or how perfect our 3-years, 1-year, 12-week, and daily deliberate action plans might be, we would find it difficult to realise them if we do not have the right culture.

Culture is the thought patterns, beliefs, values, language, and practice of an individual or group of people. It encompasses the character and competence, as well as the attitude to oneself, others, the world, and circumstances around us.

Culture consists of the knowledge, skills and, more importantly, the aptitude of an individual or the members of the group. And our socio-economic background, ethnic, education, life experiences, as well as the unspoken rules, norms, morals, assumptions, and expectations that govern the individual or group influence our culture.

Over 80% of strategic planning efforts fail due to a lack of alignment between the strategy, skills, and culture of an individual, team, or organisation. Without the people and leaders with the right culture, any organisational strategy, structure, and system are only as good as an idea on a piece of paper.

That is why, trillions of dollars companies spent on digital transformation initiatives goes into ensuring they have the right leaders, people, and culture moving together towards a common goal. Top executives and consulting firms are paid top dollars to create the right organisational structure and system to inculcate the right beliefs, values, and behaviours.

Since all living organisms, including humans, receive, transmute, and project energy from and into our environment to create our reality, a weak culture will have little energy to achieve its goals. If organisational culture is weak, the mindset, value, belief, emotion, and behaviour of its members will also be weak. Emotions of fear, doubt, anger, denial, anxiety, sadness, and blame fill the air. Moreover, when we feel that our needs are under threat, it is only natural that we strive to protect and preserve what we have at present.

On the contrary, people in an upbeat organisation are more optimistic, inspired, grateful, excited, joyful, and celebrate success together. They are more open, creative, and cooperative, and thus more inclined to achieve breakthrough results. In short, a strategy is the building block of any company, but culture is the cornerstone of success.

Our psychology determines 80% of success; only 20% of success is due to the mechanics of achievement. Even with the best technology, products, services, and the most luxurious office setups, a weak culture has weak energy to implement even the most expensive strategic plan.

That is why, throughout history, companies have spent trillions on transformations, but less than 10% have managed to grow ten times more than the average. It is the same thing in everything we do in life. Most of us would desire better health, but only 10% of us work deliberately and diligently to achieve that.

REDEFINING MOTIVATION

"What about motivation?" That is one question I frequently get from my clients. "How do you motivate someone who does not want to change?" "How do you make someone embrace change?"

Motivation is often overrated. People who wait for the right motivation to come before taking action have an inverted understanding of motivation. If we wait until "I am in the right mood" or "When I am ready" to do what we must achieve what we want, the mood and the readiness might not come. Moreover, the results in our life do not care about how motivated or ready we are.

Another phase most frequently cited is, "Do what you are passionate about." But successful people often say, "Have a passion for what you do." Results are direct feedback on our beliefs, values, thoughts, and actions, and how we feel when we are working on our goals. Hence, the short answer to the question of, how do we motivate others is; we simply can't.

That said, let us examine more closely what exactly is motivation and how we can use our natural energy in our brain, the electrochemical signals, and metabolic to generate the right motivation to propel us forward.

First of all, motivation is emotion. And emotion is the combination of energy and motion.

ENERGY + MOTION = EMOTION

All living organisms need the energy to maintain their structures, grow, and reproduce, and therefore, energy is the source of life. When we use however little energy we have to propel the right motion, we generate the right emotion to drive us forward. But when we use energy to engage in disempowering activities, it will create the emotions that drive us away from doing what we must to achieve our desire.

ENERGY + RIGHT MOTION = POSITIVE EMOTION

ENERGY + WRONG MOTION = NEGATIVE EMOTION

There are two types of energy: high energy state and low energy state. When we are in a high energy state, feelings of being happy, joyful, grateful, and playfulness increase. High energy state drives us faster with the overflowing energy in us that must be released. High energy often unleashes positive motions, possibility-thinking, creativity, originality, and solution-orientation.

When we feel doubtful, jealous, angry, sad, depressed, guilty, our fear increases, we begin to focus on protecting ourselves from external harm, including fear of rejection, unloved, not welcomed, not respected, and the fear of failing. A low-energy state causes us to procrastinate, and it could also paralyse us to the point where we become incapacitated. Medical research suggests up to 90% of illnesses is caused by anxiety, insecurity, weak perception, and personal attitudes.

One of my mentors from Sydney, Australia, Mitch, whom I hold in high esteem, often says this, "Don't trust your feeling when you're not in motion." The feeling of doubt, guilt, confusion, and insufficient trust, faith, and beliefs come from a lack of action––the lack of energy conversion from our internal world to the external world. It also comes from the guilt in our subconscious mind, knowing we are not doing what we must, to achieve the goals we want.

Our mind makes the most noise like an empty vessel when we are not in action when we are over-thinking. We find excuses to justify our inaction. Conversely, if our schedule is filled with deliberate actions, we will be actively engaging in tasks we must complete and look for solutions to the problems we face along the way.

Our emotion is often not the accurate evaluation of our results when we are not in action. But when we start to take action and experience victories, our faith and hope grow, we get more excited, and the result will motivate us to do more. Therefore, motivation comes from intentional action, no matter how we feel.

That is how great leaders do it. They choose to take full ownership, become responsible for their results and do whatever it takes, even though sometimes they do not feel like doing it. They do not allow the surrounding circumstances and their feelings deter them from doing what they must.

William James, an American psychologist and philosopher, summed it up by saying, "I do not sing because I am happy. I am happy because I sing." And, the more I feel happy because I sing, the more I want to sing because it makes me happy.

Image 9.1: Action, Results, and Motivation

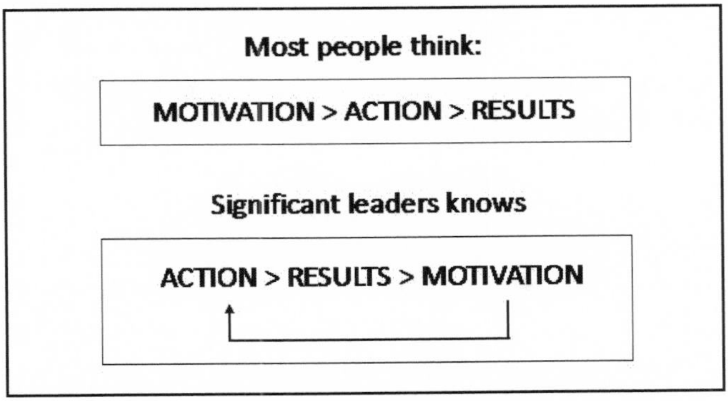

CopyRight©Shu-TzeTan

Most people could not change their current state to do what they must, to realise their desires and dreams is due to nature's law. We need force to change. Just like any other matter, as Newton's first law of motion states––every object remains at rest unless it is forced to change by an external force. That is why we usually would not change who we are and what we do today to achieve what we desire until there is an external force that pushes us to do so.

The Coronavirus pandemic, which sweeps through the world like a tsunami, is an excellent example of that force. For years, many people have debated the viability of "working from home" and "home-schooling," but COVID-19 pushed us to do so overnight. Policy-makers and enforcers that have been worrying about cyber risks were pushed to find new ways to strengthen cyber-security during the global pandemic lockdowns.

Virtual conferences, webinars, and digital signatures are now widely accepted. Many of us are beginning to realise we can achieve more with the new way of working and living. When circumstances call for it, without waiting for the feeling of being motivated, we will spring into action and find solutions.

So, back to the question, "How do we make people change even if they do not want to?" We could spend more time to find their compelling reason to move. And, we could also create a situation to intensify the pain to the point of forcing them into action. Many people who lost their jobs during the pandemic began to look for other ways to bring food to the table. Some began to provide services for last-mile delivery, some started online e-business, and others began to grow, plant, cook, and eat at home to reduce cost.

The other reason most people don't change is not that they do not want to, but because of the lack of consistent effort. We know we do not get what we wish for, but what we work for. Yet, one of the biggest obstacles we fight every day to do what we must is procrastination.

Even though procrastination causes frustration, guilt, stress, and anxiety, we still give in to it. Over a period of time, procrastination leads to low self-esteem and depression. Despite that, most of us still surrender to procrastination.

Mel Robbins, the author of the book, *The 5-Second Rule: Transforming Your Life, Work and Confidence with Courage,* said, we can fight procrastination with the 5-second rule. According to her, if we have the urge to respond to a goal, we only have a 5-second window to move our body physically, or our brain kills that urge.

We only have 5 seconds to get out of bed and put on our sports gear if we want to go jogging before work every morning. We have only 5 seconds to turn off Netflix and start working on the report we have been putting off. We only have 5 seconds to pick up the phone to set appointments with our potential clients before fear takes over. If we remain idle and entertain the thoughts of, "I am fearful" "I am scared of rejection" "Perhaps I will do it later," we would have lost the batter to procrastination.

There is always the trade-off between the long-term pain and regret of not achieving what we want compared to the short-term pain of inconvenient, sacrifice, and discipline which are often temporary. And we behave better when the consequence of not doing what we must is right in front of us, and it is clear. We tend to be a better driver and drive within the speed limit when we know there is a speed camera.

That is why most people focus on reducing short-term pain and gratifying pleasure now, which is nearer and more apparent, than focusing on lowering potential pain and increasing pleasure in a distant future. Hence, most people do not make hay during sunshine and dig the well before we need the water when we know that is what we must do.

When we focus on the pain of the discipline of action now more than the pain of not achieving what we desired later, we would not be driven to do what we must. But if we focus on the pain and regrets of not achieving our dreams in the future, more than the discipline of action now, that might drive us into action.

Once you make a decision,
the universe conspires to make it happens.
——Ralph Waldo Emerson

There are different drives to achieve similar goals. Most of us are driven to "move away" from pain or "against" pain, few are driven to move "towards" pleasure. The different drives generate different energy and cause different results.

For example, during an economic downturn, some people move away from conversations on the possibility of losing their job or business and avoid discussion on contingency plans; some people work against that possibility aggressively to keep their job or business no matter what, even if it is obvious to others, that their job or business is no longer relevant; some people created multiple sources of income to prepare for possible downturns, even before the downturn.

People who take action to "move away" from pain will avoid the pain at all costs. Potential pain stresses them and causes anxiety. They may alienate themselves from a situation, or people whom they fear could harm them or their family. They tend to avoid building a deeper relationship with others to avoid being hurt. They may come across as defensive, insecure, cold, procrastinate, and detached.

People who "work against" the pain will fight to make sure the pain they anticipate does not happen. They might come across as aggressive, confrontational, angry, hostile, domineering, and controlling. They often suppress their feelings and might appear unkind or apathy to others.

People who work towards a desire or dream are attracted to create and to increase pleasure. They are assertive, persistent, see possibilities, solution-oriented, and often come across as industrious, committed, present, appreciative, and forge strong a relationship with others.

Both "away" and "against" drives often come from the need to protect oneself from potential pain, hurt, or harm. These energies are usually pessimistic, causing a more unbinding commitment and are often disconnecting with others as the brain and mind are prepared for flight or fight. Conversely, a "towards" drive is more positive in nature, hopeful, excited, upbeat, therefore, more open to foreign ideas, creative, originality, and tend to achieve more extraordinary results.

The good news is, once we ascertain if we are driven to move away or against pain, or towards pleasure, we can tweak our minds. Instead of allowing pain and pleasure control our life, we can retrain our minds to leverage on pain and pleasure to realise our dreams and desires.

ON INVESTMENT

Now that we know the energy plus the right action generates the right motivation to propel us forward, the next question we might want to ask is, how do we increase this energy and our motivation? Newton's 2nd law of motion said, the larger the mass of an object; the more force is required to accelerate the object——to fulfil our desires, we need to create a force to propel us forward.

The state of our thinking, skills, experience we have currently and the intensity of our desires determine how much force we need. Some of us need to create more force than others. People with more limiting beliefs like, "I can't," "I don't know," "I am not born for it" need to do more to change those beliefs to "I can learn from others who know and have achieved the results I want."

Some people have a more pessimistic view of the world, and some people have a more optimistic view. Some people are currently living in deficit and have accumulated debts, and those are living in surplus and gather many assets. The different state our life requires different force to move forward.

The best thing we can do to create that force is by investing in our ourselves to grow our thinking and ability. The way we think, including our outlook of life, our beliefs, attitudes, and characters are like the software inside a machine. Our action, skills, and performance capabilities are like a machine.

No matter how sophisticated a machine is, the machine can only function as well as the software inside. When new software is installed in an outdated machine, it is of no use; we also need to update our skills and capabilities by putting whatever we have learned into practice.

We can only achieve what we want but have not reached yet, with new understanding, belief, feeling, and action. We do this with life-long learning. That is why great leaders make time to read and spend time learning from others. They are in an inner circle of like-minded people, growing together. They hire coaches and look for mentors who have achieved what they desire to guide them. Achievers believe they have control over their circumstances by upgrading their perceptions, emotions, and actions. As long as we are willing and are teachable, we can grow and learn to redesign our lives.

An investment in knowledge pays the best interest.
—— Benjamin Franklin

The other force that could empower or disempower us from achieving our desire is the state of our relationship, health, and wealth. The relationship with ourselves, our parents, spouse, partner, siblings, children, friends, and others; the state of our health and our financial situation can improve or hinder us.

The way we think, our attitude, and behaviours towards creating a healthy relationship, living a healthy lifestyle, and managing our finances are essential because the way we do anything is the way we do everything. These have implications on our belief in the role of men and women, exclusivity and diversity, justice and fairness, hereditary and health, abundance and scarcity, which influence the way we achieve our desires.

Despite technological advancement, the rise of broken agreements, obesity, and financial poverty are indicators of our mental state globally. Too many people do not have the confidence to take charge of their life despite their circumstances. Too many people are fearful of moving forward in an uncertain and unknown future. Consequently, mental health continues to deteriorate as anxieties soar. In other words, to fight poverty, we must first fight the poverty of the mind.

We are dealing with a pandemic worse than COVID-19 today. The poverty of the mind is escalating. There is still much to be done to prepare many people to cope with the smarter and faster world. If we believe we can change but do not know how we have won half the battle because we do not lack people who have gone before us. But if we do not believe we can do something to change our current state of affairs, what hope do we have for creating a long-term, sustainable, purposeful, meaningful, and a joy-filled life?

The good news is, as we have learned in Chapter 4, our brain is capable of neurogenesis and neuroplasticity. Our brain grows new neurons and forms new neural connections in response to the changes in the environment or condition the neurons are in. That is why we must get into action.

Action creates conditions for neurons to establish new connections. Action activates our five senses with stimuli that cause neural pathways to form; hence, new learning beyond textbooks.

The stress or anxiety we feel when we do the things that scare us allows our brain to build new neural connections, new thinking, and abilities are normal. These tensions are unlike the ones when we are not in action. That is why faith without work is death, but faith with work is growth.

People who are successful in achieving what they plan to achieve are optimistic, solution-oriented, and results-oriented. They have the belief, expectancy, and faith that results will come when they get into action. They have the right attitude and skills, are more resilient, adaptable, and can withstand adversity and adversary even if the results did not come through the process in the way we expected.

There are many areas in which we can invest in ourselves to be better equipped to get ahead. Skills in dealing with people, understanding human emotions, and using technology to make our work and life more comfortable are just a few of the many. These life skills go beyond technical qualifications like agile thinking, big data analysis, artificial intelligence, coaching, coding, or other "how-to" or "process" training. Life skills help us be more human than ever.

When we acquire the appropriate attitude and skills to manage our relationship, health, and wealth in the new normal, we reflect our transformation in the way we achieve what we want ten years from now. Hence, the best investment we can make is continuingly investing in growing our thinking, feelings, and actions, our intelligence quotient, emotional quotient, and also, financial intelligent quotient.

BEYOND THE NUMBERS

One of the topics which many people shun but have an enormous impact on our life is money and finance. Either due to the lack of confidence in dealing with matters relating to finance, or a belief one hold regarding money. Some said, money is the root of all evil, but the truth is, it is the love of money that is the root of all kinds of evil.

There is a difference between money and finance. Money is the accepted medium as payment for products, services, debts, and taxes. Meanwhile, finance is the study of money and how it is best used.

Since money is an accepted medium of payment, if a lender accepts a borrower's crops as repayment to a loan, the crops become the medium between them. And the proficiency of the borrower to manage his crops to repay the loan he took from the lender earlier, keep some of his crops for his needs, and some to replant new crops again, that depends on his financial intelligent quotient.

While money is not everything, almost everything in life needs money. Putting a roof over our head and food on the table, providing the best education for our children, paying the bills of our basic living expenses, we need money. We also need money to have the time to create memories with our family and help the disadvantage. When we have high financial intelligent quotient, we will be in a better position to manage the resources we have, including our income, expenses, loans, taxes, investments, and also our time, skills, experiences, relationships, and health.

Money and finance are both tangible and emotional. It is something we can measure quantitatively and qualitatively. When we learn to measure them tangibly and use them responsibility, we become financially literate and able to manage our personal finances, including budgeting and investing. We will become better in leveraging financial tools like credit cards, loans, mortgages, insurance, and investment to our advantages.

Contrarily, financially illiterate people may lead to poor management of resources, end up accumulating unsustainable debt burdens through poor spending decision or the through a lack of long-term preparation.

The status of our financial standing also brings out different beliefs, emotions and reactions. Finance is one of many forms of measurement on where we used to assess where we are now compared to where we would like to see ourselves be. It has nothing to do with how much money we have, but how we manage what we already have. And with numbers, the truth regarding the state of our life is right in front of us because numbers don't lie.

When we are financially literate, our confidence, self-control, self-preservation in handling what we have increased and are we are more at peace. The ones who are financially illiterate may have lower confidence in dealing with that they have and might experience anxiety and worry about their savings, loans, and future more.

Sadly, according to the Global Financial Literacy Excellence Center (GFLEC), only 33% of the population in the world is financially literate. And it is also unfortunate that many formal education institutions, including schools and universities, has not help prepare students to be financially illiterate. It is no wonder the global financial intelligence quotient is still very low. The COVID-19 pandemic was a wake-up call on how ill-prepared many people are to face the uncertainties and emergencies in life.

Financial literacy goes beyond learning to increase income streams, living with a budget, handling debts wisely, paying taxes in time, or setting aside emergency funds for rainy days. While these are fundamental skills we need to acquire, being financially literate also increases our confidence in setting and achieving goals. How we contain our spending within the means, save for times of turbulence in life, and invest for future gain, has a lot to do with how we manage our thinking, beliefs, values, conducts, and our life.

Being financial savvy builds the character. It trains us to live virtuously. While many people desire to be financially independent and financially free, characters of being prudence, fairness, fortitude, temperance, and living by nature's laws and universal principles are critical for getting there.

Being financially literate also helps us put life into perspective. It helps us appreciate the importance of numbers, interest and fee, time value for money, power of compounding effect and the double edge-sword of all financial tools. We learn to become more patient, delay gratifying our wants now for needs later. We learn to be more forbearing with challenges in life.

When we are financially literate, we learned to deal with risks and develop contingency plans in life. We also learn to weigh between the risk and rewards of the many decisions we make. Moreover, if countries and companies continuingly conduct financial stress-tests, identify risk and develop mitigation plans to brace through challenging times ahead, should we not do the same for our personal and family's finances?

The principles of sowing, harvesting, and preserving in our financial decisions are the same in all other parts of our life. The state of our relationship, health, wealth, and spirituality or wellbeing is the result of our financial habits, compounding over time. What we do daily will depreciate or appreciate the gains we will receive.

Financial education also teaches us responsibility and the power of leverage. When we can pay our loans, mortgages, and debt promptly, we score better credit scores, and gain trust from the financiers. When we have proven to be trustworthy with what has been given to us before, we gain more leverage. Similarly, when we take ownership of any agreements we entered and fulfilled our part of the bargain, we become more trustworthiness and have a better reputation.

As money flows like water, financial education also helps us understand how the world system works, so that we know how to follow where the money flows and navigate the rapid changes in the new world order. When we equip ourselves with the principles of macro and micro-economies, the financial impact from geopolitical influences, social-economic shifts, changes in consumer's behaviour and demography, supply and demand, fear and greed, we can anticipate how the money would flow, minimise risks and maximise profits.

When we master the skills to calculate actual returns of investment and assets against fees, inflation, taxes, and hidden costs, we can make better decisions with logic, facts, and not hearsay. The ability to understand the economic structure, systems, numbers, and market psychology is what separates professional investors from speculators and gamblers. Professional investors invest with their eyes wide open.

On top of that, when we are comfortable working with numbers, we are in a better position to protect and provide for our family and ourselves. We are also able to protect our loved ones and ourselves from the various frauds and scams in the market today. There are many frauds and scams in business, investment, dating, and romance, winning prize and lottery, shopping, tech-support, financial-support, identity theft, auction, payment, bills, taxes, golden opportunity, or even medical assistance and charity. The fraud and scam industry has caused more than tens of billion-dollar annual loss. Advertisement fraud, the attempt to defraud digital advertisement networks for financial gain alone, is already estimated to be a $44 billion industry by 2022!

Financial education helps us to appreciate the importance of strategic planning, the principle of opportunity cost or trade-off and the strategy to exit from any investment. Whenever we make an investment decision; financial investments or invest in a partnership, relationship or our health, we develop concrete plans to entry and exit that investment. We define the entry criteria, deal-breaker, and exit plan. We learn to make decisions with a clear mind and know why we do what we do.

Similarly, traders plan their trade before they buy any company shares by determining the entry, profit-taking, and stop-loss price, the deal-breaker, and evaluating the reward over risk before entering a trade. When a trade goes south and no longer yields the expected returns, they cut their loss quickly before that trade continues to lose money. Instead of looking at, "how much I would lose?" They are aware of the "opportunity-loss if they continue to hang on to the losing trade. They know they can divest the capital saved from cutting losses fast to a better opportunity.

When we are aware of the potential loss, we learn to exit a deal quickly, we benefit from the opportunity-cost and reduce opportunity-lost. We can apply the same principle and strategy to all other areas of our lives. As Newton's 3rd law of motion—there is an equal or greater reaction from every action—every decision we make has a dual impact.

Financial literacy also teaches us the power motion. Power is generated when there is movement. Many will say, "Cash is king." But in an interview by CNBC in late January 2020, Ray Dalio, said, "Cash is trash" if it is idle. Cash does not worth much, especially in a low interest or zero interest rate environment. And when countries printed trillions of dollars to "safe" the economy during the 2020 pandemic, the value of money continued to deteriorate.

Money is only valuable when it is transacted repeatedly. We can only make money work harder for us when we use it to create values. The rich get richer by getting competent in managing what they have well and increasing their wealth through investment. Hence, only "invested cash is king."

Learning the importance of time and priority also has a lot to do with financial literacy. If we made the wrong decision and lost some money, we can earn money back again. But we can never recover the time we have wasted or lost. Unlike money which appreciates and depreciates according to supply and demand, time is on a diminishing path of no return.

When we begin to look at the value of our effort and our income from the perspective of time, we begin to be aware of the income per hour or the value we create second to the hour. While we do not know how much time we have left on earth, we know everything, including our relationships, health, career, business, trust, and wealth, needs time to grow. When we are more prudent with our time and finances, we are to increase value in ourselves, in others, and for others, beyond monitory values.

Last but not the least, one of my mentors once said this to me, "We buy everything with time, not money," because we spend time earning incomes, and we use that income to buy things that we want. While many people desire to be financially free——having the passive-recurring income that can sustain their living expenses even during an economic downturn——yet more than 90% of the world population are not. Instead of getting proficient in managing their financial matters well and accumulating assets, many focus on upscaling their technical ability to secure a job or venture into business.

The ones who are financially free learned to get good at managing their time and financial matters, no matter how little they may have, and focus on accumulating assets. They raise their financial intelligence quotient on top of emotional quotients to get ahead, especially in a new world where the monitory system and world economics are changing rapidly. They become skilful in assessing financial systems and creating models which generate passive-recurring incomes, to free their time to create more memories with their loved ones, do things they love, and venture into new areas. And, because there are people who have successfully done so and gone before us, we can too.

FEEDBACKS AND SETBACKS

Winston Churchill once said, "If you are going through hell, keep going." Success is built upon failure to failure without losing sight of the end goal. We are going to face setbacks in our journey to realise our desires. Nature wills it so. It is necessary to bring us closer to what we want and to keep ourselves humble.

Setbacks are feedbacks. Setbacks tell us areas we should keep, and areas we must trim. Just as farmers and gardeners would trim or prune their plants to maintain the health of the plants, improve fruit quality, and shape growth, setback does the same to us.

Pruning helps remove broken or pest-infested branches, diseases or dying wood, also helps reduce the amount of wood, flowers and fruit to divert energy to produce larger and higher quality ones. Similarly, setbacks bring to our attention our past baggage, toxicity, and negativity that could jeopardise our results. Setbacks help us identify areas to which we need to say "NO" to achieve the more critical "YES". Setbacks allow us to filter out areas that are destructive to our goals and help us re-prioritise our thoughts, actions, and life.

Pruning also helps keep the plants in shape and grow within the available space. Setbacks make us aware of the areas we need to maintain in a relationship, health, and finances, to ensure sustainability and balanced growth. They also make us recognise our capacities, acknowledge our limitations, and resources available to us move forward. Setbacks also prepare us for a bigger and more significant role by ensuring our foundation is strong.

Whenever we pick ourselves up from setbacks, we bounce back stronger. Just as Michael Jordan says, "Obstacles don't have to stop you. If you run into a wall, do not turn around and give up. Figure out how to climb over it, go through it, or work around it." Failures are not failures if we would pick ourselves up again one more time after each fall.

When we accept setbacks as feedback to help us progress, we use them as opportune times to realign ourselves, to move closer to that one final step that will bring the quantum leap success. The only thing is, we do not know, which is that one last step that will land us on the huge success but will happen according to the law of quantum physics. So, if we take another step forward, the leap will come eventually. There are no failures, only quitters.

We might have experienced many setbacks before, and those experiences might make us feel like a failure. The fear of failure held us back from taking the next step forward. However, "No matter what our past has been, we have a spotless future," as Dan Clark said.

Some great companies and individuals faced setbacks before getting to where they are today, including breakdowns in partnership, health challenges, nature-induced disasters, and bankruptcies. But once they have decided they would not let the circumstances they were in define them, they begin to pick themselves up by doing what they must every single day to create the life they want.

Throughout human history, there are many stories of successful setbacks. Perhaps the one who faced most setbacks and eventually made a huge comeback is Thomas Edison. When a reporter asked Edison how he felt to had failed 10,000 times in his experiments while inventing the electric light bulb, he said, "I have never failed. I found 10,000 ways that won't work."

Embracing setbacks is the only way to grow towards greatness. Winston Churchill also said, "Do not let a good crisis go to waste."

GRATITUDE

There is a famous African proverb that says, "If you want to go fast, go alone. If you want to go far, go together." Getting ahead in the new world order can be scary yet exciting. While the path ahead can be full of volatility, uncertainty, complexity, and ambiguity, it provides us with immense opportunities to reimagine and redesign our life together.

With smart technologies like cloud computing and artificial intelligence, we can practically collaborate with anyone beyond our capabilities. To increase our capacity to collaborate and reach out to the resources made available to us, we must first, learn to be appreciative and be grateful.

Gratitude is an essential part of human pro-social behaviour and a social-emotional signal. Studies have found gratitude strengthens emotions and relationships between members of communities who mutually help each other.

When we are grateful, we can recognise the supports, and affirmations others, nature, and our Creator give, even when we face relationship knocks occasionally. When we are grateful, we are inspired to engage in activities that benefit other people or society. It increases our desire to give and to collaborate.

Studies have found the neural connection between gratitude and giving is intense, both literally and figuratively. At the region deep in the frontal lobe of the brain, called the ventromedial prefrontal cortex, is wired up to be a hub for processing the value of risk and reward. It is thoroughly connected to a deeper brain region that triggers pleasurable neurochemicals in desirable circumstances. It holds abstract representations of the inner and outer world that help with complex reasoning, one's expression of oneself and social processing.

Studies have also found gratitude significantly increased wellbeing during identity formation age, those with chronic pain, depression, and older adults too. People who write gratitude letters or keep a gratitude diary increase the neural modulation, which regulates brain activity in the medial prefrontal cortex of the brain. It improves the function and reduces disorder in the part of the brain responsible for emotions.

In short, gratitude activates empathy and helps reduce pain and contributes to improved mental health over time. It lessens anxiety and illness and increases goal attainment. Moreover, gratefulness generates a high emotional state. It opens up our mind to possibilities––a sure way to improve our conscious awareness level to the abundant resources available to help us realise our dreams.

FAITH, HOPE, LOVE

Technological advancement will continue to evolve and impact us, the human beings, and being human. While change continues to transform the way we live, work, play, and communicate, three elements in life remain constant since the existence of life and last forever: faith, hope, and love, and the greatest of these is love.

Throughout human history, we have learned that, despite the worst of world pandemics, wars, or nature-induced disasters, ultimately, it is the faith, the hope, and the love humans hang on to help live through the worst of time. Dwight L. Moody said, "Faith makes all things possible, hope to make all things work, love makes all things ease, and family makes life worth living."

Faith is the ability to perceive and believe in things others don't. It is about accepting all the resources our Creator has given us and acknowledging that when we participate in actions, our desired outcomes will be realised. People with faith trust and work with nature's laws and universal principles to achieve their desired outcome.

As a man reaps what he sows, faith without work is death. Similarly, work without faith is also death. Without the appropriate beliefs and behaviours, we shall not expect the outcomes we want. But, with the appropriate amount of activities and actions done consistently over time, we can expect growth and enjoy the fruits of our labour. Even with faith as small as a mustard seed, it will grow to become like a tree so big that birds in the air can lodge in its branch.

Faith is a feeling we sense in our gut when we are on the go. It is a form of energy. However, it is not easy to explain by logic. Thomas Aquinas, an Italian philosopher, said, "To one who has faith, no explanation is necessary. To one without faith, no explanation is possible." He also said, "Do not take faith lightly by believing that God will do what we want. God will do what is right, even if it pains us."

When we work closely with faith, hope is the "expectancy" that good things will come when we do the right thing. Hope is beyond all "expectation". It is "knowing the outcomes we want will happen". Hope is having the profound belief of knowing through all the darkness, suffering and failure, lies a beautiful light that awaits us.

Hope must work closely with faith. Without faith, hope is simply a wish. Faith is about trusting in nature's process. Hope is about trusting something beneficial could happen in the future. Faith turns hope into tangible outcomes, while hope provides faith in the foresight of the higher divine realm to realise the desires of our effort.

Faith is determined, aggressive, and relentless in its quest. Yet faith need hope to stay alive in its pursuit. Without faith and hope, we simply give up and die. Faith and hope keep the farmers going in their effort to tending to their lands relentlessly every day, and witnessing the seeds they have sown growing and fruiting over time. Similarly, hope keeps the patients in critical condition alive, and faith heals them faster than the scientific process of healing.

Likewise, taking the first step into the journey to realise our dreams without a complete roadmap requires faith and hope, trusting on nature's laws and the universal principles that the roadmap will unveil itself more as we do what we must, to progress.

It is also said the greatest of the three—faith, hope, and love—is love. Love is beyond a feeling. It is a choice we make in relating to ourself and others. The bible says love is patient; love is kind. It does not envy, it does not boast, and it is not proud. It is not rude; it is not self-seeking; it is not easily angered; it keeps no record of wrongs. Love does not delight in evil but rejoices with the truth. When we grow in love, we grow with these characters.

Love defines who we are and drive us to do what is necessary. Love makes a mother jump in front of a car to stop it from running over her child. Love makes a man use his body as a shield to take a bullet for others. Love makes us do the craziest things imaginable. That is why "Love is blind." It drives us into doing things we normally would not have done.

Without love, excuses grow stronger than the reasons. Without love, we complain and protest, we avoid taking ownership and responsibility for fear of failure, blamed, or unloved. When we do not have love beyond us, we resolve to protect and preserve what we have now. Hence, we do not step out to pursue our desires. We might, in the end, feel sad, depress, or sorry for ourselves.

But when we choose to love, we will do what we need to do before our current feelings. We put ourselves, and others need first beyond the circumstances we are in. Love drives us to become a better person.

Finally, faith, hope, and love must work together. They grow beyond our fear when we are in action. Faith makes us act in kindness and believing in each other. Hope allows us to seek the goodness in darkness. Love ignites a new belief of what we can be.

Since life exists, technologies have come and gone; humans continue to grow through these three elements. Faith, hope, and love make us humans and propel us forward.

GO FORTH...

The best time to plant a tree was twenty years ago; the next best time is now. The 2020 COVID-19 pandemic has brought upon us the greatest reset to most of us. That is the best time for us to redesign a new future for our loved ones and ourselves regardless of the surrounding circumstances.

Despite the significant setback pandemic brought to us, we are in an exciting new era, in which nature is revealing more of its secrets to us with the help of the smarter and faster machines. We are living in the best of times, with more than 200,000 years of wisdom passing down to us from our ancestors. We also have great leaders who paved the way before us, diligently helping us to understand better how we can leverage nature's laws and universal principles to our favours.

We have, indeed, the insights, strategy, systems, and tools, and together with the people and our loved ones to lead an extraordinary, joy-filled, and meaningful life.

Therefore, "Go forth in love. Go forth and multiply."

When we love, we always strive to become better than we are.
When we strive to become better than we are,
everything around us becomes better too."
— Paulo Coelho

INSPIRATION BEHIND THIS BOOK

As children, we grew up having many dreams. We dreamed of the kind of person we want to be, what we would like to do, what we wish of having, and what we want to accomplish. Similarly, when she was eight years old, Shu-Tze wanted to write a book. And she put that dream in her bucket list of things to accomplish before she kicks the bucket and set a dateline to do so by 45 years old. The dream has never left her.

Throughout her growing up years, she has written many stories and articles, pouring out her thoughts over volumes of journals. One of her close friends suggested her to put together a book from her journals. But that did not happen. The dream of producing her first book continued to burn like a tiny flame in her heart and started brewing in her soul.

Then, on a faithful day in August 2019, while she was reviewing her dreams, she heard a voice, "Write something the world has been anxious about and bring to lights the wisdom from the past." Ideas started gushing out with force so strong she could not ignore. Seating on her writing desk, she began to write as fast as her fingers could. Just as the waterfall cannot be silent, wisdom from our forefathers must speak.

Having lived through more than twenty years of great life under her parents' wings and another twenty years in the safe hands of extraordinary companies, industries' movers and shakers, and mentors, Shu-Tze is inspired to share with the world how great leaders become great. She is also privileged to have gained many insights from philosophers, artisans, scientists, and warriors from the past. She hopes to draw answers to the next level of human evolutions, especially in the revolutionary speed of change the world is experiencing now.

The journey of putting the materials in this book together has also elevated the author's curiosity and opened her mind to foreign ideas and has broadened her worldview to a whole new level. There are many burning questions about life which most companies and industry chiefs face during transformation and enculturation initiatives. Questions Shu-Tze wants to find answers to and discovered over the last few months of putting this book together.

She enjoyed every research done, word written, paragraph formed, chapter constructed. As she worked through the pages of this book, she took the time to reflect on her journey through life, especially the years of working with global corporations and world leaders. Through many rises and falls, tears and joys, she is grateful that there is much achieved and more to be done as her discoveries, dreams, and desires continue to grow.

She has more to learn from those who have gone before her, and a lot more to learn from people who challenged her to be a better version of herself every day as the journey of life continues.

Someone once said, "The ones who learn more than others are the ones who write. But the ones who have grown the most are the ones who rolled up their sleeves, took deliberate actions, and created results."

As she digs through the details on how smarter and faster machines are transforming the world we used to know, and how humans continue to evolve physically and psychologically, and how nature and the universe continue to unveil themselves to mankind, she is inspired to discover more, listen more, and learn more to expand herself.

The journey through her book has also helped her appreciate her life more; the family she is in, people around her, and countless blessings her Creator poured into her life and has led her to fall in love all over again on a whole new level.

She is also thankful for the time and space to write in peace, and the abundant resources today, including many smarter and faster artificial intelligence editors and data. She hopes this book will bring to her readers similar abundance, gratitude, and joy.

In this book, Shu-Tze hopes to understand how humanity has advanced since the dawn of time. Through many evolutions and revolutions, nature-induced-disasters, plagues, the rises and falls of civilization, humans continue to thrive through the worst kind of disasters.

On top of that, Western and Eastern philosophers taught us about the unspoken power in individualism and collectivism, mastery and harmony, the outer and the inner world. We are not short of resources. What we must do today is continue to get ahead like our ancestors, no matter what circumstances surrounding us.

This book does not come at a much better time as now. The first draft was completed just before the 2020 pandemic lockdowns started globally—a period where many of the "new world" we are experiencing now seem far-fetched. Few would have imagined millions of people forced to work-from-home and adapt to home-schooling instantly. Musicians performed together with thousands of viewers from all over the world, and doctors would perform surgery on their parents remotely from them. The pandemic brought the "future normal" to "now" overnight.

The term "new normal" was first coined about ten years ago to alert the world of the disruption industrial revolution 4.0 will bring. Before the 2020 pandemic, many companies knew that the urgency of being digitally readied by 2020 because industrial revolution 4.0 will transform how we live, work, and play to something we have not seen before. By 2018, global corporations and companies have invested more than $1.3 trillion on digital transformation initiatives, but more than 70% of that investment went to waste as CEOs tried to figure out how to move forward.

Many more companies are rethinking about how the industrial revolution 4.0 will transform their industries. Consultants involved in the digital transformation-related projects are in high demand. Preparing everyone for the transition to the new world of work has been a frequent topic of discussion in boardrooms.

The COVID-19 pandemic came like a tsunami, regardless of who we are and how we feel. A tiny virus forced every one of us through a "black hole" for more than nine months and opened our eyes to the brutal truth of how the new normal look like. And we have not seen the end of it yet as the infected cases are surging while the world approaches Thanksgiving, Christmas, and winter in the Northern Hemisphere.

We were literally being torn out of the daily routines we were so used to and being pushed to adapt to a new way of work instantly. Those who were prepared, survived. Those who were ill-prepared were kicked out of what we are so familiar with instantly. Yet, we may be down, but never out.

Human history has taught us many lessons of those who did not give up the fight, bouncing back stronger eventually. In recent months, despite global lockdowns, we have witnessed the emergence of new opportunities and businesses.

While the fight against a tiny virus that has brought us to our knees is not over by November 2020, an economic aftershock could be one of the longest in human history. That is a time when we must gather ourselves to prepare for the new world order.

As a curious child, Shu-Tze wondered why the world and humans would function the way they do. During the many nights she spent in the volumes of the encyclopedias in her youth, she realised that while science helped us understand how nature and ecology work, we still could not explain why they work in typical ways.

She seeks also seek to create a perfect marriage and a balance between purpose and profit, logic, and emotion, and she found the answers from nature and the universe as she pours through the pages of many books, articles, and observations done by many before her.

She also comes across the quote that says, "Thoughts are things" often. She aims to explain what this means to us, humans, scientifically––using a systematic and a logical approach to explain how the "Laws of Attraction" work to our advantages.

There are two chapters dedicated to expounding this quote further: "The Brain" and "The Mind." These chapters detail how our brains systematically process information from our environment and how our minds assign meaning to it. Our minds also compartmentalise information received and stored in our memory for later use. By that, we may leverage our physical wellbeing to affect our emotional wellbeing and our behaviours. Conversely, we leverage on emotions to transform our biological nature and create our realism in the physical world in an orderly manner.

In other words, our reality is the direct result of what happened in our brains and minds, whether we are conscious of it or not. And we can make changes even with a 5-second window. We now have a scientific method to explain why people who have created incredible success say, "Success is 100% possible, 100% of the time."

The author will not claim her perspective is the one, and only her readers need because she is not the guru. She would not claim to be a futurist, humanist, or philosopher too. For this, there are many others whose thoughts and ideas she continues to acquire. She is excited to be on the journey of life, learning, and growing daily till the last breath in her.

The paragraphs written on these pages are her thoughts from her reading, research, observation, and personal reflection, which do not represent any organisation or individual unless otherwise stated.

She believes if she were to rewrite this book five years from now, it would have evolved. She would write as a different person from who she is today because "we can never be the same person as we are now for the future we want to be."

She encourages her readers to read widely, and travel more when it's safe to do so, interact with more others, and reflect more to grow their thoughts too. Because our thoughts are potent, whatever we focus will become our reality. And this book is best used to gain a new perspective on realising desires and dreams despite all circumstances around us. The only way to make that happen for us is to test out the suggested strategy, systems and tools for a minimum period of 60 days with accountability partners to see if it works.

While we are still at war with COVID-19 and find new normalcy, we will continue to face much uncertainty in the unknown future. Yet, we get to innovate, create, and test as many ideas as possible to get ahead. And we can learn from those who pave the way ahead of us too. The more we widen our perspectives, the more agile we are in establishing new ways to get ahead in times of turbulent.

On top of that, we must know where we are going. We must focus on our purpose and find our centeredness. We must say "NO" to many temptations, shining objects and the noises that will distract us from the outcomes we want. Because "We can do everything, but we can't do everything," as Ray Dalio, the founder of the biggest hedge fund company, Bridgewater, said.

Last but not the least, David Hume, a Scottish Enlightenment philosopher, known for his empiricism, scepticism, and naturalism, said, "Be a philosopher; but, amidst all your philosophy, be still a man."

This book is a labour of love. It reflects the author life, someone who developed the love of wisdom, learning from the wise, travelling to places closest to centuries past, and having the privilege of meeting many great leaders from all over the world. She is inspired by many great scientists, mathematicians, investors, philosophers, psychologists, and business owners of the past and present. People who discovered strategies, created systems, invented tools that affected organizations, industries, culture, society and global economy. People who brought significant impact on humanity. Their perspectives and principles are what she sought to bring lights to the new reality today.

Shu-Tze has many mentors and role models throughout her life. At home, her beloved parents spend many hours reading every day before she knows her ABC. They instilled in her sister and her a life of biblical principles and inspired them to read and expend widely.

After dinner every night, anyone could see her parents holding a book or an iPad in their hands. Immersing themselves into the world of science, business, philosophy, history, and nature—absorbing in the beauty of wisdom, human spirit, and life. Conversations over dinner were never a dull moment in the author's family, with many debates flying across the table. She would say her parents have contributed to the foundation of this book.

Whenever Shu-Tze asks her mother for information, her dear mother will often reply, "Google it." Her mum is correct. With Google today, we do not lack the "know-how". But we lack the "discipline of action." There is so much more we can learn from people who went before us. We can no longer say, "I do not know how," today. Because the wealth of information and resources available to us today is immense. However, we must also choose wisely for information can also be a double-edged sword. Some learn from trusted, well researched, and respected sources, from people who created results and helped many others do so too. Whoever we mingle and spend the most time with shapes our reality.

257

Another person who inspired and kept the author at bay is her only sister, whom she respects a lot. Like Shu-Tze, her sister is also a person of high curiosity. She has a keen eye for microscopical details and digs through information most people would have missed.

During their schooling years, Shu-Tze would get all her homework done quickly so that she could go out with her friends and find new adventures every day, while her sister would spend hours going through formulas and algebra to understand how the mathematic works in real life. Shu-Tze did not realise that mathematic is a beautiful language of nature which could help us gain insights into nature's laws and universal principles. If only she had known by then, the years of using mathematics to understand the physical world and humans would have been more exciting.

Her sister is a virtuous person and a person of patience. Her ability to connect the dots and notice details beyond most people are well-known and radiated in her professional achievements. She is a respected leader in the industry, yet remains a humble soul, and that keeps the author on her toes. The author is truly blessed and grateful to be born into this family who comes from a great lineage, and perhaps, that would be a story for another book.

Shu-Tze also has many mentors throughout her life, including the ancient Greek and Chinese philosophers like Socrates, Aristotle, Confucius, and Sun-Tzu, and people who have changed the face of the world and laid the foundation for a modern society today. People like Alexander the Great, Julius Caesar, Mahatma Gandhi, John D. Rockefeller, Benjamin Graham, and Winston Churchill.

She is also inspired by many great leaders like Warren Buffett, Bill Gates, Barack Obama, Ray Dalio, people who continue to a principle-centred life and shape the world today. On top of that, she is also blessed with mentors from her business associates. People who created successes globally and guided many to do so too. These are people who set high standards and continue to educate her beyond her formal education years. People who inspired her to live purposeful, principle-centred, and extraordinary life,

There are a few award-winning authors also inspired Shu-Tze. One of whom is Thomas Friedman, a renowned journalist, three-time Pulitzer Prize winner, and the New Yoke best-selling author. Shu-Tze met Friedman fifteen years ago in a book a dear friend recommended. That book, *The World Is Flat: A Brief History of the Twenty-First Century* increases Shu-Tze's curiosity beyond the world she used to live in. Through extensive work interviewing global leaders, Friedman shared what the leaders said about the future of socio-economic affairs, foreign trade, policies, and globalisation internationally. That opened up a whole new world of opportunities to Shu-Tze and brought tremendous impacted on her career, life, and her writing today.

Friedman continues to contribute to the world through his journaling career, interviewing leaders worldwide. In his latest book, *Thank You for Being Late: An Optimist's Guide to Thriving in the Age of Accelerations*, first published in November 2016, brought glimpses of another new world with invasion of smart technologies, and many of the predictions in that book are unveiling rapidly as we speak today.

There are many other great books which tell us stories of how many people survived the worst kind of illnesses, war, and nature-induced disasters and emerge stronger than before. People who are living in war-torn zones, among the poorest of the poor, and the cruelty of the underworld are creating lives they could only dream of in the past.

The books like *The Fortune at the bottom of the Pyramid* by C. K. Prahalad, *Riches Among the Ruins* by Robert P. Smite and Peter Zheutlin, *The Secrecy World* by Jake Bernstein wrote of those. Shu-Tze concluded the ones with the highest propensity to grow would develop in them the human spirits which breakthrough all impossibilities to create new opportunities.

One of the many must-read books for Shu-Tze is *A Man's ßSearch for Meaning* by Viktor E. Frankl. In this book, Frankl detailed the events in Nazi concentration camps during World War II. He observed how millions of prisoners of war helped on to the hope of reuniting with their missing family again. That hope has kept them alive despite being subjected to the most the horrid physical and mental torment.

According to Frankl, the last human freedom——the freedom to choose——is deeply embedded in each of them and helps them through every bruise and bitter winter cold, extreme hunger, and death around them. Visit the Nazi concentration camp in the Auschwitz at least once in your life. Feel the human spirits who thrived and survived the worst of human torture and choose to be better for the human race herein.

"If you are in your 40s like me, we still have 50 wonderful years or more ahead of us to live fully and extraordinarily," Shu-Tze often says this to her audience in her speaking engagements. With the advancement of smarter and faster technologies, superintelligence artificial intelligence, there so many ways we can reprogram our DNA to get ahead. Today we have access to abundance resources to form better a relationship, better health, be in a better position of wealth, and living a meaningful and joy-filled life.

She also says, when you have the privilege to travel, travel far and wide, to the many places you would have read and the amazing historic sites around the world. Behind every gap between the walls, every alley, down in the marketplace, try the cuisine and talk to the local people. There are pearls of wisdom waiting to pass to us—— stories of resilience and tenacity, even in the face of fear of possible death.

Therefore, despite the pandemic and technological revolutions which brought upon disruptions we have not experienced before, let us still be a good steward of our lives, our relationship, health and wealth. When we do what we must according to nature's will, we continue to create a life worth living. As many of our forefathers and ancestors have lived through the worst of time and emerge victoriously, so will we.

—————————————— THE END ——————————————

Made in the USA
Middletown, DE
01 May 2021

38822341R00175